The One That Got Away
The Truth Revealed, Volume 2

Syeda Anese Majid Khan

iUniverse, Inc.
Bloomington

The One That Got Away
The Truth Revealed, Volume 2

iUniverse books may be ordered through booksellers or by contacting:

iUniverse
1663 Liberty Drive
Bloomington, IN 47403
www.iuniverse.com
1-800-Authors (1-800-288-4677)

ISBN: 978-1-4620-3307-2 (sc)
ISBN: 978-1-4620-3308-9 (hc)
ISBN: 978-1-4620-3309-6 (e)

Printed in the United States of America

iUniverse rev. date: 1/20/2012

Dedicated to my beloved husband

Group Captain Majid Khan

BECAUSE

The year has swiftly slipped away from me,
Because you are ever here and dear to me.
Your tender smile, is a heavenly light for me,
Because your unbound spirit, still resides in me.
Memories recall, thy flood of tender care for me,
Because with devotional love you nurtured me.
I walked alone, until your beguiling smile enraptured me,
Because, I came to you with naught save love for thee.
You held my hand and raised my eyes, so I could see,
Because, you brought a world of hope and joy for me.
You always spoke tender and compassionate words to me,
Because, you dispelled the darkened swirls, engulfing me.
I found roses, growing round my lifeless feet so free,
Because, your gentle smile, poured sunshine over me.
I silently await, the "Call from Him" to be with thee
Because I know, you will be waiting there for me.
In life I treasured most, your unconditional love for me,
Because through tears and joys I was drawn to thee.
Through life and death, through all time to be,
Because, He made love divine, for you and me.
Through light and darkness, I have cleaved to thee,
Because, through time He made thee, one with me.
God made thee mine — I have life-long cherished thee,
Because, beyond your love, there is no other life for me.

~ ANESE MAJID, 2008

Biographical Overview

Born in India in 1928, Mrs. Anese Majid Khan migrated to Pakistan in 1952 and settled in Lahore where she established the famous Esena Foundation School on most modern lines. She belongs to the famous Imam family and is the daughter of Late Syed Jaffar Imam, the Chief Justice of India Supreme Court. She is a scholar of great prominence and has authored, knowledgeable books on Islam: "The New Arab World" and "Insight into Islam". Being herself a poetess also, she has beautifully translated the Quranic Verses under the title: "Poetical Echoes of the Eternal Message". She received the Award of "Saint" at the International Religions Conference held in Tokyo, and the award of "Jerusalem Star" from Mr. Yasser Arafat for her services to the Palestinian cause. She has also been the recipient of "International Merit Crystal Award" and many other National and International Awards for her services to the cause of Islam. She has had the honour of delivering lectures on Islam at Islamic Schools, Islamic Centres in Canada, Research Centre at Dallas, America and at Church of the Savious and Temple University of Florida. In 1993, she was appointed member of the Board of Directors of Global Stewardship Core International and subsequently the Vice Chairman. She worked as Trustee for the Welfare of the Bosnian students. She has the unique distinction of distributing free of cost thousands of video cassettes of the English translation of the Quranic Verses. In 2008 the government of Pakistan honoured her with the Award of "Pride of Performance" and also "The Presidential Award" for her services to Pakistan for over fifty years.

★ ★ ★ ★ ★

Table of Contents

JOURNEY TO A NEW SCHOOL
I Developed and Matured: Reaching the Merit Command

My, all important education had been severely interrupted, from the moment, when Britain announced that World War II had been declared. After a break of approximately six months, I found myself preparing to rejoin my educational classes. So I wended my way up to another Convent in Mussoorie, where I had been enrolled from England, at a branch of the convent of Jesus and Mary, which was to be my new school. I was tense and apprehensive, hating the very idea that all around me would be people and a life style that would be unfamiliar and alien, all would be new, strange and in all probability I would find myself unversed, struggling at the lowest end of the class. I also wondered about what other co-curriculum activities would be available to me. This kept my head spinning around in circles, but the more I lent thought to it, the further my dejection kept sinking, I became thoughtless, the more I failed to concentrate. My mind raced in concentric circles of doubt and despair, the cobwebs of my brains required to be swept away, it was imperative, that I pull myself together and muster some vibrant restoration of positive thinking. Thus compelling me to concentrate with this effort. I regained my optimistic attitude towards life and a few sunbeams once again appeared to filter through, in a progressive order, for which I was truly grateful. This gave me the impetuous, to urgently acquire, and summon all my faculties, to assist me to hasten my progress.

Syeda Anese Majid Khan

With amazement, I encountered the growing discovery of life in India, bringing with it a great many unfathomable surprises. I was amazed and marvelled with shock and perplexity that both English and Urdu came to their tongues as their natural language, for nearly all the family members, friends and a great many members of the staff, all spoke in English. The official and social life at that time was very anglicized, especially the elite of the upper class society, as if it were the threshold of modernism. Life, at times presented an English sway of mannerisms and codes of living, there was no such notion or presentation of a stand up dinner – it was all very formal. Be it lunch, tea or dinner, the tables were laid, covered with damask, Wedgewood or Daultlan china, were laid out in a formal presentation of a given menu, monogrammed silver cutlery banked on three sides of each place, set like surgical instruments that are correctly laid out for an operation according to its requirement. The sparkling crystal cut-glass, were all of a single design, but the similarity ended there, as they varied in shapes and size. At the upper right hand of the place setting, stood an array of glasses, that were a medley in shapes, each according to it's own function. White wine was held in a wineglass nearest to the right hand corner, as it was to accompany the first course, an appetizer or the hors d'oevres. The next stem glass which was slightly larger, held fragrant dry white wine specifically used to accompany the first course, which in all probability would be a fish presentation, when the fish plates were removed, so were the two white wine glasses. Next came a deep red wine with a decade or more of vintage behind it. For this the glasses were larger and almost tulip in shape, these held a fair quantity of sparkling red wine, with an aroma and bouquet that was fragrant, and spicy holding a subtle smooth persuasive quality, the bulbus glass was filled and refilled with the main "entree" course of red meat or "game" that was served as the main course of the meal. When the red wine had been consumed the glasses were lifted, there emerged a brief interlude of conversation which was more animated while awaiting the service of the savory course. Once more plates were lifted and a delicate sweet white wine filled into long fluted glasses, as a prelude to the desert, small sips of delicious sweetly subtle white wine carrying an evasive fragment "bouquet" enhanced the delicate flavour of a deftly created desert. Anyone could swear that a 'formal' elite English dinner was in progress right there at an Indian residence.

At this stage an "accomplished" hostess using a silent code of eye contact, rose and ushered the ladies into the drawing room, where black coffee was served in demitasse coffee cups, accompanied, by the famous after dinner chocolate mints, marzipan or other very appealing crystallized fruit. When the ladies had sojourned to the drawing room, the decanters of Port and Brandy were passed round to the male diners, who still remained seated at the long dining table, drinking hand warmed port in very large bulbous brandy glasses – cigars were brought out and passed around. The evening turned into a life of no worries, as peace and contentment descended with relaxation. That was when male jokes were making the rounds, political discussions lacked serious verve, while harmony and repose made an entry, and formal social constraint fled to return with the sunrise.

I need to return, if I am to make progress with my story, instead of dashing off at a tangent to reveal my thoughts, and my re-actions to the conflicting social lives I found confusing. These formal occasions must be revealed for the sole purpose of proffering the double – standards and style of lives we led. Our homes and residences were planned and decorated in the English style which was a classic British Colonial elegance. Our food had incorporated the basic style of an English menu, soups with Irish stews and roast beef, Yorkshire pudding, bread and butter pudding, and dumplings entered our menus. French and Italian fare, had not yet reached our colonial tables as a matter of course in any large measure before World War II.

Yet with all of this somewhat anglicized semi-colonial imitating style of life we had embraced, we had not substituted our national attire in favour of clothes from the west. The saree was a Hindu form of dress and the Mughal outfits were "Ungarkha" and the "Gharara" that were handed down, by the Muslim kings and the Begums of Oadh.

The majority of the society thought in and spoke in English, and even wrote in English. All letters and invitations were documented in English, yet we were actually truly modern, and educated Indians of our homeland.

We had not forgotten our national language, nor our values albeit that we had slept for over a hundred years covered by the English blankets. But late in the 19th Century and definitely in the early days of the 20th Century, Indians were stirred, awakened, and assessed the unacceptable subjugation of our converted homeland. The highest

Indian bloods of the country such as the Princes, Rajas, Nawabs and highly educated lawyers and even the men at the top cadre, who had been knighted and were "Sir" this and "Lord" that, forgathered to form a platform for the repossession of the homeland and relinquished their "titles" repudiated their allegiance to a foreign flag. It took almost fifty years to achieve their goal, to raise the national flag above the two new countries, that emerged as a result of a division and partition of the sub-continent, that stands today as India and Pakistan.

But here I have once again digressed from the memories of my induction into a new type of Educational System which I dreaded. If I had been a lesser person I would have just side stepped the issue, but because I am the person I am, I shunned the very thought of such a decline in the power of my self control. My answer to the problem was, that I needed to stand up and assimilate the conditions round me. Then pick up the gauntlet, unafraid, then go out and meet my challenges.

I was perfectly well acquainted with the knowledge and accepted the common consent that my sister and I be admitted to the school in Mussorie, that was a branch of the Convent of Jesus and Mary in High Barnett, which had been my academic institution in England. I realized that the type of living would be different, but wondered what mental gymnastics I would have to perform and what summersaults awaited my attention. Not knowing is the worst part of life. Unsolved thoughts kept turning like a ferries wheel, I always returned to base without a direct comforting answer. I kept thinking and re-thinking analyzing, but getting no comforting impression, I learnt to promptly, switch off negative thoughts I was incapable of harnessing any worthwhile answers that brought comfort.

Eventually the day arrived when we were to take our train journey from Patna to Dehra Doon, where the railway-line came to an end, as this last town lay at the foot of the very high rising Himalayan range of mountains. From there travel had to be made by car, or by bus climbing the steep slopes to Mussorie. Travelling by road was approximately eight hundred miles which was impossible by car with trunks and baggage, so we made the journey by the mail train of the East Indian Railway, arriving at the terminal of Dehra Doon early next morning, hundreds of miles away from home.

Disembarking from our train at Dehra Doon, we proceeded by car to climb, travelling upward to 7500 feet we ascended the lower slopes of the mountains of the Himalayas, our destination being Mussorie. As we negotiated our ascent of the steeper winding bends, the gradual grassy slopes, we had wound our way through occasional bends, but the further up we moved into the hills, the slopes ceased to be grass like terraces, they became steeper and steeper, the bends more acute and the roadway narrower than before and bordered on both sides with tress and shrubs. The higher we climbed, the twist and turns converted into hair-pin bends, becoming sharper and much more frequent, that soon they hung to the hillside almost in quick succession. On both sides of the road the pine-trees, were inclined to get taller and heavily grouped and the juniper forests became denser. This projected the views as even more beautiful than the picture cards one receives. This beauty was to be seen, from both angles, on looking down into the valley, as well as scanning the views, above where the terrain ceased to be hills with mild slopes, there were rock mountains, as we entered the steep mountain areas. Here they claimed their prerogative, as soaring high mountain peaks that towered far into the sky. From these great heights silvery streams of gurgling water tumbled gushing down the mountain between gutted rocks, creating a waterway rumbling and tumbling as it plummeted, downwards in a frenzied gush, toppling over satin smooth rocks, only to collapse as it joined a steady stream flowing in natures natural course.

Two hours into this picturesque drive we began to observe a few tin-roofed huts and cottages, but within the next half hour we entered a beautiful hill town with scores and scores of red roofed cottages, that studded almost half the country-side, making it appear as a vast green bed-cover printed with an assortment of multi-sized strawberries. The pines were hung with dark clusters of woody pine cones, white chestnut trees were in bloom. I had seen plenty of pine trees in England, but could never have envisaged the size and grandeur, that these stately majestic alpine trees presented as we drove past. These were the parental plants of, the symbolic wood clusters of cones, that decorate the Christmas trees as they nestle after being painted in silver and gold, taking their place amongst twinkling fairy lights that adorn the household Christmas trees, turning bleak cold evenings into festive ones, while hot spicy mulled punch and roasted chestnuts contribute warmth and peaceful satisfaction, to the family hearth on snow-bound, blistering cold ice chilled nights, the family members sing beside the warmth of love and relaxation.

Arriving at Mussorie our hired cars stopped at the bus terminal, after which there was no possibility for any motor vehicle to proceed further. The cars were unloaded and a series of rickshaws were hired, this was to be the new form of transportation. I was told these high wheeled boxed carriages were rickshaws, but they bore no resemblance to the rickshaw, I had seen pictures as vehicles of the same name in China and Japan. The rickshaws I knew and was acquainted with were co-related to China – a canopied seat, rested on two large wheels, that were joined to two long shafts with a man in front wearing a cone-shaped hat. The man centred between the two shafts, taking one in each hand, ran pulling the rickshaw along the streets, conveying people to their destination. But the rickshaws in the hill stations of India was quite a different vehicle. It was built as a two seated coach covered by a canopy, with the front shaft built like a coach, with two men harnessed to the front shafts like a pair of horses. To assist the strenuous act of pulling two to three passengers, there were three men at the rear clinging to the cross bar rail as they pushed, running with co-ordinated steps. This mode of vehicle moved at a fairly good speed, but the men really did earn their meals by the "sweat of their brows". I could not find myself approving of this as a means of transport, but I could not object, as all decisions were the domain of the elders. I realized that I must adhere to "do in Rome as the Romans do".

After another half hour we arrived at the arched gate-way of "The Convent of Jesus and Mary." My heart jumped a double beat – here was the branch of my school in England and I was thrilled to look up and see the Convent Crest riveted in gold to the overhead archway.

The driveway was gravelled and quite wide presenting us with a chance to walk which thrilled me indeed. Both sides of the driveway were lined, not with pine-trees as one would expect, but cherry, peach and pear trees in blossom, with other flowering trees that were in full bloom, as spring had already dressed the hills in an abundance, of beautiful flowers in a variation of colours with healthy bushes of hydrangeas in colours of blue and pink, were interspaced, with ivory cream in snowy white clusters. Oleanders were blooming in various shades of streaky peach forming clusters, clumps and bunches, while the ground was covered with wild violets, giving the effect of rolls of green and purple carpeting. The artist in me was arrested immediately, as I stood soaking up the beauty, the harmony of colour and the gorgeous benevolent gift of nature, so generously splashed in the circumference around me.

Just lately, for months I had been living on a wobbly sea, where there was no water "water water everywhere" as Coldrige had written "but not a drop to drink" it was not water that we needed, we desired terrer-e-fermer beneath our feet at that moment of time, but here was green in every shade to soothe our eyes, coloured flowers exuded their charm for our vision while aromas of a mixed wide spectrum of fragrance assailed us with a perfumed bouquet that filled the air. The natural charm of the spring flowers was a scenic beauty to behold and my own inner tranquillity had been amply fed by the soothing harmony and unrivalled presence of nature.

A sudden call from my sister brought me back to life on earth once more, "Anese why are you just standing there, we still have a way to go and are expected, to present ourselves at the Convent office – do hurry up or we shall be late."

Without looking up or replying, I hastened my steps as I came abreast with her. I stopped to take another look and to take stock of my surroundings, then I almost went into shock saying, "I don't believe this – I really don't", my sibling sister said, "You had better believe it, there is no other way up this mountain. And for God sake don't try any of your funny tricks, or try to find a novel way to ascend, so we reach our destination."

I wished then that I had wings – I knew what was going to be her reply "If wishes were horses." I don't think that even a horse would be stupid enough to attempt that perpendicular ascent. If we owned horses, at least we could have made the attempt. My sister used her usual brusque tone and said, "Hey stop that – you are supposed to be the athlete, a sport's brat, a tomboy, so stop your unbecoming mooing."

I said, "Fathma do you realize, that we have never even been for a walk since we left High Barnet. It is, cars we ride all the time, as though we had no legs. I'm out of condition for this climb."

"You can do all the walking, your heart desires to be content, do whatever you want, but don't think I'll be with you, catering to your whims and fancies, or your up and down moods, "nor your conquest of the miniature "Everest" you were born under. That birth in Darjeling and our Mother gazing up at the "Everest Peak" was our Mother's folly".

I was too angry to pursue the bitter one sided conversation.

Looking at the large rambling house above, that covered extensive areas across the hill. I was impressed and I remarked, "I wonder how they managed to carry all those bricks, wood and steel up these hills while they were building the convent, that now appears to be sprawling all over the place, in unrestricted freedom. Yet it looks quite at home where it stands in congruity with the landscape."

I could see that the sheer force of gravity had been challenged, or was I at first being negative. The slope up was almost at a right angle, or that is what I felt at that time. I wished that I knew more Physics or Newton's Law of gravity better, so I could have planned a formula of gravity to work out a plan for us. I presumed, that there had to be some other way to bring the building material to the summit of the hill, where the main structure of the Convent obviously had basically been planned. This was not the Egyptian Pyramid where enormous rock slabs were moved by sound.

A few minutes later, I saw two gardeners as they walked up a zig-zagging track that crossed and recrossed the road many times, advancing further up the hill. They reached the top, where the building was actually situated, the unconcerned men kept on talking, while they ascended the broad path, but they were ascending at a somewhat quick pace. I called my sister to attention and said to her, "Look Fathma, at those two men they are making their way upwards pretty fast, even if they have to climb by zigzagging across the track that ran from one side of the gravelled road, only to return and re-cross, at a point that was elevated by three to four feet. But even this method of slow progress is marvellous". The possibility made me excited "I'm sure, we have found this as a plausible answer, to our problem to negotiate the ascent. Let us make the attempt. So lets go." I said in haste.

We started to climb forward, working at it slowly or rather very very slowly, then our progress became, faster and still faster. It had been hard and an unforgiving task, as I became aware of this devilish punishment. My undesired combat with gravity was unevenly poised, leaving me at the wrong point of the receiving end. Sometime later we had almost achieved our task. At the top where the main building was guarded by another gate, that gave direct entrance to the grounds of the Convent. We stopped our climb, taking a rest to catch our breach and a few moments also, to tidy ourselves, presenting a groomed look, for the climb had been very hard indeed. Despite it being spring, at the cool height of an eight thousand feet high mountain range, we found ourselves with small beads of perspiration across our foreheads and around our necks. This needed attention at once, our hair needed combing and re-arranging.

Since we had been on the ship for nearly two months, with no real programme of exercise, we were unfit for this undesired hitch hiking thus we required to rest, to compose ourselves before attempting the last assent. We needed sufficient physical form, and some regulated exercise had to be reintroduced with a planned regime that we had previously been accustomed to. As we neared the summit, we were once again almost huffing and puffing and could hardly carry our toilet cases leave alone "blowing the house down." This necessitated another stop for us to get spruced up. What caught my attention, that Fathima refrained from saying one word leave alone her caustic remarks that were mainly directed towards me. I suddenly realized that she too felt out of condition.

The steep climb had left my leg muscles strained, accompanied by aching sore feet, and a long rest was overdue – apart from this I had an overwhelming desire, to take a scrutinized assessment of my surroundings, I decided it was a comely building with captivating and picturesque views. The building was over-hung with climbing roses in pastel colours, gorgeous displays of fuchsias in large dark green baskets, that hung midway between the pillars, bridged by oak carved railings that circumvented the wide verandas, which extended itself to almost the entire perimeter of the large spread out and rambling building, that stood out, like a disproportionate oversized white honey comb. Three enormous gravelled playgrounds, could be observed at three different levels and was clearly visible from where we stood. The building had no symmetry, no sized co-relation, no architectural balance, no specific design. It belonged to no era, it belonged to no designer, it belonged to no architect. It was neither a mansion nor a cottage it belonged entirely to itself, and it became for me "a self presentation" that I loved as a home away from home.

The Convent stood nestled, or rather rambled across the expanses of the unlevelled earth, to create the varied ground levels of the building, leaving the slopes of stately pine and juniper trees that stood like sentinels, swathing the hill in protection from a woodman's axe. Behind this special home I had acquired, I had learnt to love the rising and distant majestic mountains of the Himalayas, capped with snow and in the distance beyond, stood the ice-bound snow ranges that would have appealed to any artist's brush or mountain climber.

Many years later I myself produced an oil canvass of this scenic majestic beauty. The building itself, ran in every direction, as the need of expansion demanded, fighting its way for the construction of another building. These mountain ranges, were a sight of magnificence to behold and fortunately, could be viewed from any one, of the many buildings that comprised the convent's estate. The hillsides had been terraced at many levels, being put to use as gravelled playgrounds, orchards in bloom, vast flower gardens cultivated for the sole purpose of decorating the alters of the Church, the maroon carpeted corridors, and the graceful guest parlours delicately emblazoned for visiting parents, representatives of authority and the members of the clergy and other distinguished visitors.

I had been accustomed to contemplating and admiring the trimmed look of the English gardens, the vast rolling lawns, smooth manicured hedges, meandering walkways, rosaries of hybrid roses, woods with nature's wildflowers, daffodils swaying in the breeze, climbing primroses and even mushroom toadstools clustering around the moss covered roots. But despite this apparent disarray of structural planning, the convent still came together as one unique entity, complemented by its own individuality. In fact to me it was a place of tranquillity and natural beauty. My memories are ones of happiness, growth, hoards of cultural opportunity, and an abundance of wonderful kind disciplined, ethical yet benevolent nuns. They carried their black habits with grace, dignity and respect. To this day I see them as personalities of purity and I remember them for the love and the training, they imbued in me and still after seventy years and fleeting time I thank them for the initiation into a productive world that they instilled into me. "If you must do something then you must do it well, taking full responsibility upon yourself." This is what the nuns taught me, and this is how I have endeavoured to live my life.

After being received by Revd. Mother and ushered into the decorated "Parlour" that could have graced any well placed household in England, which in fact appeared out of place here in a simple convent , except that it had the addition of several gilded items, a crucified Christ upon the cross, a gold framed picture "The heart of Jesus" and a statuette of "The Virgin Mary." The room boasted of gilded chairs, Grecian urns filled with Red Easter Lilies and giant sized creamy- white St. Anthony's lilies, these were to be seen in abundance, in this tastefully gracious room. What struck me most at that time was the highly polished "baby grand" "Steinway" piano, that elegantly occupied one corner at the rear of this formal room, with its highly polished "Parquet" wood floor, that shone because of the devoted care it received. I was intrigued by the enormous porcelain Wedgewood container, that monopolized the main space on the mahogany piano, which contained blush cream roses tinged with a dash of sunshine, the effect of it sent my heart spinning to a home I had just left ten thousand miles away – I almost felt I was back home at Cedarwood in High Barnet. Unfortunately I had to drag my attention back to the parlour, so I admired, the pale pastel biscuit beiges that set out the basic colours of the room – the same hue ran throughout from carpet to sofas and even to the walls. The blandness of the room was relieved by the softly blended salmon and peach, contrasting ever so tenderly in the curtains, the cushions with dark peach fringes, tassels and thick satin shiny cords were in evidence, wherever I grazed around the room. I was lost in the colourless beauty that blended purity of arrangements, profusion of flowers and the religious paintings mounted on glided frames, rendering the room the result of a real dedicated artist. I was once again to wander off into a world of profusion lost in my own thoughts that I can hardly recall Revd. Mother's welcome, and her gentle smile, endeavouring to make us feel at home in this strange abode, and yet not so strange, the parlour as I had seen was spectacular, so much on the same type as homes I had visited during my years of sojourn in England.

There was a russel and movement around the entrance door, it was gently–pushed open, but the sudden noise jolted me out of my lost revere. A nun entered soundlessly and behind her two lay sisters of the Convent, who carried in silver trays, set with a tea service, cups and small silver spoons. Sugar was present here, but I do not think Britain had yet gone on to a ration card system for almost everything. That was yet to come – it was only seven months, since war had been declared. The other trays carried in were laden with, what I recognized with nostalgia, home baked scones lavishly spread with clotted cream and strawberry jam. Later I was to learn that all manner of jam and fruit preserves were available at the convent, due to the vast orchards cultivated by the nuns themselves. Along with muffins there was toffee fudge, peanut brittle and an assortment of small cakes, delicately made cucumber, cheese, and tomato sandwiches, sprinkled over with water cress.

The students benefitted from these bakery products, as every Saturday afternoon we could go to the "Tuck Shop" of the convent and buy a fairly good variety of tempting "goodies" that we enjoyed over the week-end. Almost all the girls waited eagerly from Friday afternoon, for the Saturday afternoon sale. A group of friends would pool their weekly pocket money for purchases, a school level feast, then get down together to play monopoly or some type of board or card game enjoying the freedom of "free play." The weekends were full of fun and many of us forgot that we were in school and home was so very far away. It was an antidote, to brush away the blues of home sickness, experienced every Saturday morning, while we penned our weekly letters home to our parents, relatives and friends. Few girls failed to remain dry-eyed after these sessions. Saturday afternoons were a reviver and to some it was almost mesmerizing, creating a baffle-wall against a negative emotion of separation, that could lead to a psychological problem.

After my elder sister had finished her tea, since I had demurred to drink it, which surprised Revd. Mother as nearly everyone in India was a tea drinker. But I really did enjoy the pastries and tiny sandwiches of potted salmon and butter spread on brown bread. There were delicious soft slices of current loaf lightly spread with golden butter. I could have eaten more, but held back, refraining from displaying any bad manners, or giving the impression that I was hungry, for hungry we were not, because Mother had sent with us ample food and "tit-bits" for the long journey we had to undertake.

I had sat wide-eyed at first and excited about the tea service – and the profusion of delicious, and skilfully produced confectionary. I was later to learn that the convent estate, owned nearly most of the hill on which it stood, enabling the many terraced slopes to produce an abundance of fresh vegetables that were grown for salads, plus what was used to enhance the taste of what would have been termed "plain" English food. Since we had several French and Belgium nuns their taste for delicate flavours, touched the kitchen menus – as a result we also benefitted by the presentation of herbs, roots and spices, that made simple fare into one that was flavoured and well in demand.

As Revd. Mother stood up, she asked my sister and myself to kneel down on the thick piled carpet so we could receive her blessing. Mother St. Clare who was to take charge of us presented her with a small bowl of Holy water – she dipped her fingers into it and sprinkled the water as she flicked it round us, banishing any evil that may have been present, then dipping her index and fore finger into the water she anointed both of us on our forehead with a small sign of the cross. It didn't occur to me then, but later it appears to me as a miniature "Papal blessing" I suppose that would be the nearest, that anyone could come to such a blessing.

As we rose we thanked Revd. Mother, then Mother St. Clare led us away to the apartments and dormitories where the children slept.

Since the Convent estate covered a very large area, it was not built as a large single building, the sleeping arrangements and dormitories were grouped in different areas, according to the age group that encompassed the child's age. Because my sister was over four years older than me, she was taken to another building, while I was escorted to a primary school building which was called Belmont Hall.

The way down to Belmont was strange, as it had not been constructed as a part of, one of the main buildings. First we walked through carpeted corridors where the religious statues stood as spiritual sentinels, but leaving them in our wake, we negotiated long lengths of oak railed verandas, from where the mountain scenery was visible, then we descended a long flight of steps, walked across an enormous hall that was in fact a Junior School playroom on rainy days. At one end stood an upright piano, long benches lined the walls and cupboards full of balls, bats, drums, percussion instruments and skipping ropes could be found. This room was used essentially for activities on cold and wet days and after dinner as a playroom for the junior students, but most of all, it came very handy, on rainy days and winter nights. Leaving the hall behind, we walked down another long corridor, then another long flight of steps, before we came to the passage way that led directly to the entrance of Belmont Hall. It was here that my dormitory was located and where I slept for the next four years. Due to my good and responsible behaviour, I had earned respect, so I was moved to a large cubical providing for me privacy and supervisory authority. Every dormitory had one large cubical that was reserved for one of the nuns who supervised and maintained the discipline, welfare, timing, and order of the children of Junior School. Children were to be woken up on time, herded with persuasion to wash not only their faces but also behind their ears and across their necks. It is amazing that we think we know nice clean children, but they quite often want to play truant with ablution duties in front of them. Their bodies are at the sinks with running water but their minds have already raced off in some other direction, that suddenly appears to be urgent. The system of hygiene and cleanliness is not an attribute or a gift at birth, it is a cultivated mode of living, that becomes a habit and eventually it becomes an essential part of one's life.

From the cubical that had become my own room, I could see through its high wide window the towering Himalayan ranges behind which, elevated ice bound peaks formed the hinterland of this magnificent view. The mountains from this distance appeared as shades of blue tinged with mauve, while the white capped snowy ranges caught the peaks of pink at sunrise, fading away giving place to the creamy rays of the rising sun. The snow cased mountain ranges, were not white or cream, nor salmon, or even creamy gold, it could never boast of being a single colour, yet it is claimed by all the world that it is a sight of great beauty. This benevolence of nature became the recipient of my morning worship, as it is the only place of worship that exists in such purity. No Church, no Temple, no Synagogue, or Mosque is as pure, for sinners return again and again seeking forgiveness. The unblessed enter to make an outward show, the blessed struggle to attain His favours and live in a hope to enter Paradise and others fall prey to the dazzling sparkle of depravity and drugs.

I was not unaware of the special status I had been given by the nuns and I worked to be worthy of the trust they endowed on me. As time moved on and I advanced in ability and prestige I wore the ribbons of monitor, then the badges of captaincy and eventually, in my last year of schooling I stood as the Head Girl of the convent.

Being the "Head Girl" of this particular prestigious Convent was a very high honour indeed. This Convent of Jesus and Mary was not only an educational centre, but was an acclamation of a polished "finishing school." The school was known all over India as "Waverly" situated on the hills of Mussorie. The accommodation had originally been built for only eighty students, but when World War II struck Britain in 1939, it became essential for children to be evacuated from Britain to other peaceful countries and in our case it was India, where a number of Englishmen were in the service of the British Government. Their children returned to India for the period of the war to be with their parents. All the good top missionary schools, prepared to augment the accommodation facilities for the duration of the war. As "Waverly" received its influx of evacuated children the student roll went up to one hundred and six. This was considered as overcrowded and with it came bigger classes, more competition blazed, but less delicate in manners. As the new entrants settled down, class competition were challenges, on the games field more teams developed, the gym turnout expanded and drama aspirants, worked harder to keep their places.

All in all the added students brought with them a diversity and a boost of a more lively nature.

I cannot say that we students who were coming from Britain were better, we brought a different western approach to a group of girls that were not Hindu, Sikh or Muslim, they were mostly Anglo Western by culture, but Indian by nationality. More than half the original students were the children of British couples posted to India and some from France.

In 1939 when World War II commenced, it was considered, that the children, must have to be evacuated from Britain to external countries for their own safety, so a number of children were sent to India where their parents resided. The convent chosen for us to continue our education was a Jesus and Mary convent, and a branch of our school in High Barnet. The school catered for a small number of students, and their tuition accomplished by very highly trained teachers, hence the Cambridge results of the Senior Cambridge and the Higher School Leaving Certificate which was equivalent to the "A" Level of today were exceptionally good. My sister and myself were the first and only Indian girls to be admitted to "Waverly" at that time.

Over the seven years I spent at "Waverly" I passed through many changes in my character, apparently it appeared that I was some type of chameleon. My boisterousness, impieties, my unpredictable actions and then my long periods of withdrawal, must have been the bane of many a nun's existence. My music teacher Mother Eugene had great hopes for me, but she was unable to make me play the piano in conformity as required for the Royal College of Music in London. Once my fingers slipped across the ivory notes, I flashed them across the keyboard, in my personal rendering, rather than the sensitive composition of the composer himself. I remember choosing for one of my exams a piece composed by Dr. Lovelock in his lively "Scarve Dance" which flowed and sparkled with life. Much to the irate chagrin of my piano teacher, I made my way into the exam parlour to render the chosen pieces for my exam under Dr. Lovelock, the examiner from the Royal College of Music conducted through England. The visiting examiners came out from England, twice a year and toured the important European schools throughout India, to examine the practical rendering of each student judged by an English examiner.

I entered the examination reception room and wished the examiner a polite "Good Morning Sir." He glanced at the music sheets before him, while he kept me waiting.

At this point Dr. Lovelock looked up at me then indicating for me to sit down opposite him at his table, while holding my music sheets in his hand.

He said, "Who chose these pieces of music for you to present for this exam."

I replied in a very soft voice, "I chose them myself Sir." Dr. Lovelock looked surprised, "What made you choose them? Was there something special that attracted you?" This was not the way the exam was supposed to be conducted.

"Yes Dr. Lovelock I did. I've really enjoyed learning how to play them and somehow I seemed to identify with them." Keeping a very straight face Dr. Lovelock asked "Did you know who the composer was?" Very quietly I replied, "Yes sir I did know that you had composed it – but I enjoyed the challenge working for a good rendering."

"Were you not afraid to play a piece of my work in front of me? Not many would be that daring" came Dr. Lovelock's comment.

By this time I had recovered from my nervousness and said, "Mother Eugene my music mistress, made every effort to dissuade me from choosing them, but much to her displeasure I remained resolute. As time passed I took it as a challenge and put every bit of emotion I could summon, to aid me, so I may succeed in my determination to learn it."

Dr. Lovelock was a bit surprised and remarked, "I'm afraid that perhaps your teacher may have been right. No pupil has ever played my work while I have sat as the examiner."

By this time I was beginning to regret my impetuous choice. I hesitated then explained "Dr. Lovelock when you were here last year for the music exam, you gave us a recital of several renderings by a number of outstanding composers ending the recital with your "Hungarian scarf Dame" I've been living in a dream since then. By some unreasonable desire I chose your work for my exam because I liked it, but perhaps I have over stepped my abilities, trying to render the music as I feel in harmony with it. Maybe I shall play it in poor form and certainly not as you meant it to be played when you composed it."

Feeling a weakness in my legs I dejectedly asked him, "Is it possible that I may leave and not take the exam. I would rather not take it, than that I should fail. Perhaps it has been most presumptuous on my part. Please may I leave."

Dr. Lovelock sat back in his chair saying, "No young lady, you may not leave now, it is I who am curious to find out what you have done to my work. I'm intrigued – how old are you?"

I replied, "I'm nearly sixteen sir."

I think Dr. Lovelock realized the obvious disappointment in me. He said, "Lets forget all about this and begin with the sonata that you have chosen. Go and sit down at the piano while I observe your rendering of Mozart. He is one of my favourite composers."

As I sat down at the piano, all the fear that had built up in me, left me and I became impatient to begin. I ran my fingers across the black and ivory keyboard, in a scale that he required me to play, then the few music exercises as was the requirement for the exam.

I moved into the beginning of the Sonata and time just flew past, I had played for less than half an hour loosing myself emotionally into another world of melody, tones, notes, semitones and chords following each cadence with another in quick succession, I was lost in Mozart's sonata and the Hungarian Scarf Dance. I was unaware of the presence of my examiner. As I completed the assigned pieces I rose and sought his permission to leave – he looked up smiling, tapped the fingers of both hands in soft miniature clap, which I dared not to interpret, and with his head he nodded his permission that I could leave.

Mother Eugena was standing directly outside the door of the exam hall. She grabbed me by the arm pulling me swiftly away down the carpeted corridor saying, "What was all that about? You were a very long time with the examiner. Did something happen before you started to play, the time lapse before you started was a long one?" I remained silent as I had no intention, of giving her a birds eye view for my indiscretion, which was personal and related only to myself.

The next day the exam results were pinned up on the school notice board for all to see. I refrained from going to view the board, as I had not been able to determine the examiner's mood as I left. Some of the girls came crowding around me, congratulating me, for I had not only passed, but I was in the honour's list. Tears smarted behind the eyelids of my eyes, but I recalled a trite saying "Nothing ventured nothing gained." My love for music and its rendition on both the instruments I play, namely the piano, and the sitar always had my personal emotions mixed with the originality of the composer.

I regret to confess that in my busy life I failed to play the "Piano" as often as I would like to have done and in the last forty years I have wasted the training I received, as I have ceased to play nor practice.

The playing of my "Sitar" was an intense emotional replacement for the Piano, but now since the last thirty years it has been taken out of its box and shroud so that I may play it, but only work, my writing, World Conferences that I attend, and the time given to travelling. This is at the cost of these my dearly loved instruments.

I cannot live without music so very conveniently, my homes in Lahore and London are equipped with the best sound system and I can find the unlimited music discs of every kind particularly by Beethoven, Mozart, Chopin and Litze. Spanish and South American music, Hawaiians and Strauss and even the "Dixie" West Indian music. But while I am engrossed with writing, it is only piano music that fills my background. I have mentioned several times that I have tried to live in the best of both worlds. From this written picture that I have painted, it would appear so, at least for my living and emotional needs.

There was much I acquired in the way of learning and life during my developing years at the Convent. My love of drama found its place in the heart of Mother St. Teresa, the eccentric but dedicated drama mistress. She for some unknown reason took me under her wing, worked with me, taught me the rudiments of acting, impressed on me the need for good elocution with slow clear annunciation, the call for perfection in good delivery and skilled presentation. With hard work and practice she raised me to heights of performance in singing, my favourite being the amusing plays of Gilbert and Sulivan and some operatic arias. Our ballet mistress taught me ballet, the sequences of the Hungarian Dances by Litze and Bulgarian country dancing and a number of round the world folk dancing. I was thrilled to once again pick up the movements and lessons of ballet, which was a part of my natural musical diversion. The grace required in "Copellia" and "Gisella" the dramatic presentation of "Swan Lake" entered my soul and still lies there to be resurrected by my never ending rows of tapes cassettes, disc and now D.V.D"s. Stage shows and ballet production take up a great deal of space for DVD discs.

The Pastial Symphonies of Mozart, the "Moonlight Sonata" of Bethoven, the Ave Maria by Bramhs, almost every symphony of Chopin became a part of my training. I took up the difficult challenges, held out by the intricacies of the Spanish Flamingos, with their numerous romantic Spanish serenades, as a result my development raced on and I soon found myself also singing in Latin, as a prominent member of the

Church Choir and often, I was their soloist especially during "passion week" when the Church organ remains silent, I needed to know Latin and pronouncing it well was essential, but not easy.

My musical heaven was all wrapped up like a huge unknown New Year's gift waiting for me to go into action to subdue my fears. I proceeded into the new arenas of instruction with a gladness in my heart, as I discovered the frisky steps of my feet. I became almost one with the school and its generous patience, that opened the way for my training. I have loved my "alma mater" for all the years of my life, in grateful thanks for laying in me the foundations of the vast accomplishments, for which they had prepared me. I bow my head in grateful thanks to each of the nuns of my developing years and also to the teachers and professors I had the fortune to meet and work with later, when I entered college.

My Mother never left anything out, when she planned our training with each detail that was given it's due importance. Apart from these elevated accomplishments she also encouraged us to express ourselves in paint, to be capable needle-women, prepare meals of creditable presentation with elevation in taste and food value, such as nourishment and food content, for she truly believed, that the best way to a man's heart, was through the pleasurable care of his cuisine and tasty morsels of delight.

My long period of residency in "Waverly" was like any student's life, except that I appeared to have picked up quite a number of coveted prizes, designations and awards to the chagrin of my competitors. The award that I proudly cherished was the one that Revd. Mother decorated me with, when I became the Head Girl of the convent. With broad smiles she presented me with my Head Girl badge and the certificate that read "The model School Girl". I constantly wore the broad, dark and light blue corded ribbon from which dangled a silver medal. At that stage of my life I was young, impetuous and idealistic, but there was something within me that kept me bridled, so each morning in the privacy of the Head Girl's own room I admired it, touched it to my lips and smiling put it over my head letting it fall in a V to dangle from my shoulders. With each morning, I made a fresh vow to be worthy of the medal. I'm almost certain, it put springs in my feet as I left my room.

No matter what kind of a day it might turn out to be, I was convinced that I could cope with it.

It was time for me to leave school, to cut the ropes of bondage and sever the cords of dependency from the nuns. Crutches were a disability, prolonged protection sowed the seed of dependency, and this I learnt that the world made no place for the weak, the dependent or the disabled.

★ ★ ★ ★ ★

NATIONAL AND INTERNATIONAL AWARDS

1. Awards from Greece
    Three Awards for the promotion of International Culture, Education and Human Rights.
2. Awards from U.A.E.
    For the Interpretation of the Holy Quran into English and education.
3. Presidential Award from La Roche U.S.A.
    I served as a trusty for Bosnian students at the "La Roche" College Pittsburg University U.S.A.
4. Educational Award from Dubai – The "Diamond Award"
    In appreciation of Educational Performance and human rights.
5. Pride of Performance and Presidential Award of Pakistan
    For Education, Islamic Dedication and International Recognition.
6. Pride of performance for 50 years of dedicated service to Pakistan.
7. Educational Awards from Pakistan
    For Education and Welfare Developments.
8. Islamic Awards from Pakistan
    Human Rights, The Eternal Message of Islam and Educational level for five decades.
9. Countless Bolan International Awards.
10. The village Tubewell Water Projects.
    The large number of Educational Scholarships given by Esena Foundation.
11. Several Quranic T.V. Programmes of the Holy Quran in English.
12. Developed Modern Educational Programmes
13. Upholder of Human Rights.
14. As a Writer and Poet.

★ ★

★

ISLAMIC DEDICATION

1. Group Captain Majid Khan,
   My beloved husband and constant supporter who was ever at my side.
2. Mr. Hanif Ramay, Chief Minister of Punjab and Syed S.M.Zafar, Law Minister of Pakistan.
   I received their respect and hand of friendship unstintingly for several decades.
3. The Translated Light of Islam. "The Eternal Message".
   My singular dedication and submission to Islam. – my aim in Life.
4. Miss Shaheen Ajmal, Supporter and Editor of "The Eternal Message".
   Throughout, at my side in full support and encouragement surrounding unstinting time,
5. Inauguration of "The Eternal Message" and Volumes of "Insight into Islam".
   My Islamic Books carry the Message of Islam around the world through the lecture tours I present for over a decade.
6. Mr. Daniel Samuel, my patient and dedicated computerist.
   Without his dedication to me, perhaps my work could not have been completed.
7. Anese Majid Khan, 'The Author'. SAIF (Syeda Anese Imam Fatima)
   My pen is my sword, injustice my enemy and my victory is through "SAIF"
8. Inaugurated by the Honourable Justice Sardar Iqbal, Chief Justice of Pakistan.
   Blessed and inaugurated by my devoted "mentor" my untold gratitude – a man of incomparable status.
9. Mr. Liaquat Chaudhry, and Mr. Riaz Baloch,
   The T.V. Producers of "Quranic Light" 114 Suras on T.V. "Royal" Channel.
10. Members of my Secretarial staff, Mr.Mohammad Hanif, Mr. Yousaf Gulzar, Mr. Daniel Samuel and Mr. Farooq Francis.
    Without this team I could have been a lame dog. I give them my thanks.
11. Special guests at the inauguration of the Eternal Message.

THE PARLIAMENT OF WORLD RELIGIONS
WORLD PARLIAMENT

1. Dr. Rustum Roy University of Pennsylvania a world renowned scientist and a dear friends.
2. The World Parliament of World Religions, San Francisco U.S.A.
   An Epic experience for which I would have traded ten years of my life.
3. Dr. Revd. Don Conroy.
   The dedicated upholder of modern and moral spiritualism.
4. Mr. & Mrs. Mikhail Gorbachev and Anese Majid Khan.
   The privilege of dining with a great leader at the "Millennium 2000" New York.
5. Red Indian Chief Mr. Alan and Anese Majid.
   The Red Indian Chief made me a "sister" of the community blessed by a burnt feather.
6. Dr. Rudd Lubber, President of the Netherlands and Anese in New York with Mr.Mikhael Gorbachev.
   A great "Human Rights" supported for justice and a member of "State of the World Forum".
7. Queen Rania of Jordan "Millennium 2000" in New York.
   A queen but a working lady of distinction.
8. Sardar Singh head President of the Sikh community
   An esteemed gentleman of honour, presence and humility.
9. Mr. Kofi Annan, General Secretary of the United Nations with Madam Mico and Myself.
   In New York at the "Millennium 2000"- A friend of great ability and dedication.
10. Dr. Revd. Don Conroy, Dr. Allan, Red Indian Chief and Myself.
    Respected and devoted friends beyond the duties of a Parliament. .
11. The South American Red Indian, Chief of the Azeet
    The chief, with members of the team and myself at the World Forum San Francisco.
12. Mrs. Anese Majid Khan speaking at the "Millennium 2000".
    I was privileged to be a speaker at such an "Elevated Forum".
13. Mr. Rehman Ghanni of the Graman Bank, Bangladesh.
    The "Noble Prize Award for human care and development was awarded to him. A man born to uplift the conditions of the poor and especially poor bonded women.

WORLD RECOGNITION

1. "The Spirit of Islam" – Awarded in America 1954.
2. "The Dome of Al Aqsa" – Presented by Mr. Yasser Arafat 1972 at the "Islamic Summit"
3. Dr. Alexander John Malik, Bishop of Lahore, Col.Roy working with us at the Inter-faith Conference.
4. Monsignor Kerr presented me the "Presidential Award".
    I worked with him at the "La Roche" College as one of the trustees for the Bosinian children.
5. Myself dedicated to expose the true peaceful concept of Islam.
6. Monsignor Kerr and myself at Pittsburg "La Roche College"
    Awarded the "Quranic Award" in Dubai for the translation and interpretation in English of the Holy Quran.
7. Dr. Rustum Roy and myself at the Parliament of World Religions – San Francisco.
8. The Bosinian senior students of "La Roche" College Pittsburg U.S.A.
    The brave student group of whom I am very proud.
9. Mr. Allen the Red Indian Chief working with me at the "New World Forum" in Washington during the session of "Millennium 2000"
10. Natalia and Majdoline my grand-daughters stand proudly with me holding the "Spirit of Islam".
11. Adeel Burki a famous singer from Pakistan holding a mike for me.
12. Dr. Rita Yeasted and myself with the gift of a "Teddy Bear" which says "We at La Roche love you".
14. My Islamic tour that teaches student to know and understand Islam.

★ ★

★

THE WORLD FORUM

1. Dr. Kofi Annan, General Secretary United Nations, guests and myself..
   It was refreshing to be with elevated people across the globe.
2. Anese Majid Khan.
3. Monsengar Kerr, President La Roche, Pittsburgh, U.S.A.
   From him I received the 'Presidential Medal" for my services in Bosnia.
4. Dr. Revd. Don Conroy.
5. Dr. Rustum Roy, Dr. Don Conroy, and myself.
   My mentor, my friend and my International benefactors. .
6. Anese Majid speaking at a lecture session at the "New World Forum" at the "Millinnium 2000" in New York.
   I have had the privilege to stand with world speakers – I do not know if I was worthy.
7. Dr. Tony and myself at the "Parliament of World Religions" San Francisco.
   An important member of the "Parliament of World Religions" platform in 1979.
8. Dr. Rustum Roy, my mentor
   My childhood friend, my lifetime "Spirit bond" and my educator for International work.
9. Members of the Parliament of World Religions dining together.
10. Delegation from India, U.S.A, Canada and myself.
    I met thousands of people from almost every country of the world.

★ ★

★

CLOSE FAMILY & INTERNATIONAL FRIENDS

1. Dr. Roy, Dr. Don Conroy and friends in the U.S.A
2. Mr. and Mrs. Eric and Antonia Payne, London
   Over three decades of love and friendship that never wavered.
3. Dr. Roy and Della, Penn State University U.S.A.
   A life long bond that needed no face-to-face presence came together at Niagara Falls.
4. Majid and myself framed in harmony.
5. Peggy Dean and Christopher Waymark.of Toronto, Canada.
   Partly sister, partly daughter and Christopher a son. I almost brought them up because we cared for each other.
6. Mr. S.M. Zafar and myself
   My old friend and Buddy of ages past- We tread five decades together.
7. A group of friends in Washington.
8. Mr. Fakhar Majid and myself
   My Auditor and a five decade friendship.
9. Mr. and Mrs. Magda Azhar in Cheam Surrey Britain
   Good friends of nearly five decades a devoted couple with a sincere friendship.
10. Stewant Granger and Ave Gardner when in Pakistan
    For the shooting of the film "Bhawani Junction". They became friends but did not fade in my memory of friendship.
11. Asad and Meena Thakur with the family from Wimbledon.
    A wonderful sincere Indian family settled for half a century in Wimbledon.
12. Christopher Waymark and myself with a life time bond.
13. Peggy Dean with the poodles in Canada.
14. Mr. Johr Willmot, Begum Raza and Majid in Windsor.
    My old old but now deceased friends are not forgotten but remembered in love.

★ ★

★

Truth Conquers the Universe

MY DRAMATIC
CHARACTER CHANGE
A Rapid Growth in Height and Maturity

My character had undergone several unbelievable and dramatic changes. From a harum-scarum tom boy who was not a lady, but a very unsuitable girl. I stood five feet seven and a half inches in height, wearing size five in shoes, heavily braided coiled hair remained styled upon my head, making my amber eyes fringed with dark lashes appear larger with a wider look. My finger nails were never short or cracked, instead they were long and tapered, finished in a dark carat shade of pale amber, defying the festive colour of "firefly" and "ruby" that were the prime colours for usage of that era. No I was not a boy, but a most "unsuitable girl" was the general opinion of the ladies.

Those were the days when it was the fashion to wear jewellery, from the start of the morning, till late into the evening, as jewellery was a regular part of the outfit. One wore it constantly even for day use. I could admire the designs and workmanship of any jewellery, but to use it, I had no need. I never used any jewellery myself except the occasional broach at the base of my neck and that too, only as an accessory to dressing, but not as a piece of Art made by a jeweller. One elegant piece to be worn by me for a dinner was more than sufficient. The adornment of bangles, bracelets and ear-rings were for the dolls of society. Even till today I hardly wear any jewellery only a watch, my wedding, and engagement rings and one large diamond ring a gift from my parents on my marriage day. Two plain gold bands both were from the "first salary" of both Tahira and Natalia in appreciation of the love I bestowed on them.

In an effort to assess myself correctly I needed some deep thinking and I had needed to make comparisons. I had been quick tempered, now I was silent and tolerant, I had been swift tongued, but now I was calm or spoke with gentle permission. I dressed as I chose for myself, I considered it to be my right, I used clothes befitting the younger modern fashions, my clothes were made and stitched at home under my personal supervision, by our resident tailors. The styles I chose for myself remained elegant, well cut and excellently stitched, but all were designed on very simple lines, yet they were modish and chic. Button, bows, lace and frills were for other delicate girls, but for me it appeared that the use of frills and trellises, were the frosting and silver bells on a New Year's cake. Since I was not seeking to be sampled and appreciated for my sweetness and quality, I had no desire for decorative dressing, it was superfluous to my requirement.

In recall I have traversed multiple areas of my past life and I believe that I turned out to be an observant observer. I am now able to sit back smiling, at all I have seen, believing that I missed very little and yet kept my silence. My dearly loved daughter Tahira christened me "Madam Hawk Eye" perhaps it is true that I have observed, retained and recalled when needed to do so, as a result, all that I discerned I locked away in a vault, to fade into the dim past, as time flew past and I moved on. Through the years there have been untold secrets heard by me, but never were they ever divulged, they were safely buried away forever. Perhaps that is why so large a number of people, have entrusted me with emotional secrets and problems. I have not yet broken a trust that was entrusted to me.

During my growing up years, I had but only a few girls or lady friends, during my college days I played by the grounds rules of the boys. In practice I played hockey, tennis, riding, squash, gymnastics, archery and sometimes even billiards, which was exclusively the realm of boys and men.

Invariably when we went shooting, I was the only lady amongst a hunting group of twenty to twenty-five men and was always at peace and comfortable in their company. In the matter of physical activities, I was an extrovert, in matters that were emotional or personal I become an introvert, depending entirely upon myself. I took up psychology with an in depth interest, so that for many past decades, I have acted as a councillor, leaning back to listen, to observe, translating actions and behaviour patterns, or lack of them, enabling me to comprehend the depth of concealment, stressed emotions, psychological denial and so many other emotional syndromes. It has enabled me to put, not only two and two together to make four, but it also enabled me to add halves, quarters a few decimals and still come up with four. I have read deeply and extensively, which has enabled me to comprehend human behaviour, human desires, truth and prejudices, to decipher what lies in depth or below the surface, to sympathize with a self destroying hatred, screening off gross ambition, as a sad human control power and a host of other devastating factors that encompass the unwary, that brings a disability of the human mind, scared emotions and self abrasion. Turning what could be a stable life into one of devastation.

At the opportune time of birth there comes with it a purity, of circumstances, conditions, later people become the product of their own environment, commencing with turning a "blind eye", allowing discipline to slip, forsaking principles and ethics, which gradually vanish, and self indulgence creeps in with stealth, to cripple the conscience, where the norms of conduct take flight into oblivion and the reins of life goes on as desired and individuality of self becomes their creed.

I am basically enterprising by nature, I speak my mind only when and where there is a need to do so. I ensure that I keep the power of control over my words, my actions and my self-desire. There are numerous ways I exercise to handle a situation, perhaps considered as eccentric by some, due to their own imbalance in the understanding another's life. With my advanced age, I suppose that my forthright manner of speech could be referred to as feisty by some super sensitive person. But because my real worth is unexposed I have no occasion to grieve regarding myself. I endeavour to approach matters under humanitarian circumstances. I suppose I have embraced a form of life for myself through the annals and medium of spiritualism. I decry the use of "salt and vinegar" in thought, word or deed. To know and experience the joy of laughter and giving, creates a bonding, because it has the capacity to enliven a saddened world, to fill and enlighten, a dread of darkness that is falling round the world, when life should embrace the sparkling stars on a midnight sky, even on a moonless night.

I learnt to sing, yet shade my eyes while holding a broken heart; I learnt to hide behind my vocal chords, so I don't cry, I encouraged my legs to dance, performing with leaden feet, I've performed as a theatrical dramatist veiling a hurt and unshed tears, I learnt to accept and live through broken dreams, but the best of all I learnt was how to attain the "sufi" state of mind leading me on to spiritualism. It kept me afloat, as I re-discovered the beauty of life and the benevolence of my Super Power the Holy Quran. Since then I have found peace.

I've demurred several offers of political forums, a reserved seat for women in the assembly, the senate and even the post of ministerial advisor. None of these elevated posts could beckon or possess any allure for me. I desired to work directly with the people, who needed immediate sustenance. I have lived in simplicity, leaving the creditable desires to others who 'man' the prestigious and "elevated" chairs.

My work has taken me, from the gleaming glittering capitals to villages across globe, as a member of several International Boards, I have met a vast number of highly placed personalities, I've been presented at Court to her Royal Majesty Elizabeth II, in July, 1952 I have been a guest at many homes of the nobles of the Royal Court, and Lord Ironside was my one time guardian. In the long list I can mention Queen Rania, Queen Mother of Jordan, Yassar Arafat the Commander of Palestine, Mr. Kofi Anan Secretary General of the U.N.O. who is a friend, Dr. R. Roy and Dr. Don Conroy and Mr. Rudi Luger ex-president of the Netherlands, Mr. and Madam Michele Gorbochev and countless others holding highly designated positions. I've been right down the line even to the refugees in the Palestinian camps, I've worked for flood victims, in earthquake refugee camps and a dozen other places where I put my best foot forward. If given a choice, I would still opt for the same life I have led, because in it I found my own fulfilment, through the trials and tragedies I have had the courage to face and to bear my own burdens. This is the "freedom" for which I fought.

I can easily state, that I embarked upon the strange life that I have led since I was fifteen years of age. Looking back now at eighty-three, I can admit that I have enjoyed His Benevolence bestowed so generously on me.

I've fought arduously for my freedom, but with it came enrichment and contentment, I can regale an audience with truly bizarre stories that are in fact true, not fiction. I have heard and seen across the span of over half a century, captivating episodes and very often mind boggling, but whatever they are, they are an integral part of the truth. Sometimes truth can be dubbed as "far – fetched" and "fiction" but when true drama becomes so scintillating, belief is shaken and the integral essence of veracity is questionable, even truth then wears a darkened veil and a dubious crown.

The stories are so profound that they are enthralling, perhaps, even mesmerize a sensitive audience, particularly if they are divulged by a narrator who delivers the story like a professional story-teller. Geffery Chaucer with his "Canterbury Tales" added picturesque words that vitalized the truth. A good teller brings a hint of colour, a sense of awe, or perhaps the ambience that creates empathy. The story emerges, bringing a new spectrum of emotions, giving birth to many questions that are raised in regard to the related bondmanship of the human brethren.

I had built for myself a little niche, a life of self dependence since the age of fifteen. In the fleeting years I became an unbridled and an exacting master to my own slavery to duty, to responsibility, to honesty and integrity to comforting and generosity. These are the virtuous I learnt though the decades of month long fasting and pray. In fact the constant examination of my own conscience urged me on, to be fearlessly proud and oblivious to the opinions addressed in my direction – perhaps the most I feared was my own fall to a complex – I had seen enough of needless "guilt" complexes, behaviours of the "psycho" destructions donning armour, by going into "denial". In each one I saw a warning signal for myself and endeavoured to side track it.

Now in my later years, I've been more silent than before, thinking before I speak, often sad at what I see behind the "dry eyed Bess", so much pain, or much sorrow, so much disillusionment sometimes hurt and even anxious apprehension. I want to reach out and give them hope and courage, but the norms of society do not condone entry into the private domain of others. Sometimes I hear the beginning of an appeal and then it stops, I too must stop, often the choice of a word tells me much, and I know I have the answer, so I spend a long night in wakefulness trying to kill my own desire to reach out to a phone so I can council. The night passes, the day moves on without any action and the moment of verbal exchange recedes into the dark and distant past.

I've learnt over the years to live two lives at the same time, I've learnt to smoother my desires, to live at a distance even if the mileage is close, the distance is my call and need for privacy. I thank my Maker for teaching me how to go to "confession" with myself – I cannot give myself "absolution", but I've learnt to recognize my faults and my weakness, thus I do my penance in silent modulation and heartfelt remorse, trying to overcome any weakness that lies within me.

Before I move on to write about myself, I have to introduce my parents, my family and my background.

★ ★ ★ ★ ★

Truth Conquers the Universe

MY LADY MOTHER MRS. ASMA JAFAR IMAM
The Greatest Lady in My Life - I Owe Her What I Am

As I write about the greatest lady in my life, Mrs. Asma Jafer Imam, for me she was a sparkling jewel and well loved. I remember nothing but the strength of her goodness, in the very fibre that ran through her and the blood, she sacrificed for others. The composition of her mind and heart was priceless. Despite her size, she was a "great-ball of fire, in a very tiny capsule", but all precious things come wrapped in small parcels. She was a direct descendant of a wealthy vein of royal blood, but she cared nothing about it, for she developed her personal self, ideologically maintaining, that what she had been endowed with, was a sacred trust, not for the benefit of herself but for the requirement of others. No one ever went without, if the required assistance was genuine – always ensuring that being taken for a ride, was not her type of open handed succour. All assistance had to actually reach the destination she intended.

Despite the open handed benevolence she was famous for, she observed the social and moral duties as the norms required, by the aristocratic class into which she was born. She had a rare mixture of presentations for all special occasions, and her society was made up of a plethora of individuals who were not socially bonded together, even if they varied in their religious persuasions. There were basically the English, as members of the British Government, Judges of the Upper Courts, and the Bureaucracy, with many Muslims and Hindus educated in England that also manned the bureaucracy. The professions of doctors, architects, lawyers and often professors were also manned by Jews, Parsies, Buddhists, and even some atheists, but socially all well-behaved with acceptance of one another's religious beliefs, thus they were always welcomed and entertained by my parents.

A great deal of talk existed, with regard and appreciation regarding Mother's ever-ready generosity, sustaining a consensus of opinion with praise-worthy anecdotes, that floated through the drawing-rooms, of the informal society meetings, at the clubs, the coffee parties, even the groups who met together doing war-work during the World War II. Everyone loved her smiles, happy nature, generosity of spirit and selfless attitude. She scintillated with life making any party a place of joyous fun. Her ballroom action accomplished, her contralto voice melodious and her comforting words soothing, as they flowed from her lips. People inevitably remarked that she possessed a "Golden Heart". Mentally I could not accept this type of mundane classified statement, regarding, this outstanding special lady for she really was praise worthy. It had no 'in depth' meaning, to me she was a lady with a "Heart of Liquid Gold".

I had watched my Mother, through clear open windows, of my mind for a life time, I had witnessed her humility and her heart rendering reactions, when there was a merciful appeal, I had seconded her comforting condolences, I had helped her to nurse ill friends in hospital, she was always present at the hospital to help, when babies were to be born, fearsome mothers to be walked up and down for forty-eight hours and sometimes more, when they struggled to endure distressing labour pains. She was always at hand with something to drink, some joke to be cracked and quite often a scolding to a non co-operative mother, struggling with her own personal dissatisfaction at the prolonged labour. In those days, pregnancies, deliveries and labour, received no aided medical assistance to kill the labour pains, or hurry on the deliveries with the magical epidural of today, or a quick Caesarean operation for easy delivery by busy doctors, who these days are "scalpel happy" for quick results, like the cowboys of the past who were "trigger happy" and anxious to move on, to other pastures, Reviewing my Mother's past actions and way of life, I undertook and did a mental autopsy on her sainted character, which unfolded before me a beautiful sincere lady embodied, with a heart that was a stream of liquid gold, trickling down in streams of purity unafraid of obstructions. She recognized no such word as "inability" always available to quench a thirst, to give succour to those in dire need. This was the fundamental pattern of her life. She was a queen with a beauty of face, but far more beautiful, were her deeds as she carried the vitals of "bread and water" to the needy.

At the benevolent age of almost eighty-one she breathed her last in my arms, saying her last prayer and looking at me, when the light left her eyes and her spirit flew to God, by cherubs on the wing. I am grateful to Allah who brought me from London, to nurse her in the last two months of her life and allowed me the honour, to bathe her precious body myself and lay her out ready for her Eternal rest.

Before my mother died, she once again repeated to me the story of the mendicant before I was even conceived, that I would stand by her with love and care, even into death.

With both my parent's departure, those chapters of my life closed. I began to embrace the many other chapters of my life with undivided attention, true dedication, with greater spiritual humility. My footsteps were unplanned, yet they took me to all parts of the world, spreading the doctrine of "PEACE" as called for by the Holy Quran. I attended World Conferences for nearly two and a half decades, during which time I learnt to live out of suitcases – Now I am adept, at packing suitcases and being a one night stop-over traveller.

Being a descendant of such an elevated background from where we emanate, our responsibilities, our duties and our cultural guardianship is required above the usual, it becoming an important part of our educational training.

Mother inducted the norms of gracious living, the arrangement of flowers for different occasions, the unusual decorative presentations in areas of a room that needed high lighting. I was to learn in later years that the magnificent arrangements of flower decoration were contrived by Constant Spry of London. I was so taken by her style that when I returned to England a couple of years after World War II, I went to Constant Spry and took a week of lessons based on her flower presentations and formal decoration. Every important hall of prestigious Hotels, and even some of the elevated banks, consortiums, high grade commercial houses boasted a Constant Spry's welcoming flower presentations in their entrance halls. Conversely the huge fascinating imperial presentations were challenged by crisp diminutive flower arrangements that were the model outcome of the Ikabana Creations. In later years when I visited Japan I took a special tour, that revealed scores of shapes presented by the Ikabana style created with wood, twigs, the odd leaf here and lacy ferns there, wires, sponges, shells and coloured stones from the quarries, stood side by side with waxy flowers and flimsy blossoms sharing the flat wood base on which the arrangements were anchored down and held with green cord, olive wiring and damp mossy sponge, that kept the presentations of leaves and flowers free from sagging. I could not really say which style of presentation was the best, both styles were master pieces each in their own world.

Mother was a fine painter herself, she had us taught art, the piano, she even yielded to my own desire to learn the violin. In later years I learnt to play the "Sur-bahaar" a type of "sitar" but with very much more elevated tones and the texture of vibrations. It is not often played with a group of musicians working together, it has a vast dimension of notes, cords, cadences and tones and even semi-tones, enabling one to produce a deeper and more appealing melody with scintillating, muted, soft and subtle melodies that enrich the presentations of compositions. It carries several wires more than the ordinary "sitar" aiding the player to enhance the performance with double tones played at the same time keeping in harmony the beat and the rhythm of the original composition. This I learnt to perform well, because my heart and soul were in it, and because a part of my inner-most emotions were involved with that great big pumpkin from Africa, that forms the heart of the instrument. The wooden shaft that holds the wires and bars for the scales, run the length of the shaft coming to a halt, where a beautiful tail flows upwards, forming a graceful elongated curled scroll turning inwards. The scroll was as beautiful as the ones that are to be found in the Regency and Georgian Architectural pillars, which grace London's streets. The scroll architecture has been borrowed by the British Americans, who migrated to America, years later long after the pilgrim Fathers, who took their life of simplicity to the new world. But as years fled by the New World changed and once again looked homeward and brought the style of elaborate living to the New American World. Time moves and modern glass has taken over the high rise buildings in America and many parts of the great cities across the continents.

Whatever I have become today I give the credit with deep gratitude to my Mother for bestowing it on me. She was my Mother, but more than that, she was my friend and teacher. She sowed numerous types of seeds in me, she encouraged me to be unafraid, to face the world bravely, never to deviate from the truth, to defend what I believe in, and defend it with courage. She taught me the pleasures one obtains from the act of giving and sharing with selfless motivation. She exhorted me to exude strength, to protect the weak, to cook and feed the "have nots", but for ones self, one must devour only enough to keep body and soul together. I learnt from her the art of gracious giving, in a manner that brought no distress, of being beholden to no one, I learnt the happiness that comes with sharing, but more than that, she taught me to be a slave to my conscience and she conveyed to me the need of "submission", the need to accept the Divine Will, the obligation that I must be generous to 'His' children. Leading me to recognize the merciful Benefits He bestowed on me, the Generosity and Graciousness in which He has enfolded me. Mother still lives in me with every action I render – at the moments of my happiness, my awards and my earthly rewards she stands silently with me. She was indeed a worldly woman, but a saintly one. Her pilgrimage to the Holy Kaaba at Mecca was performed three times. She refused even the barest suggestion, that she should go to Saudi Arabia by plane, she refused to go with the Ambassador, who went to receive her at the ship. She travelled on the bus to Mecca, but not by car, she explained the reason for her refusal. The Pilgrimage is supposed to be performed with humility in simplicity, without the comforts and ease that is now considered normal.

It was for her, a true spiritual submission, with each "Haj" that took her five months to complete. She lived in the pilgrim camps, ate only boiled rice and a thick lentil soup twice a day. Only one cup of tea at dawn, a little fruit at mid-day or some plain salad with lemon and water, this was her daily routine where her food was concerned. She boarded the boat from Bombay to Jeddah as an ordinary deck passenger. From Jeddah she travelled to Mecca by the public bus service, that is used by the common pilgrims to cross the desert. It was no air-conditioned limousine for her. A small mat to lie on, a tiny piece of foam acted as her pillow and a pair of sheets and two towels made up a small utility roll strapped with leather which she carried on her back. A small convase bag, contained her special "pilgrimage robes" and her basic and limited toilet possessions she carried, herself – no porter or other pilgrim did she allow to carry anything for her.

On her return her face shone with radiance, her health was stable and her speech was mellow, as she always believed in the existence of "Heaven and Hell", so she was naturally gentler, kinder, more generous, more enduring, and a total giver. For more than thirty years, she filled her "Heavenly Treasury" with the favours that Allah has commanded as the spiritual and human roll for mankind.

In hindsight when I review the past decades of my age, when I weigh the circumstances that elevated me to the position which I now hold, and the worthy trust of International World Communities, I need to assess and recognize the pivot point of my development and acknowledge, that it is due to the diligent teaching, care and the rich nurturing given to me by my devoted, honourable, dearly loved and beloved parents.

It is amazing that two people, so poles apart in their characteristics and personalities, could join together to form a union of such compatibility when joined in marriage, each using their individual responsibility, to cement the bond and together becoming a single united entity, from whom we their off springs derived, the benefits of their example of integrity, ethics and graciousness on which we developed our own lives.

My Father, was not only an intellectual, but a giant of a highly elevated and potent law giver – his innumerial and monumental judgements, are quoted widely even today in the esteemed law courts of both India and Pakistan. Every senior judge and superior lawyer respects my Father's name and his remarkable clarity of judgments. The pivot point was not just his legal knowledge, but his highly elevated awareness that constituted his distinctive legal mind. He possessed, prowess and the intellectual expertise of a brilliant brain, that placed him on a pedestal as an outclassed man of excellence. His elevation to the position of Chief Justice of India, placed and confirmed the mark of his competence, and ability in the field of litigation, where he had tough competition as a member of a minority Muslim Community. He was surrounded by highly developed and sound legal minds of a majority Hindu community and that too in a Hindu oriented country. My Father was amongst the last of the British peers to be knighted in India – but the Indian community gaining independence rejected and returned the British knighthoods and all the awards at the end of World War II. It was a movement of defiance and a non-aggressive battle for self rule, and the call for Independence of the subcontinent. Non co-operation had become the paramount point of resistance, for the vast population of the sub-continent. It had become a civil war of silent protests, silent processions and hunger strikes, a large number of politicians and Mr. Mahatma Gandhi himself were incarcerated in jails and 'force feeding' was the "modus operandi" taken by the Government itself.

My father Syed Jafar Imam was a man of unflinching honour integrity and principals, this time-honoured man was my Father, it was due to his interest that I was inducted into the process of my mental training. With my mind that was extremely fertile, he recognized this ability, despite my young age, thus he planted the seeds and implanted them well, because he was a caring gardener, he nurtured my mind, leading it into the numerous paths and avenues that I was to traverse. His guardianship over my mental process continued even after I was married.

Father discussed and taught me the law, the power of deduction with all its practices, he tutored me, leading me through the tangled web of philosophy, he introduced me to the plots of Plato, Aristotle, Shakespeare and to the biographies of some great men such as Danta, William Pitt and Galileo. He guided me through the ever changing knotty strands of politics, imparting to me the assessment of screening situations and even the hidden personalities of those who I met. I soon learnt to decipher and detect from what I observed, I ceased to take everything at its face value. I gradually attained the ability to analyze comments, interpret gestures, evaluate expressions, to assay glances, thus I never passed judgement, but smiled at the social-climbing statements and manoeuvres for advancement.

Father was not a man to smile, or silently ignore what he believed was an incorrect statement, sometimes he held his peace if the occasion demanded it, but if defence was needed for the honour of someone else, or something important he would make a serious defence statement. He would excuse himself from any company that failed to display respect for the principals of truth. He believed that there should be room only for honesty and justice, it laid the foundations against the decay of moral responsibility. If there was error of judgement, or plain misunderstanding, much could be condoned, but not as a shield for protection.

I remember an occasion when I was home, as Father and I sat in the shadow of the high hedges and beautifully sculptured trees, making a peaceful backdrop at the rear end of the garden, from where we observed our mansion house, surrounded by velvet rolling green lawns, mauve flowering jacaranda and yellow laburnum trees. We peacefully sat in reclining deck-chairs, drinking cold lemonade with freshly squeezed lemon and orange juice. We both fell into contented silence.

The morning sky had an azure hue, with a springtime transparency of the palest aqua blue, birds had stopped their morning twittering, bees their humming drone, and tittering crickets snoozed after a mid-morning snack of insects. Our half a dozen dogs were sprawled out on the grass nearby, with eyes closed, but one ear open keeping guard for the faintest alien sound.

Such a calm and friendly peace reigned over us, that perhaps I too could have dozed off, but my ever alert brain kept ticking and I knew that sleep was only a far off desire – but I, being the slave to my forever searching mind, posed my father a question, "Father would you be able to tell me where fact ends and fiction starts. Is there really a turning point?" Father came alert saying, "Anese I thought you may have dosed off for a catnap snooze, you have been so quiet today. Is there something that is troubling you? Life is a checkerboard of night and day, as Omar Khayyam tells us in his "Rubiyaat" so if we have a problem today then I assure you there will be a sunrise tomorrow.

I was not surprised at the similitude as his command over the English language was phenomenal "No Father, nothing is really that wrong, or troubling me, but all the conviction that religion holds for us, makes me think of the unknown. How can we actually know what is fact or for that matter what is fiction – there is no proof. If we fail to obtain proof where there is none, then how could we know what is to be done and what may not be done."

After a few moments his unexpected answer came "Anese this is a very profound question and I admire your courage to speak so openly regarding your search for the truth. Fact is "truth" and "religion" is belief, so when one believes, then there is no requirement for proof. Belief in itself is the foundation of "belief". In a way one may consider the facts that have surrounded, the great men of their time and what they later passed down in documentation, then those after them termed it as fact. Even the visions they received as such, which they in turn instructed to their followers and then, their followers who have taught it down through the ages, from generation to generation, thus we accept the spiritual belief of yesterday as a fact of today.

I had been listening very intently so I said to him, "Father I am able to accept and follow this theory, but I cannot accept it as a fact in the normal sense of the word, hence I prefer to consider it as "Belief" with no proof, no strings attached and no conformity. I have given it an immense amount of thought and a great deal of research to find a substantial reason to call it fact, but have not yet found one. I have come to the conclusion that within man, the marks of good and bad already exist from the time of birth, or perhaps even earlier. I see religion as the honest and the pure, I see the cruelty in man and his injustice, I see unabated greed, yet I observe that there is humility, there is a great deal more of beatitudes in man, which fans out from magnetism that ousts oppression .

In my reckoning I have discovered that I prefer to liken man to children, who need to be taught to recognize that there is a system of "Reward and Punishment" for their actions. The world would be a better place if we awarded degrees for the practical".

Looking at me intently he remarked, "Anese are we the evidence of our own behaviour? I am amazed to see how simplified you have made the greatest of all philosophies. It is true that there is a "Heaven and Hell" or even the dreaded wave length of "Reward and Punishment". Man in the final analysis, is his own keeper."

After awhile Father continued, "I really desire that life could be that easily simplified, but since we deal with human beings, who are created in very large numbers of different modes, we cannot approach everyone with the same brush and in the same way. It is also absolutely necessary to look at each person as an individual, many are strong and wend their way through life, creating their own formula of living, others are effected by their environment and the company they keep, while others are sadly the victims of a debilitating sell out. The selfish greed of materialism and it's allure can be resisted by far too many, but it's sparkle is like the beckoning glints of gold, and the enticing ripples on a ensnaring lake, creating a pivot of irresistible desire. The changing process gradually emerges as a challenge over a period of time, then later emanates to a point of no return".

This was a new tack Father had moved onto, so I said, "Father I have always been deeply interested in philosophy and the works of Plato and Aristotle, but I have not yet learnt enough or the in-depth meaning of life – and perhaps death too. There are several missing vibes somewhere and I keenly desire to find them. How shall I seek them out? Must I seek them out by practicing them as is the way of the sufis. I've read about the Zen philosophy, but not enough to acquire the depth of meaning that is meant by the arches of life. I've read and understood the basic philosophy of the Holy Quran, but I have not yet co-related it to a way of life and living. It has to have something deeper about life to be the Masterful Book of the World".

Suddenly Father raising his hand he stopped me, "Anese hold it right there! The time is far too early for you to develop that understanding. You are only now entering the gate of spiritual norms and values. You must have to live in this world before you can talk of philosophy, life and living. You have a long journey ahead of you – there is much to learn, philosophy is in fact a basic of the "modus operandi" by which man may comprehend the conduct of his life, fulfil his aspirations, enjoy the beauty and the free benevolent gift of nature. You have to learn to honour the ethics of the great men, procreate the generations by loving and giving. This is indeed the philosophy that wise men seek. They have mastered control over their minds and bodies, abound with fortitude, are bent without complaint, accepting hardship with sacrificing, and bending in submission themselves, mastering and marshalling their desires, at the alter of obedience to the law giver of Life. They emerge as great men of wisdom being powerful men in the fulfilment of their own duties, lives and emanate as an example for others to follow."

My mind was turning into new avenues so I asked, "Father do I need so long a time to comprehend the spiritual "saga of life." With a benevolent smile he slowly said, "yes my dearly loved daughter, I sense the birth of inspiring spiritualism developing in you, you are on the right path of what we both seek, you are about to enter the gates of the true philosophy of living – The base words here are "life and living" when you have attained the heights you seek, your pursuit has begum to have meaning, you shall aspire for entering the boundless sphere of the beyond, then life will take on a new meaning. The landscapes will emerge in varying hues, blended with subtle co-related colours that will harmonize and sooth your heart, it will sparkle in the brightness of your eyes, your days shall be cradled, your nights spent in sweet peaceful slumber and your spirit surrendered to Allah.

Go after what you desire, nurture what you have attained, forsake the company that clutch to hold you back, fasten yourself to the truth, anchor your soul with the chains of prayer, truth and submission, only then you shall emerge victorious."

I was relieved that he understood my requirement for inner peace, "Then you do approve that there is some hope for me to receive the "Greatest of all Lights" that I'm searching for. I sometimes see a ray of hope and then it vanishes, to return at another time."

Father caught my hand pressed it saying, "I believe you are on the right path. If I doubted your ability to cope I would have refrained from encouraging you. Because you are different, I have encouraged you to read, given you free reign in my vast multi-dimension library. When you were only fifteen, I was aware that you were reading a series of books written by Radcliff Hall. I found a postcard addressed to you, that you probably used as a book mark. I frequently wondered if you understood the underlying meaning that rested between those pages. Perhaps I had been wrong, to permit you to get acquainted with some of the books that lined the shelves of my personal library at that early age."

I quickly interjected, "No Father, I did not really fully understand at that time, many of the very sensitive books in your library like the "Well of Loneliness", "Lady Chatterly's lover", "Sons and Lovers", and even the "Dark Romances of a King". But one thing you can be proud of is, that what I did learn, prepared for me the stance I took regarding the morals of my own life and I also learnt not to censure the immoral behaviour of others. From those books I learnt the power of psychology, the power of sex, the debilitating power that works on the weakness of human beings. Due to my early reading, I learnt not to condemn, but to find reasons to exonerate what society calls "shameless deeds." I cannot condone them nor accept them as right, but I cannot condemn them, when in actual fact the weakness and flaw of nature, or the weakness of character, or just a weakness and acts fulfilling desire, for infact the acts are of what is termed as "immorality"

There are no hard and fast rules, for they change according to culture.

> *There is no good, there is no bad*
> *It is the twist of human will*
> *The things we weal we term them good*
> *The things that hurt we call them ill.*
> *And in the various span of time*
> *Each vice has worn a virtues crown*
> *Each virtue dabbed as sin and crime*
> *They change with race with time and place*
> *~ Haji Abdul Salam*

Strongest of all the senses, often over-powers the strongest of men and the weakness of submission in women."

By this time Father had the chance to observe my many facets "I marvel at your generous approach regarding the vices of man, but I am indeed pleased, in fact very pleased to share your moral understanding of others, while you have your own morals well adjusted and kept reined in well, at the same time. Your ability to comprehend the forces of nature, and your search for the "light" is commendable, you know well that I'll always be there for you to speak to me, you are still very young.

I'm hoping, that from time to time we have the opportunity to sit together like this and discuss such elevated subjects. I'm interested in the path your mind is taking and the road of your philosophical and spiritual leanings."

★ ★ ★ ★ ★

Truth Conquers the Universe

READING BOOKS ON
MANY TOPICS
A Penchant to Read Expanded
My Library Very Rapidly

This conversation took place many, many years ago. It was after my marriage when my daughter was approximately only four to five years of age. Subsequently I rammed my head into all kinds of books, I did a great deal of in depth reading from every philosophy I could lay my hands on. Books from the Zen Philosophy taught me to look through seven arches, one within the other before I make any serious decision, for in a way man has to follow the decision made by previous generations. The arches represent seven generations of man, all acts should be conducive and beneficial to the coming generations that are connected and on whose shoulders the burdens fall. I've been through the Bhagvat Gita, that consistently forbids the destruction or infliction of harm to any living thing. The Hindu philosophy indicates the fact, that, roots that form our food, may not be consumed – because in doing so some worm, small insect or even their larvae may be disturbed and die, if the roots are pulled out of the earth. The Hindu diets cannot accept the presence of garlic, onions, ginger, carrots, radish and peanuts in the preparation of their food or a number of other edible plants that are normally consumed in vegetarian dishes.

I've read through the "Ramayan" and read the Gita of the Great Buddha several times – it is written by a Prince of great spiritual strength, possessing will power over his desire, for which he has to be greatly admired. Therein is a light so pure, it is adequate for human philosophy at its best and at the same time it declares his vast generosity bestowed of nature.

The Jewish Toras is a combination of ancient history with a developing code of "dos" and don'ts" coming down through the ages, expounding the Gift of Jehovah and the history of punishment for desecrations of the Holy Orders brought down from the mountain by Moses one of the oldest Prophets of the Jewish scripture and acknowledged by the Holy Book of the four Revealed religions, Jews, Christian, Muslims and Sabions.

The Bible conveys the creation of the world by a Powerful God, it divulges the loss of Heaven and the state of grace by Adam and Eva, and it warns of Satan's Hell. It tells of love and hatred between Cain and Able. It enumerates the Generosity and the punishment delivered by the Master Creator in the devastation of the tribe of Noah, the Pillars of salt for the rejecters of good, in the time of the Prophet Lot, it divulges the Benevolence bestowed on Joseph and the destruction of the Temple of Soloman. He is a God of love, but also a God of Justice.

The Pharoahs suffered from rivers of blood, seven years of draught and seven years of famine, while King David the gifted Prophet of God was forbidden to touch the tabernacle, for the grave sins he had committed, until his prayer for forgiveness was heard and he was granted forgiveness, then he was once more raised in status.

The Wisdom full of sound philosophy, was a blessing given to King Soloman, great men from afar, came to his court to hear him propound the wisdom gifted to him. He spoke and they came, even the Queen of Sheba could not resist his wisdom she came to bow before him.

With vast reading I appear to have gleaned the fruitful benefits of my reading habits, so when I developed the urge to make an in depth search for greater Islamic knowledge, I turned to the Holy Quran, at first I found it appealing and as I delved deeply, I did not find it difficult to comprehend, or co-relate it with my life. The philosophy of good living is a fundamental and basic requirement, for man to live within a community. The philosophy of life is to be found between the pages of the Holy Books.

During the decades of reading, I acquired an appreciable amount of knowledge. I have taught myself, the purification of my spirit and during the past years as I kept up my progressive reading, at a ferocious and relentless pace and I feel my worth has magnified. There are ups and downs in every sphere of life, yet I see life in its multiple and diverse forms. There is no sea without ripples, but tidal waves appear without apparent reason, the sun rises bright in all its glory, yet at dusk it leaves behind a trail of total darkness, again to be revitalized by the rise of dawn. Life is full of summer draught and winter ice, the spring blooms are riotous in colour, yet they shrivel and whither with a short spell of summer sun. Rain descends to feed the crops making fields verdant and green, spring showers are needed, thus man's faith is his survival. But those who imbibe the drunken power that comes with material worship, are soon victims of a flood that washes away the power of man.

There was much to learn and even now, in my octogenarian years I am still reading and learning, the process never ends.

My years of education moved on from school to college, from college to marriage and motherhood, but I was adamant to continue, to learn through the process of reading which I devoured faster than a book-worm in a Library. I spent money on books rather than fruitless entertainment, I sought out the great books of philosophers, of Plato and Aristotle, the great works of Danta and the emotional theories of Freud. Also the Roman, Egyptian and Islamic histories, graced the shelves of my library, the revolutions of the Saracens also, the inquisition of Spain, and the Revolution of France captured my mind. I once more turned to the East for knowledge, in my search I was enthralled by the conquers of the East, such as Changez Khan, Tamur Lane and Alexander. The Philosophies of Buddha, Zen and Rumi began to take their place on the book shelves of my study, which month by month expanded as I began the transformation of my mind, being a voracious reader, it gave me intense pleasure. My conscience refrained from conceding me any time off, from my encumberent house-wifely duties. To a great extent it was difficult, but I made the time, I had to surrender the needed hours of my nightly sleep to acquire the knowledge I hungered after. As a rewarding result of this nightly flagrantly blatant indiscipline, I become a habitual night owl, not hooting, but dispassionately scooping up the contents with compelling avarice, the medlay of volumes that lined my book shelves.

In the past two to three decades, these hours burnt under the midnight oil have unstintingly aided and bequeathed to my diverse topics. Copious pages roll off my pen on winged feet, the material issues of my books are the product of my vast reading and search for knowledge. My work covers a number of books and endless educational books that range through spirituality, poetry, English Literature, Philosophy, a series of Urdu Books and last but not the least, infact the most important of all is my work on Islam in English, dealing with the commonalities of the Revealed religions. Now at eighty three, I still have my pen racing at two o'clock in the morning in an attempt to conclude my biography.

My educational years became one long crammed event, where I quaffed, gorged like a glutinous gourmet, guzzling every article in print that bore the aura of self expression. I challenged the strength of my augmenting courage, that was developing at a fleeting pace. At the same time that this change in my individuality was racing ahead, I found new dimensions working their way into my sub-consciousness, generating in me a maturity that was urgently needed, if I was to maintain my freedom and my independence. I was very much aware that women were being prevented from attaining their natural potential and their human rights. Infact men held such dominance over women, which was an unacceptable act of human bondage, and men who endorsed this were slaves to chauvinism, misusing their physical male strength to subdue the frailty of woman, giving men illegitimate power, to boost what they themselves lost in a variety of self weakness of their own conditions, passing on to women their own ailment in a state of "Psychological denial".

I had barely finished my college days, when I was made up to be the bride of a husband of my own choosing. I embarked on the voyage of marriage, being launched into a totally new and unfamiliar society, where parties, and dinners were attended almost on a nightly basis, drinks and cocktails made the rounds of almost every social household. Club functions and gambling rooms, from card-playing, to horse-racing, to the antecedents of prized live stock, were of paramount importance. Stud farms dotted the hinterland of Bombay, Madras and other important cities. Each club had a stream of memberships from the Princely courts, big bosses of large commercial firms and well endowed landlords could be observed in almost every sector of the club.

Billiard rooms were never vacant, bridge rooms boasted a full capacity of gamblers, who played at a guinea a point in the early fifties. No one went to the bar, the bar was brought to a member, served by uniformed waiters glamorized with red and gold or green and gold turbans with glittering breast-plates and wide cummerbunds to match. There were 'swimming galas' and horse racing seasons, there were hunting safaris and grey hound racing. There was far too much of dissipated time, wasted energy and worst of all squandered money, while the poor and villagers could hardly make ends meet, leave alone the absence of a full or decent meal. The fate of the poor was to serve, they never lived, there was no acknowledgement of health requirements since the topic never surfaced they got no chance to heal – they just died – burnt on a funeral pier and sent down the river or buried to be soon forgotten in an unmaintained graveyard.

Those were the days when I learnt to listen, to watch, to absorb and to relegate to my memory what was around me. I learnt to keep silent, to sift, to refute and to plan my own life, in the way I felt and had been taught what was morally wrong and what was religiously right. One most important factor that I did learn, was not to judge or condemn – each man is entitled to plan and live his life by his own design. The right and the wrong was not my concern, no condemnation fell from my lips, but I assiduously learnt how to mould and groom my own life. This early experience that opened my eyes, gave me even a greater determination to be mistress of myself and this strength has served me well.

My life has been a checkerboard of happiness and sorrow, of hopes and then disillusionment, of trust and betrayal, of hurt and forgiveness, of hunger and fulfilment that played its part in the drama of my life. Today I have been rewarded with success in many fields. I have educated the children of four generations, I have re-established a "living" life for a large number of paraplegics and drug edicts while I served in the army. Allah granted me to bring water with my "tube-well" scheme to cover a vast area of arid land, comprising nearly one hundred barren villages. I've written books on Islam, Spiritualism, Education and poetry. I have lectured on Islam from one end of the globe to the other. All this has brought me acknowledgement which I never sought, but the honourable reward of my country, now most of all, I am at peace with myself with my total submission to Allah to serve as His hand-maiden.

In the process of learning I gradually rid myself of dogmatic views, I acquired the sense of acceptance of human rights, of weakness and debility, I absorbed philosophy, enabling me to see the gentle dawn that rises after every midnight of storm, I was attracted to reach out to ascend beyond the stars, all be it that my journey has been a lonely one. The galaxy abounds with sparkle and allure, but that journey through darkness has to be travelled alone, star-work is more or less an opposition, they form benevolent triangles, create difficulties and disaster in forming the squares they make, they never move in parallel unison as their transit is singular. Thus my journey through life, made me emerge as a singular aspirant, on the ghost train that moved through the dark tunnels of the night sky.

Today I am alone, as I have been for the past five decades, which commenced as I read the spiritual work of Rumi, the Masnavi and other Sufi poets. I stepped into a "mental sufi" mode, I withdrew for the social world of pleasure, clubs and finance. Plain white and that too in cotton, was the only apparel I donned to cover my body for two years. My mind and emotion got wrapped up in the printed pages of the Holy Quran, that advised me to share, to fast, bestow benevolence, to practice charity, donate help for the stricken, to feed the hungry, to worship deeds of kindness, instead of accumulating wealth. In the process I saw the tiniest vestige of self gratification. The besetting problem of poverty, had the poorest of relief. The upper class didn't even have the perception, or the awareness that, the basic citizens who were in the majority were going without a square meal. Those who lived in the villages consumed the natural food the earth provided, but they could not consume what was meant to be sold as crops, or what was gleaned in at the harvest. Fruit from the orchards were forbidden for self consumption, as the substance or product represented sale and sale, signaled more money, money was to be reinvested, not to be eaten to argument a sub-standard meal.

The search for knowledge, this left me as a hungry beast searching for relevant matter to augment my knowledge. I burnt the mid-night oil with such regularity that it became my second skin and a part of my natural physical routine with sleep only for four to five hours at night, with several nights in a row of three to four hours. I gleaned much by day and wrote by night, but my writing could only flow, to fill page after page in the stillness of the night, in an acquisitive peace of mystic silence. It is a time that must be used, for if not harnessed one could sink into the soft appealing folds of day-dreams, spinning words, weaving a story of oneself that is fantasizing, or surrendering to melancholy. Night is the richest time for provoking thoughts, summoning words, recalling situations, is addition the world's problems are wrapped, shrouded in the mantle of a long dark night.

I had married early and gave birth to a daughter who I named Moniba when I was only nineteen and a half years of age, but my mind and maturity was very advanced and far ahead of my years. I surrendered my one dearly beloved daughter who slipped away on an angle's wings at the tender blush of her birth she was only six weeks old. It was my experience with death and my first encounter with tragedy, but I had not much time to mourn her loss for once again I found myself pregnant. It was an easy pregnancy, thanks be to Allah, as I did a great deal of travelling across India. I returned home often to see my parents who were now living alone, in a sprawling house with acres of marble flooring. Hugh slabs that covered the floor space, that even ran into a never-ending marble terrace, bordered by an almost unblemished black marble perimeter. Dozens of marble pillars supported the high roof of the spacious verandas and the terrace that descended covering the sweeping expanse of shallow Grecian steps, flanked by slender urn shaped railings of the descending steps, where it met dark green lawns that rolled out, down to the flowering shrubs at the rear of the garden. A red bricked path that circumvented the entire building, exhibiting the beauty of the well planned, proportional architecture that gave it the appearance of grandeur.

This was the official residence of the Chief Justice of the Bihar Court. My Father a few years later went to Delhi as a member of the Supreme Court of India and later took his place as the Chief Justice of India.

Mother and Father lived alone in that dazzling white historical colonial monument that had always been the abode of the Chief Justice of Bihar. We their fledglings had fled the nest, to live and create homes with our marriage partners while a growing generation of young chicks of our own were keeping us busy. My brother Akbar was still in London completing the required three years of law practice from Middle Temple after leaving Trinity College in Cambridge with an M.Sc. honours in Science, then "called to the Bar" from Middle Temple of the Inns of Court in London.

I could not accept calmly, that the now empty home of my parents was a soundless mausoleum, so I returned every few weeks to spend a fortnight with them, or a week at some celebration time. The opportunities that I had during these sojourns with my Father gave me plenty of time for appropriate discussions, I learnt a great deal from him. Our week-ends were a period of great delight for him, we relaxed and yet he taught me law, in which he briefed me well, it comes back to me from time to time, by some natural instinct, but his meticulous grooming conferred on me a depth of understanding and the polished presentation in which I even now convey myself. I often have a renaissance of the past, as the years and decades roll back with fleeting time that slips away.

But to my regret and aching heart my idyllic time with him was cut short. He was at the height of his career as the Chief Justice of India, when he was struck down by a cerebral stroke. It was not long after that he breathed his last, but I was not there with him as I was living in Pakistan, and residing in Peshawar where my husband was a very high ranking officer of the Pakistan Air Force. That was at the end of the 1965 war with India, when diplomatic ties had been severed and any communication across the boarders was impossible. I learnt of his demise from a "News bulletin" that was broadcast from Radio India declaring a period of three days of "mourning" as a respect due to him. All the courts of India had closed for that period of time. Ministers, Ambassadors, the Prime Minister Jawaharlal Nehru himself with Mrs. Indira Gandhi and a host of others high ranking dignitaries came to condole with my well loved and respected Mother. As an Air Force Officer's wife I was debarred from making that trip home, to see my Father's face, or mourn alongside my Mother, to give her the comfort she needed. But in my mind and heart my Father never died, I live in memory amongst his souvenirs of words and wisdom he ungrudgingly taught me. I was blessed and fortunate to have him not only as my Father, but also as my teacher and devoted friend.

Perhaps it is at this stage that I should present my Mother's participation in my life. I would be unable to proceed unless I presented, a minute character sketch of the great lady and humane woman that she was. She was diminutive in size and in statue, just touching five feet, very slim and petite into her late thirties, when after a series of surgical operations she put on some extra weight. She may have been "little" but she was a very large and effective cylinder of dynamite, and a whirlwind of activity plus a quick but competent fighter. There is an expression in the Urdu Language that would reveal the dynamic quality she possessed it says "A small little chilly, but burns like a scalding flame". But I prefer to dub her with "All precious things come wrapped in small parcels." That is my incomparable Mother.

It is amazing the versatile power she possessed, her attributes were countless, her beauty a petite "French Poupa Doll" with her beguiling smile, bright eyes that were alert but sparkled with mirth, good cheer and happiness. She was a lady of dauntless courage, unafraid of the devil himself. She tread with confidence where "even angles fear to tread." She was too alert to be caught in the mesh of any spider's web. Her love of music and song was inherent, her voice melodious and her happy singing melodies filled our home.

Mother loved the tasteful apparel that hung in her wardrobes. She had an eye for elegant and chic outfits and the quality never fell below the elegant. Clothes and accessories had to be well matched or she refused to call it "good dressing". The colours she chose for herself were never plain, bright or garish, yet the colours she wore were alive and blended with becoming hues. Mother had a fascination for the superior and original texture of fabrics. It was from her that I learnt to dress and mix my outfits, till my entire wardrobe spoke of an elegant and a chic mode of apparel. In streamlining my attire to simple lines without frills and bows, I acquired a reputation of being individualistic and paraded as a model of my own fashion, yet everything I wore had been in current fashion, apart from the usual run of what the society ladies favoured for wearing. This individualism I owe to my late mother's example – I followed the trend in fashion but kept my individuality, because I stand at of five feet seven and a half inches which was a good seven to eight inches taller than my Mother.

Mother inculcated in me the love of poetry, she inducted me into the pages of Tennyson and Browning, to the verses and philosophy of Omar Khayyam. She introduced me at a very early age, to become acquainted with the teachings of the laws of the Holy Quran. She encouraged me to learn to sing, to dance, to paint and even knit, crochet and excel in needle-point. But my instruction did not end there, for she herself was a fabulous cook, thus she instructed me on how to cook, to make menus, match the appropriate drinks, to the food that was served, the correct dressing of a dining table, that was an integral part of a competent and accomplished hostess. There was so much else to learn during the several years that followed my return from England. She passed on to me all that I needed to be a "Hostess with the Mostess". It makes me remember her and be grateful almost everyday and several times in a day as I go about my duties as a housewife. I send her a silent prayer of thanks every night – My Beloved and Sainted Mother lives ever at my side.

As you would have assessed from the previous pages that at a very young age I cultivated notions of my own as to what was best for me. But unfortunately in reality this is a self deceiving notion, I to my unexpected cost found that life could shatter and it does not bestow the fulfilment of one's desires, or dreams on the basis of one's own singular concept of life. There are mountains and valleys to be traversed, there are oceans and seas to be crossed, there are huge wild areas of forests and even wider stretches of desert to be negotiated, there is happiness and rewards to receive but they all fall in together to paint the personal canvas of each one's life. These emotional pictures give life, lights and shades and are the meaning of life and existence. Some canvases are barren and others emotional, some are just pleasant scenes in passing, while several are dramatically breath-taking and scintillating with power and beauty, some presentations are harmonizing and peaceful. But my life's "Canvas" is not in the style of the old master painters, or the productions by abstract artists nor the "new age" splash and contours of modernism.

My life's picture according to precedents was basically poised to be classic, but with the swift rotation of eras it incorporates the world of today, into which I found myself. Despite the modernism, this new world that beckoned was a farce and far from anything remotely trendy. For all my independence, I wove a canvas that blends in colour the tissues of the life, I have woven with the colours of my own, discriminating in my choices, but in the field of my unprotected destiny, I have reaped as I have sown. I pause frequently, to stand back to gaze and assess the events of my life. I evoke the words of a great poet "Oh great God this gift to give us to see ourselves as others see us." I am unable to assess my own worth, but my effort has been to serve my inherent aspirations, I have endeavoured to present the best of my abilities. If I have been found wanting it is not due to lack of effort, but perhaps my personal inability to accept the unrestrained bondage that man puts upon his brother.

I have sincerely served and dedicated my life to some "extra sensory perception". It steeled me to embrace the truth giving me the courage necessitated to me stand on my own, despite the insecurity of being a "Loner".

My Canadian friend Peggy once discussed with me the concept of having the courage of one's convictions, in the belief that life is one's own, if so, does it become mandatory to live with a balanced vision of life, keeping in view, not the clarity of one's desires and its outcome conversely rejecting blindly the decisions of others. I told Peggy that I had made myself my own witness in my demand of plotting and planning a life for myself, but inevitably I also took the compiling and crucial responsibilities that would devolve upon my shoulders. Thus I unsealed the dedicated chambers of my associations and withdrew from the secure nest of a gracious and protective homestead, at the tender age of eighteen, expressing that I was a major and therefore free to rule my own life. Becoming a teacher at a pastoral nursery school, introduced me into the followed chains of convention. After five months. I missed the security of my ancestral haven, my defences were aroused I discovered that there was sagacity in persuasive words of deceit. It is unwise to take flight from the Cuckoos nest, my friend Peggy also had flown from her cuckoos nest. The trials and tribulations that both of us faced, have not been insignificant, but infact today we both stand firmly on our own feet, facing the challenges and undertaking the full burden of responsibilities on our own shoulders, still living with the wrong or right decisions, we took upon ourselves, living by the commitments we made, but most of all neither of us became the pawns of others, nor extend our hands for aid. Both Peggy and myself made a success of our lives, all be it that life was demanding sometimes and daunting, but we both have the perception that even if life had posed us stiff challenges, our lives have been most fulfilling.

In hindsight I acknowledge the consummate and the misconceived egoism with my determination to adjudicate my "right" to marry for the first time, was a blind show of independence – my parents advised, my Mother warned not to be impetuous yet gave me formally in marriage, but I basically declined to repudiate my arbitrary decision. I had rejected to contract a marriage alien to my wishes, for I presumed they would shackle me with their choice. My elder sister as a more respectable girl had accepted their choice, which she conformed to as is the way of proceeding in all the marriage requirements of the upper nobility of our august society. For us with our noble ancestral background, only a princely groom could be suitable, but these human trade agreements were conversely alien, in my opinion and unsuitable for marriage, particularly for me, as I could not willingly submit my "personal self" in surrender for the wishes of others, or because there was a formal document with a name bestowed on me, making me another man's property. I could not and would not acquiesce, to my being the formal possession of another human being. I was born to be free and it was my birth right, but I had not yet learnt the security of parental backing, nor the many many obligating benefits the girl receives, through these arranged marriages of convenience. I was not prepared to vow a questionable commitment, of "honour and obey" under conventional conditions, because I wore a wedding ring on my finger.

Marriage for me was love, a prince with charm, a dreamy eyed romantic poet, murmuring under a silver moon, a caring nurturing lover under stars as witness, but I was soon to learn to my detriment and dire emotional cost that my ideals were only dreams floating like dandelion puffs upon the wind – reality was extremely different in size, shape, form and colour. Little did I know or envisage that I was to become merely the social partner, a hostess of consequence, an efficient and exemplary house-keeper at my personal residence, the mother of my only daughter, the nurse-maid when illness knocked on the family door. I was the manager of a well run establishment, a free of cost interior decorator ever present and to serve with perfection and grace. In less than six months after my first marriage I was confronted with these facts and I had to face up to the reality, of a malevolent marriage and that I must take care of myself, to make my own arrangements, to bear my troubles in the unknown world of a new bride. For my confinement I had to be responsible for the care of myself and my yet unborn baby. I was nineteen and a half when I gave birth to my first baby in a strange town amongst strangers in Calcutta. I knew nothing about babies and birthing, as I was the youngest of us siblings, but I had been left on my own, so I had to go out to discover the process of child birth.

My baby – a little girl I named her Moniba – after my maternal grand-mother. I refrained from going to my parents for the confinement, since I had no dependable husband, I would depend entirely upon myself. I rented an apartment in Calcutta – I engaged an English speaking butler, I had an automobile "Thunder Bird" car, a bank account, money to spend as I required for my babies layette, medical services of the best of doctors, but no adult matured person, to care for me or to guide me. Being alone, I endeavoured to search for a good gynaecologist, a well-reputed nursing-home, an experienced baby nurse – last but not the least a Swiss doctor, who was highly recommended by everyone, when I was making inquires in an alien city where I did not belong. Colonel Fisher took me on as his patient, but was rather surprised to discover that a young girl having her first baby, was alone without a husband in sight, or for that matter no elder relative, dancing attendance as was the usual scenario of the East. He soon enough discovered that his patient had some very independent views and if my absent husband did not see the requirement of taking responsibility, his patient had enough courage, sense and pride not to need outside assistance. Since my absent husband did not deem it fit to take the responsibility for a child he seeded, then I did not need anyone else to take on his duty.

I was alone when I went into labour, I phoned my doctor who advised me to move to the Reidon's Nursing Home of gynaecology, where he had made all the necessary arrangements for my admission and the delivery of my baby. I myself drove the long graceful "Thunder Bird" to the nursing home and placed it in the parking lot. Entering the reception room, I made my way to the reception desk where I was expected. I attempted to check in to find the nurses looking for the pregnant mother. It was without sense, for everyone was surprised and shocked to learn, that a young girl was to be alone for the confinement of her first baby – there were many many negative remarks regarding this unconventional situation, but I never let it touch me. l returned from the hospital with my baby alone, my husband duly arrived from Karachi, six days after the birth of my daughter. Her father came to celebrate New Years Eve. We went dancing with his many business associates to the most exclusive "Three Hundred" club of Calcutta, with a limited and strict membership, making it a highly elite and exclusive club. I imagine (but do not know for certain) that since, he was a member of all the exclusive clubs in India in the pre-partition days, he certainly had his membership with all the important and exclusive clubs in Pakistan. Once again, after the New Year festivity, he left me in Calcutta and flew to Delhi, then he sallied forth on his repeated flying trips. I once said to him that his status and name should have been the "Flying Dutchman" and when any forms were required to be filled out, his home address should be recorded as "The BOAC" or "Indian Airline". Within the new state of Pakistan the national airline had just been established, bearing the name of "Orient Airways".

When my daughter was thirty two days old, I took her home to visit my parents in Patna, till then I had no home. My husband arrived a week later and took me with him back to Karachi. I endeavoured to make him recognize the essential need of my baby, who was by then only six weeks old, but he insisted that I must go to Karachi, he thought that since my daughter had an English baby nurse who could take care of her, and my baby was safe with my Mother and Father who would take in hand any problem that might arise. I left Patna, my parents and my daughter as he had insisted, but returned in haste five days later, when we received a phone call giving me the stunning news that my precious baby had passed away, turning over while she slept and was smothered by her small soft pillow. I returned home dry-eyed silent from shock and perhaps guilt – I had obeyed my husband, but lost my daughter. No one gave a thought to the Psychological trauma, and the anguish that overtakes a bereft mother – I had to handle this in my own way, even if I did not know how to handle it. The way was very hard and I was quite alone, and unable to divulge to my parents the state of my marriage affairs. I had made a wanton marriage for myself, so the gravity of the situation I must handle. Since I was unaware of how to handle my "trapped in" marriage I remained silent and just let the time pass. For the independent person I am, it was my entrapment and a disaster.

It was some months later that I found myself once again pregnant, there after I followed the same routine of residing alone in Calcutta, with the repetition of the same story as the previous year, I gave birth to another daughter the night of Christmas Eve who I named Tahira Nazira. God in His great mercy blessed me to enjoy, to love, to cherish and look after her. She was not the gift of "love" but the bright pure star of my life. I enfolded my daughter with devotion and pride for thirty-six years. Her tragic story is another episode to be presented at another time.

Reverting to the hypnotic issue of a love marriage, it belongs in the world of dream, at that young age it is a magical situation, it has no experience or worldly exposure, no real concept of meaningful love – there is a wide chasm that divides love from marriage, for love is a warm tender emotion, while marriage is a commitment and a legal bond, nearly all our young brides grow into young mothers two to three times over, if one stripes the festivities of marriage, the love play of a honeymoon, a new world of clothes, jewels and physical satisfaction, combine to evolve into a deep love that becomes the core of a sound attachment with family bonding as the result. The husband is a singularly and unique man as she has never known any other, for her he is the beloved father of her precious children; he is the sole benefactor of her subsistence, her security and an able provider. This is "Love" it comes with attachment, is sound in bonding, it makes a unit, but not a romantic type. From it as one learns to love, to compromise, to surrender on the wheel of worldly reality. For myself I thought it was love, my late husband saved me from being shot when I was declared as "Beauty Queen" in June, 1947 at the popular hill resort of Mussorie. He wooed me, he professed love, he promised to nurture and cherish me, and I put faith in his words. He romanced me with flowers, chocolates and perfume – nothing more, as I made it clear that I take nothing from anyone.

It was only after I met Majid that I realized what real love really means, what devotion it creates, what care it bestows, what nurturing it provides, what a relationship of tenderness and what a life of sacrifice. These virtues blend together for the sole purpose, of imparting joy and contentment, presenting and cementing the bonding with consuming a "Love Capsule". Love is not derived from the diamonds and jewellery that is bestowed on one, as money can purchase a stupendous amount, but not love. Love is the graciously given gift of space and peace that one lavishes on another, love lies in the core of welfare, it exhibits itself in the small gestures of thoughtfulness, the honouring of total trust, the fidelity in freedom, and the thoughtful responsibility to diminish any burdens, thus in love one finds the negation of self. My emotional wisdom is what I learnt from my beloved Majid, this is what he endowed on me for forty-seven years. He consistently put me before himself. Even on the last morning that he was still at home – before he was struck down by a paralyzed spine he said to me "I told Nawaz (our cook) to get a dozen marrow bones and have them cooked for you, I am extremely concerned about you, you fail to accord time to rest, you do not consume enough nourishment to sustain your day's work. You are extremely weak, and your platelet count has fallen far below the danger level, so please take cognizance to plan your rest, see that your diet includes the type of meals that would help to raise your platelet count." He told me "You are precious to me, you must learn to take care of yourself, time is running out and I may not be here to watch over, or minister to your needs, you are aware that your health is fragile." Even in those last days he thought about my welfare. No better love could I have had, nor a more accommodating partner could I have wished for. Always loving, always giving, always caring, always generous and always my pillar of support. My body goes on to do the work I am destined for – it is my responsibility, but my heart flew with him with the last breath he took.

A true devotional love, an exemplary guard, a kind compatible husband and a human partner has been Allah's gift to me for forty-seven years. Can I manage to live without Majid – I wonder if I can – I do not know as yet. Perhaps the early tragic foundation I have had with the loss of two beloved daughters, has prepared me to face the long lonely hours of the remaining time, that Allah has ordained for me.

We imagine that we possess discernment of ourselves, but do we really perceive such cognizant values – no body can be astute enough to make a complete assessment of one's self, nor can we observe ourselves mirrored as in a portrait. In the images we point out for ourselves, are the comfortable confident elevations we think we have achieved, or the depressing swamps we appear to have waded though, or even the swirling whirlpools that drag us down into oblivion. In fact, do any of these rocking see-saws really matter – the pace of life goes on, sometime melodramatically slow, sometimes racing like a tempest, while we are unable to keep the pace, it appears that all is lost. Time! what is time? It is now, it is tomorrow and time was yesterday. Unavoidable changes come with time, with age and place – virtue has been condemned by another time, another race, and even vice has been extolled and it has worn a golden crown in another time, in another race and also in another place. Time rolls on and waits for no man. All one can question is "time where has it gone?"

I have become what I am today, because I took time and life as the master of my conditioning, I have had no cause to regret it, being at peace with myself, because the path I opted for was one of sincerity and truth. I employed my conscience as my master in life, and Allah the Master of my being. I have endeavoured to tread the path He ordained for me – I have been at peace with myself, even when harsh and raging storms battered at my door. I held on to the hem of the Master's gown – I submitted my faith and He lifted me, giving me courage. I occasionally bring to mind King Bruce of Scotland as he sat dejected in defeat, he saw a spider that attempted to scramble up the wall a score of times, falling each time but in vain, with repeated efforts it did eventually succeed. Doubtless the spider taught a king to persevere and achieve success. I have always been consistent and well aware, of exactly what I have worked for, this is probably the reason for my success, but I am totally unable to assess the elevation, the depth or the measure my own worth.

The Web

Wont you come into my parlour
Said the spider to the fly.

It is the prettiest parlour
You ever did espy.

The way into my parlour
Is up a winding stair
And I have many things
To show you when you're there.

★ ★ ★ ★ ★

Truth Conquers the Universe

FIRST HUNTING EXPEDITION
Hunting Tigers and a 'Rogue' Elephant

When I was first married I discovered that it was, to a man who lived by the worldly trappings of the rich which they found exciting. Exciting perhaps it was, but there are an abundant pleasures and situations in life that rank far above the killing of wild-animals. Wildlife is essential and should be preserved, not a source for the gratification and pleasure of hunting, regardless and unconcern guarding the explicit need of the conservation of wild-life, despite the knowledge that numerous species are dying out and are becoming extinct. There are hunting laws, but strict laws of conservation are violated without heavy penalties. For desecrating the laws, there should be the confiscation of guns to save the dying out of animals – killed by man for their skins, their tusks, their special feathers and many more useless trophies.

I must admit right here, as I begin this topic, of preservation of wild life, that when I was newly married I too went on quite a few of the local hunting trips, but after shooting my first and only tiger, I laid aside the guns and turned away. I shall never forget the look of complete helplessness and pathetic surrender I saw in the eyes of my wounded tiger.

But I must start at the very early days of my induction, to the forests and streams of the "Tari Bhavar" forests that lie at the foot of the vast and almost never-ending Himalayan Range, which forms the hinterland of India. It is a fortress barrier that starts at the Suliman Range in Pakistan, moving North to the Pamir Knot on the borders of Afghanistan, then turning due East, at almost a right angle to stretch Eastwards forming the hinterland protection of India. It is the great unconquerable Himalayan mountains that divides India, changes its course to run down South forming the central spine of Burma, but loosing its height as it moves southwards. It is "built by nature against pestilence and the hand of war" in the famous words of William Shakespeare, spoken by King Henry Fifth before the attack of France.

The Tari Bhavar is the forest area in which the world famous hunter Jim Corbelt did his shooting. He knew every inch of the land, he could identify the size of a tiger just by looking at the tiger's pug mark in the mud, or track a wild animal by the spoor they left behind. I do believe he knew almost every tiger in those forests. His hunting, in later years became a type of protective hunting. He only went after leopards and panthers that raided the villages, stealing the cattle, and injuring human beings. He hunted "man eater" tigers on foot in an effort to capture and bring them down unaware. As his years advanced and his hunting life matured, he traded his own life for protection of the weaker animals, cattle and the safety of the scared villagers.

The shooting parties indulged in by the "crème de la crème" gentry were a far cry from Jim Corbelts motives of hunting. Those dramatic shooting parties were a social phenomena and at the beginning I too was enthralled with the reconnoitring, the novelty of challenges, the survey, I had not yet learnt some of the unworthy acts. I must confess it was not true sportsmanship and I leant to deny them. It was dishonourable and unfair to conduct a shoot, that is literally managed, planned, baited and then shot from carefully pre-planned, safe and secure places. But there is more that I shall divulge regarding ethical and the grossly unethical manner of this sport.

My own story needs to be disclosed first. A group of about twelve to fifteen participants and I was the only lady who participated in this my first shoot. I must declare now, I had no idea of the terrain, conditions nor the appropriate clothes and no one, not even my husband thought I aught to be briefed on what to wear.

The shooting arrangements for our stay had been made at the government's rest house at Harduwani. It was late spring and the summer had not yet fully set in. After a good night's sleep and a satisfying early breakfast, the jeeps had already been loaded with water, food, guns and rifles and plenty of ammunition. Each gentleman sported his luxurious hunting equipment, double-barrelled gun, his Holland and Holland rifle, his 375 magma rifle, his double –barrelled guns, his special Smith and Wesson revolver. Who needs cross belts and cartridges for a single shoot, I'll never understand, except if it is a subtle way of advertising to the rest of the company that one has the material resources to buy such equipment, that would fit a gunnery. Be it as it may, I am not here to record any criticism for I believe in "Each man for himself and God for us all." The jeeps were also loaded with things called "machans", these are in fact small square wooden frames like cots, their space woven by ropes to produce a suitable and reasonable sitting place for the hunters. These cots are lifted high up above sturdy branches of strong tall trees. They are roped and harnessed to the branches of the trees, standing at appropriate places where a tiger is likely to come in search of food, for a goat or a calf, that the hunters have already tied up and secured to a tree. The unfortunate bleating animal has a fair length of rope about ten to twelve feet long encircling its neck and the other end lashed around the trunk of tree. The "bait" can move around a bit, even tries to escape and when it fails to free itself, the bleating begins and a tiger hearing it easily wends its way to where the scared and bleating animal's distress rises into terror. This I suppose is considered good sportsmanship. There is more but it must wait till later for the telling.

Since I was inexperienced, I was oblivious to the activities of the shoot, but most important of all was my balance on Jeep and Landrovers. My clothes were totally inappropriate for climbing up onto elephants. As I moved slowly through the tiger forest, I observed that there were no deers munching grass, standing, or wild animals in sight, the forests are full with monkeys forever chattering and prattling, but here of monkeys, there was no evidence. The forest should have been crackling with wild sounds but now appeared to be hushed. Being a novice I had no idea what this actually meant, but I followed the shooting team that moved very slowly and carefully through the bushes and trees. I was walking ahead without the slightest apprehension of danger, when I observed a stream between the trees, flowing through a rocky area. It had caught my attention, so that is where I turned my direction and arrived at the bank of the gushing stream.

Syeda Anese Majid Khan

Looking downwards from where the water was flowing, between smooth rocks that bridged the two banks, with a series of smooth boulders, rocks forming stepping stones, I proceeded to cross the stream. My skirt was long and I needed both my hands to hold it up, thus enabling me to step onto one rock at a time, then on to the next. As I moved forward my eyes caught sight of a number of fish swimming in a natural deep pool as though nature had provided a special swimming pool especially for their convenience. In that split second of my distraction my foot slipped and I fell into the pool and joined the fish in their swimming gala. At that close encounter, their wide and large open mouths and eyes that stared at me, swimming round and returning to take another look, I was not confident that I would not be attacked. I was an alien in their pool and had no business trying to consort with the fish in their exclusive swimming pool. If I could have spoken their language, I would most certainly have assured them, that I was as much disconcerted at having them for company, as they were displeased at my presence. I had no way to communicate with them so I was obliged to keep my peace.

Picking myself up with my skirt and cotton blouse drenched in fishy water I made my way with great difficulty, I crossed to the other bank of the stream. Just several yards away, there was a huge slab of over-hanging rock creating a shallow aperture, forming a cave where I could sit, stretch my skirt across a sunny patch that lay under the slab of rock, where I was planning to sit. Once I had got to the cave I arranged my clothes as best as I could and I waited for the rest of the hunting team to arrive. Time passed and it was quite awhile before I saw some movement amongst the bushes on the opposite bank.

Four or five of the hunters carrying their rifles emerged and then some others. Something very odd had caught their attention and the scenario they put on appeared to be an over excited pantomime. There was total silence, not even a call of my name. Some of the men put their hands up, like policemen in a gesture to say "stop" using their hands, except here, there were both hands giving me a signal to stop. Some others kept their hand on their lips signalling me not to speak or move. Three or four of the men were holding up their guns and pointing to something way above the slab of rock that was giving me some shelter. I really didn't catch a full translation of what was being enacted, but this message of "don't move there is danger" came through loud and clear. Except for my breath I kept everything else under check and didn't move, but all my senses had been alerted to the danger that surrounded me.

Out of the blue, three shots blasted the silence and then another three in quick succession. I was stunned at this turn of events and wanted to scream, "What the hell do you think you are doing?" But I did not dare ask at that distance, but what I did see was that the dramatic pantomime had ceased and everyone was hurriedly wading over the rocks, scrambling splashing water, from the stream and coming straight for me. When they got near enough I did say, "What the devil are you people up to?" A very indignant Rupert, who was the Director of the Forest Rangers said with great exasperation "Look who is asking the question. Its more like "What the Devil are you doing splitting from the group on your own. You are supposed to stay with us, in fact you were to stay far behind us. And if you really must know, what the devil this is all about, I'll tell you, Mr. Unworthy Tiger, was about to appropriate you after his sunny siesta and sun bathing session on the rock slab above you when he awoke, he would be ready to feast upon you, sitting back to lick his chops and then indulging for himself another tender hearty meal before sun down, and you have the gall to ask us what the devil happened."

I think Zaki tried to bring the situation back under control because by this time I was as angry as Rupart, but for different reasons. My racing mind objected to the way he spoke to me, and Zaki understood this and said "Anese Rupert's only concern is your safety. You have no idea how terrified we all were, looking at you sitting peacefully under the slab of rock, with a hungry tiger lying right above your head."

I turned round and said to Rupert "Why didn't you shoot it then" still with a touch of annoyance in his voice he said, "I think I ought to teach you, that you don't shoot a tiger, leopard or panther unless you are sure of a clear shot that will kill. With a tiger at that distance I could not be sure to kill it. If we left a wounded tiger in the vicinity, it would surely become a "man eater". A large number of villages in this area would be targets for a tiger to find a meal through true necessity. No responsible hunter could ever make that mistake. You apparently have no idea of how much danger you put yourself into. You must never be in tiger country unless there are four or five people together and at least two or may be three guns, who can perform with those guns or rifles a clear shot.

The day was far advanced and the sun was well past the zenith and approaching the horizon, so we decided to call it a day and returned to the rest house.

The next morning we returned to the tiger forest area and started to reconnoiter as to where the "Machans" were to be erected and secured with ropes. There were to be five "machans" with three people to each, two with guns and one forest gunman experienced to conduct the correct procedures in case of an eventuality or any mistaken action taken by the people on the hunt. There are quite often one or two people like myself who are inexperienced, creating such dangerous circumstances, so a highly experienced and competent "shikari" meaning hunter must always be in attendance.

After duly erecting all the five "machans", tied to strategic trees, we once more returned to the rest house. A postmortum discussion of issues regarding the activities of the last two days, made the evening conversation very interesting. Even as early as that time, when I was not even twenty years old, I had the ability to remain silent, listen, absorb and learn from the wisdom of others. We ate an early dinner, just before sun-down, then getting into the jeeps we went back to where the "machans" had been erected. Each one of us took our guns climbed the trees and sat on the mats covering the "machans". The seating arrangements were comfortable, flasks of cold water, finger food, coffee and tea rested on the mats. The waiting could be any number of hours as there is no knowing when the tiger would appear. A small calf was tied to a tree at a distance of fifteen to twenty feet, but a good and comfortable distance from each platform, where all the shooting parties could readily shoot the tiger before it could kill the "bait" that was the calf.

I suppose this is the honourable sportsmanship that there remains a chance that the tiger won't harm the animal. If it does not die by the teeth of the tiger, it would probably die of terror and an over active heart beat.

The calf kept trying to free itself and when it couldn't it started to "moo". Then there was silence for awhile and once more the "mooing" would commence. This went on for a couple of hours without any indication that a tiger might be at hand. Rupert who was my partner, suddenly stiffened and pressed my hand to indicate that I shouldn't move. I didn't and then I realized that the "moo" of the calf was getting frenzied. This, itself told me that the tiger was in the vicinity and getting nearer all the time.

Rupert picked up his rifle and indicated I pick up my 375 magnum. As I did so I slipped the safety catch open and put the gun to my shoulder. Suddenly the "Shikaris" light went on, straight to the tiger's head. I aimed between the eyes I got the shot but not in a vital spot. As the roaring tiger turned to run Rupert put into him two quick shots in succession. The tiger was badly wounded, but had not fallen. This meant that we had to follow it up, as a wounded tiger must be totally finished by the hunter, so we had to plan to go after him. This cannot be negotiated by jeeps, elephants or horses. The only way possible to go after a wounded tiger is to go on foot. It needs courage, stealth, purpose with conviction and no return till the job has been successfully accomplished.

We could not start the search before day-break and Rupert refused to allow me to go with them. I challenged him fiercely by saying "What kind of a "shakari" do you intend to make me. You of all the people, so if you are a real teacher, then you should be teaching me the right way. But more important is that it was my tiger, it was my bullet that wounded it – it is my job to finish what I started." He replied, "I am worried about your safety." I simply said "Don't worry I have the courage, the stamina and the will, plus there are two of us" Then Rupert said, "There will be three of us, our "shakari" will also come".

As day was breaking all three of us had coffee, tea and sandwiches. Taking our rifles, we descended from the "Machan" and looked for pug marks and blood. We soon found the blood and followed the trail. As we came nearer we became slower and more cautious. Suddenly we lost the blood trail, it had got mitigated due to the heavy bushes. Rupert was ahead of me and slowly kept parting the shrubs, before taking one step at a time, then the next step slowly forward. Suddenly his forward movement faltered and he stood still, I came abreast just behind him. What I saw brought tears to my eyes. I was emotionally shaken. There in front of me lay a beautiful "King of the Jungle" beast

– no longer a beast, with the sun baring down on his ochre fur that looked like burnished gold, his black stripes shone like rich ebony, his long tail stretched out behind him, his enormous paws spread out in front of him in docility a beautiful specimen in all its richness. I saw all his beauty, but I had no time to admire it, for my eyes were arrested by the expression in his eyes. His eyes were soft and gentle, helpless, yet not a pleading, he was defenseless, his life ebbing away in gentle sweet surrender. Even as he lay dying, he was still the "King of the Jungle" Rupert indicated that I was to raise my riffle and finish the last bullet, but I couldn't, so I took a step back and Rupert himself finished the job that I couldn't or rather did not have the heart to do. This happened sixty years ago and I can still see the gentle dignity of my wounded tiger his eyes and his sweet surrender. When I remember that I took a life for no good reason, except what the world calls sport, but I cannot call it sport, it is a destruction of a life. May God forgive me as I still feel the remorse. I never touched a gun, a riffle for shooting or a hunters knife since that day. Life is for the living – death should be when the Lord wills it so.

There was no routine to my life as I wondered here and there, in no particular way. In some odd way this was because in the following year I somehow found myself resident in Nani Tal, living in a rented cottage by myself. The same as before, my mornings were occupied leaving for the Boat Club to sail Molly, my two sail yacht on the lake. Being a lady the club rules did not permit me to negotiate the yacht alone. I needed another male to be with me. I was careful, never to sail with a member of the club as the majority of them were male, lest I earn for myself the erroneous reputation of being a flirt, or even worse still a "provocative coquette". My boatman named Punjoo maintained the care and condition of Molly and could be the best sailing partner I would have asked for. I was relaxed gratified and content, safe from flirtatious and indelicate propositions, insinuations under the cover of "romantic prattle". Punjoo and I sailed for a good two hours every morning, then leaving the club, I rode out on one of my Arab stallions over the hills during the afternoon. I traversed the mountain paths, made by the constant use of mules and other horses. I often took a book with me, then dismounting and harnessing the reins of my horse to a sturdy tree I would choose a place that provided a very beautiful scenic view. I spent the afternoons sitting under the trees alone, which for me was heaven itself. The deep blue cloudless sky, sun drenched foliage, and delicate wild flowers growing in perfusion, often delicately swaying in the breeze, the aroma of flowers filled the air.

I hated the moments when my watch indicated that it was time to leave and return to the cottage. Mounting my horse I would ride back to the cottage at an indolent and leisurely pace. Once back at the cottage, I bathe and dressed for my evening return to the Boat Club, to show my presence, joining the social activities listening to the mundane, banal and terrestrial world of trivia and trite social euphoria, sometimes for some, this was arrived at through the assistance of inebriation.

I enjoyed the music played by a professional five member band. After a couple of hours at the club, I would then set off briskly, wending my way home, where I burrowed like a worm into a book, it was book, after book. By morning I was once more looking to the sky for a sign of the sun, but I was denied the gratification of my desire. The sky was over hung with dark and heavy grey clouds that vowed nothing less than rain, thunder and storm.

Sitting in the lounge on the window seat gazing across the lake, I lazed for a time creating day dreams, as I was sunk in the doldrums of another monotonous tedium. I was conscious it was late spring and the forests must be heavy with foliage, and the simplistic flowers of nature would be in full bloom. The gay clusters of lantana bushes forming bouquets that garlanded the forest. Here I was sitting at the window seat of a dreary cottage, when infact I craved the generous beauty that was splurged by nature. I had no word, nor was I acquainted with any suggestion, or hint, that there was to be a hunt that summer, not even through the grapevine of the club, had I heard any rumours of a shooting or a hunting programme.

The lure of the jungle was incessantly calling and I presume that my inner soul was quickened and responded to that call like the mating of desire.

The call of nature, had enthralled me, that was very obvious, but worse still my own desire of being totally free was being frustrated. I wondered if I could go for a whole summer without a reasonable sojourn in the wild beauty of the jungle. The wild animals were my friends, so I refrained from eating meat that had been shot. The meat from a shoot is coveted fare, filled with venison, partridges, grouse. But to me, even the wild duck which came at a high premium in good and special restaurants was for me unacceptable. No amount of high priced value should be put above the unnecessary annihilation of wildlife. None of the gentlemen of leisure required the meat, or game for life support, but since the fanciful concept expounded, demonstrated and propagated by the elite, shot meat had become a delicacy, thus provoking the indiscriminate urge to kill under the guise of "sportsmanship", but infact it is to display and prove ones marksmanship.

I had a hankering, in fact, a deep yearning and the ardent desire to be once more in the haven of the habitat that nature provides, so generously to all manner of living things. I was smarting with the depression, that the summer would have fled and any hope of a vacation in my natural habitat was about to remain only as a day dream.

Very late that nigh my husband phoned to inform me of his arrival on the following day, as he was coming to make the arrangements for a tiger shoot and that we would leave in four or five days, driving back to Harduwani to stay at the regular Government Forest Rest House. He instructed me to arrange for all the guns, rifles, search lights and all the hunting paraphernalia and accoutrements that were to be carried on two land rovers, as we ourselves moved by car into the Northern area of the Tari Bhavar Forests.

My pulse raced, my head cleared, my day dreams banished, my depression soared and my impatience mounted. Surely we did not require five days to arrange the shoot, but my reverie was about to become real, making my spirit race swiftly, dispatching my black depression to wing itself across and over the lake, loosing itself in the thickest of the evergreen mountain, amongst the alpine trees. I was too elated with enthusiasm, it was propelled with a flurry of sensational stirrings that evicted sleep, so by dawn which comes late to the hills I was already dressed and making lists for all the requirements that were to be assembled for the shoot. I abandoned my yacht and sailing routine, dispatched the horses for stabling and their afternoon rides. My books lay unopened piled on the table, my exclusive thoughts were mustered around the shoot. I had to mobilize the gunmen, select appropriate clothes and toilet equipment for a ten days "shooting party".

Apparently, all else was to be arranged by Rupert at the guest house, the elephants, the shikaries, the jeeps and more guns, plus a contingent of beaters with their local drums. All this was conducted on the phone. Rupert phoned and instructed me to deal with arrangements he left that for me to organize. These were not difficult or problems for me. I think Rupert felt sorry that I was not twenty yet, but had heavy responsibilities dumped on my young shoulders.

My husband duly arrived very late the next day and within two days, all had been prepared and he only had to pay for the show to be orchestrated. The labour positioning and accommodation arrangements had been done at his bidding. In after years, I often wished, my life had been as simple, but perhaps my reward was that I had found my fulfilment, but of this I am certain and very much, aware that his life had no fulfilment. By early morning we piled on to the back on the jeeps, winding our way down-hill to enter the Tari Bhavar forest, at the foot of the mountain beyond Harduani.

As our itinerary had no special agender for we were not after a "man eating" tiger, a "Rogue" elephant or a wounded leopard, creating dangerous problems for the villages, this shooting trip was to be an ordinary trip, taking our hunt and action, as we confronted each episode or circumstances.

Once again a young calf was purchased to be tied up for the night, as bait for the tiger, making me incensed as I found my heckles rising, but I was badly out – numbered, in fact I was the only one to be a veto factor. As my husband, bluntly informed me "If you don't like to shoot why are you here." I retorted "I didn't come here to shoot, I came because I love the bounties of nature and find the jungle beguiling." his retort was "If you don't use a rifle you are no use on a "machan" we need the action of guns from all who sit on the "machan", he snapped". I wasn't going to take that lying down quietly and with a none to gentle protest I scathingly replied "You need not worry your head about that, or me, as I shall be advancing on an elephant along with the "beaters", who would be beating and driving the tiger into the semi-circle formed by your "machans". This information really surprised him.

Rupert could clearly comprehend where this would lead us, so catching my hand he maneuvered me towards his jeep. A jeep is able to go only a limited distance into the forest areas, once we entered the forest and a grassland area we are obliged to leave the jeep on the sides of the rough pathway. This is where the waiting elephants and beaters awaited our arrival.

The four "machans" that were loaded on the jeeps were off loaded and carried by the porters to suitable trees that were chosen by Rupert. The "machans" were to be erected in limited time. Once this task had been completed we climbed onto the elephants and took an elephant ride trying to locate a young deer, as the men dreamed of "spit roasted" venison for the night's dinner. There was no thought or indication that we were in some hungry tiger's private domain. With his sudden and unexpected roar he made his presence felt, but by this time we had only two elephants with six people and the porters, who had been walking and the rest of the men on elephants had made their way back to the jeeps. As the roaring went into an angry crescendo the porters flashed past in reverse gear, leaving just our two elephants and hunters to deal with what was coming. What was coming was an angry, hungry beast in a golden coat stripped with shinning black velvet streaks.

"Jugnoo" was the name of our elephant, she also made a hasty half turn in order to get away from the angry beast and her greatest concern, was the preservation of her trunk and her sensitive snout. There had been a great big log of a dried out tree that had fallen and now lay stretched across the long grass. The tree was completely dry and in full decay. In her attempt to turn around she placed her heavy ton weight leg on it and with a crash the log split, its splinters went flying in all directions. As the log broke apart it smashed the beehive that had been built by bees inside the hollow and decayed interior. It was split apart with swarms of angry, very angry bees attacking us and the elephant. We hardly had time to draw our head nets over our face, when we first saw the tiger running towards us, furious in his attack. He leapt high with his great big paws extended and his mouth widely open, giving a ferocious roar displaying his four teeth like large thick tusks.

Rupert lifted his magnum and pressed the trigger, nothing happened, he tried again and still nothing happened. He must have realized that the rifle for some reason was jammed. All he said, "Take this and give me yours", we had hardly exchanged guns when the tiger went into a ferrous attack on the elephant. Jugnoo kept turning partly in half circle, giving her broadside to the tiger trying to save her trunk and also her effort to rid herself of the bees that were making mince meat of her head which the tiger kept attacking her from the right shoulder. She kept repeatedly moving in an arc but the tiger also moved with each move that Jugnoo made.

It was I, who was sitting above her right shoulder, so it was I who received the attacks of the raving tiger. He was a big tiger and his springing leap was high. He kept on attacking and I kept on shoving my right leg into his open mouth, with my very heavy riding boots as protection, as he charged again and again mauling my boot, making quite a few rents with his mauling claws. My mutilated riding boots had split and ruptured in many places, I prayed that it could stay on, as it was a Duncan and Duncan boot that is the toughest of all boots, but my knee and leg remained seriously undamaged. Jugnoo had also lost her bearings and all she did was to move round in circles.

I had been using my left hand to hang on to the ropes that harnessed the padded seat to the back of the elephant on which we sat, while my right hand kept shoving the butt of the gun into the tigers open jaws. Rupert's gun had a heavy butt which I used. Suddenly two loud shots blasted from almost under the elephant and Rupert shouted, "For God's sake don't shoot" but I had not fired the rifle. The gun had fallen from my hand, as I fed the butt into the tiger's mouth, and as the gun fell it had hit a very large boulder that was lying almost under Jugnoo. With the jolt the jammed trigger came unlocked and the two shots in the chambers blasted out automatically one after another to the surprise of all including myself and the tiger.

In the confusion that followed, the blast had shocked the tiger, so he pivoted and set off at top speed in the opposite direction entering the heavy forest of trees. Rupert lifted his gun to shoot but the distance the tiger had covered was beyond my rifle range as Rupert had changed his rifle with mine. We collected his rifle and walked back to the waiting jeeps.

Our shooting trip for the day had been aborted, but the experience had been perhaps one of its kind.

Rupert took my boot and had them build a glass box around it . . . the words read "Boots of the Jungle Princess".

Being the daughter of nature, sometimes showed through in my actions, at unguarded moments. Different members and friends of the family dubbed me with a variety of names from time to time. Uncle Ash called me his "water nymph", my paternal aunt hung me with "elusive sprite", the boys at college termed me "Gipsy Wildcat" but from my immediate family I had less endearing names, I was the "Ugly Duckling" the "Black Sheep" of the family and my loving sister referred to me as "Red Indian Squaw".

I didn't mind and never felt the pinch as I believed I was and am what I am, and names would not change me or have me comply to the undesirable demands of others. Perhaps I was as free as any squaw can be.

Such a daughter of nature had to be quite at home on this natural habitat – the jungle, the forests, the tumbling streams and the multi-shaded rocks.

So here I was once again on another tiger shoot, but this time it was different. I had no intention to shoot and kill, I once more desired only to roam the forests of the Tari Bhavar area, picturesque in its beauty and peaceful at the same time, powerful and dominating. The stately alpine forests standing erect in their grandeur, made harmonious space for the valuable graceless deciduous forests. My shooting equipment on this occasion was the multi-equipment of my camera. Lantana bushes were to be found growing at all heights, but their colours were limited to mustard yellow fringed with Vandyke brown, others with yellow ochere fading into lemon, touched with deep dark burgundy, while the others had clusters of white lantana flowers rimmed with sunny lemon blended with deep salmon. The vast variety of forest flowers, had escaped my training in Art class. Almost every flower in the "Sutton Seed" book was known to me, but here in the jungle I was a complete ignoramus in regard to forest foliage. There were hawthorn berries and small blue berries growing alongside orange and yellow snake plants, and small bushes with spring time flowers, stretched widely across under the shady protection of large leaf foliage. At this time which was late spring the forest was verdant and presented a colourful landscape.

I had gone on that shoot not for the sport of killing but to embrace the bounties of Nature with my cameras, to drink in the silent harmony extended by the forest, and the mysterious appeal of shadows created by the contrast of wood lichen and bark, sinister branches and devilish ominous shapes.

Another shoot was to be very interesting as we had been alerted, that there was a "Rogue" elephant expelled from the herd of wild elephants roaming in that part of the forest. No one is permitted under the law to shoot, an elephant under any circumstances, but in the case of a "Rogue" it had to be shot, for the safety of the herd and the many villages that have no protection. The word "rogue" here implies that the elephant for some unknown reason, has turned "rogue". In fact it is a type of mental derangement, that when it is advanced it reaches a frenzied, berserk stage that makes it run wild in an indiscriminate stampede destroying all that comes before it. There is an urgent need to "put it away" so that the damage caused would be of the barest minimum. Only special groups that are professional at this type of shooting are entrusted to receive a "permit" for undertaking this dangerous task.

As Rupert himself was a Director of the forest rangers, he received this "special permit" at once without any problem. Once we had the permit we hit the road and moved to Hardowwani at top speed. All the equipment needed and especially the heavy bore guns were made available in the shortest period of time. We set up base at the rest house, planned how to scout the area, search for any elephant droppings or "spoor", as it is called to indicate the vicinity in which he was now traversing. The herd had now fully separated from him and were claiming another suitable expanse for their temporary residency. Elephant hunting is a day time job, the sun needs to be out, the trees widely spaced with large fields of long elephant grass, which is their main diet, added to this there are certain types of trees that have suitable food value for their heavy and bulky bodies.

Getting into our jeeps we went driving, skirting the grasslands, we drove between clumps of young trees but were denied the sight of the "rogue." We stopped for a quick mid-day meal and were once again on the move. By sundown we had not been able to trace a single bit of evidence, that there might be a "rogue" in the area, as he had not dropped any calling cards along the way. The sun had dipped below the horizon when we made tracks back to the rest house. All the exuberance and high spirits of the morning had been deflated and the occupants of our four jeeps were in very despondent and somewhat depressed moods, so then our exhaustion was evident. For myself I had enjoyed the whole day, it had been stimulating, every once in a while my pulse quickened in expectation, but was relieved we had seen no elephant to kill. I had no awareness or estimate of the damage that could be done by a"rogue" elephant.

When we arrived at the rest house we took a quick bath, changed into loose cool cotton clothes and sat on chairs on the grassy lawns discussing the plans for to morrow. Ash caught my eye and said, "Don't move keep very still" – then, I really froze, my instinct told me why I had to remain still – this was a throw back to the time when I was attacked by a king cobra, when I was only five years of age, before my sojourn to England for my schooling.

My blood ran cold, my breathing almost stopped. They say, I faded out like a white marble statue. After a while Ash rose crossed the distance between our chairs and held his hands out to me. I was frozen with shock and could not respond nor could I speak. Pulling me up he turned me round to witness the new commotion that was going on behind me. The "Shirkaries" were busy clobbering something with their poles made of bamboo. I knew without looking, that I had once again been saved from a deadly snake bite, this too was a cobra, but not so large. It just made its peaceful way between my two legs encased in trousers.

While I sipped cold water to regain my composure the rest of group had drinks in their hands, each to his own taste and enjoyment. Once more the sound of voices grew and talk became animated.

The next morning we arose and repeated the drill of another time. It was like replaying the tape of yesterday. Deers and gazelles, sprang up and over the tall grass, sometimes they stood poised like deers in a painting. Blue buck or "neelgie" as they are called, roamed the grassy areas in their search of food. Birds were on the wing, monkeys chattered and the pale grey long tailed languor (a special type of monkey) hung by their tails swinging from one branch to another. That was the total action we witnessed in the whole day. Another defeated day had flown past. I wondered how many days did it take to find an elephant. I did not make the query because there could be no answer.

While we were driving back to the rest house we had to cross the railway line that went to Hurduani. As we waited for the train to pass we were fascinated by the occupants of the train. There were large cages of lions and tigers, horses and seals. Two elephants and some baby elephants. It certainly was not the one we were after. These inmates were travelling on their own sightseeing visit as they were a part of the circus "en route" to Harduani, where their tents and living arrangements were underway.

We enjoyed this diversion from our aborted hunting day, so our spirits were again revived and a laughing, bantering mood returned, to re-activate the usual enjoyment that came to us, in this free unsophiscated homestead of nature.

While we sat killing time in the evening breeze Terry volunteered a suggestion. It was wild, it was crazy, perhaps as crazy as Terry himself, but he put it forward. "Why don't we get in touch with the circus and borrow their tigress for a night." I thought he must be quite out of his mind, so I asked "What are we to do with a tigress for a night she certainly won't go dancing with you." With widely set eyes he said, "No, No! Anese we are not going dancing, we'll put her on an open truck and take her into the jungle at night." I thought he was quite mad, so I enquired "And what is she to do there. Call out all the male tigers to come and join her." With a big broad smile he said, "You see you got it right – so you agree with me?" With indignation I retorted "I most certainly do not concur with such a far-fetched idea. You must be out of your mind."

By this time everybody had become a part of the conversation and paying avid attention to this new turn of events. I vetoed it completely. To me it was unfair to lure a tiger into a situation, then in cold blood and blind fulfilment of self desire to shoot it to kill, without a chance of combat or sagacious confrontation. But when excitement is high and one's sense of mastery becomes paramount, no amount of reasoning, persuasion or the denouncement of ethics and values of fair play, can find its way to reason.

Since Terry had given birth to this unmanly dishonourable suggestion, he and his friend Hari were dispatched, to negotiate the hiring of a tigress for one night and he was to bring back the entire caged tigress and all other requirements on an open truck. Terry, who had by this time grown to become ten feet tall, proclaimed in a loud and electrifying voice, "I swear I'll bring the bloody tigress back even if I have to pay a couple of thousand bucks to buy it." I was mad at him and I ejected a barbed ill disposed arrow from my lethal verbal bow "Oh! Sure you would! What I'm afraid of is, that you may become the blooded man from Niger who went in the search of a tiger, the tiger came back from the ride, with the man inside and a grin on the face of the tiger." The entire assembly of hunters guffawed at the humour except Terry himself, who had been my target, spat out words in high dudgeon that were to have insulted me in front of his audience, "This is what comes for bringing a woman on this shoot – She is nothing but bad luck."

Well I wasn't going to take that lying down quietly. In a flash my repartee came "Oh! So now I'm bad luck! You didn't think I was bad luck, when I joined the group, then it was showering me with compliments and drooling over me. I'm bad luck because I brushed you off to go play with your own kind – they are accustomed to one night stands and a slip away week-end."

Terry was shocked at this open disclosure in front of my recently – wedded husband "good Lord, can she keep nothing secret." I interrupted him with "I kept it secret as you call it because I can look after myself. Since your tongue has no control, you asked for exposure."

Things were getting rough and out of hand so Rupert gave a strict command. He said, "Terry leave at once and go about the business all of you are after. See you return in good time. Call me from the station if you have made concrete arrangements with the circus people, and I suggest you bring the tiger – trainer and ring master with his whip just for good measure" Taking the jeep and two shakaries Terry went on his way, to do his erstwhile and deviant errand.

The evening slipped away as we all spoke of different subjects, none of it political, none of it social and certainly none of it financial, as we chatted recollecting episodes from the past and our personal experiences.

I noticed Rupert glancing at his watch several times then sometime later with a frown and I wondered why he appeared to be so anxious, so I asked him "Rupert is there something wrong or is it dinner time already, the sun set less than an hour ago." Kuran Singh took a sip from the glass he held in his right hand and remarked "It cant possibly be dinner time, I'm still on my first drink" Rupert gave him a broad grin saying, "Relax old boy, dinner is a long, long way off and you can nurse your heady nector for quite a while yet. I've been looking at my watch and waiting for Terry to return. Its three and a half hours since he left and he should have been back by now. I suspect he has been able to negotiate something with the "circus management and perhaps he is now making the suitable preparations that are required to bring the tigress here.

I could hardly believe my ears, that this crazy conversation was being conducted, to use a circus tigress for such an underhanded purpose. In that early stage of my life, I had not yet learnt that money could buy almost anything if the price was "Right". The current interchange and dialogue of arrangements I found despicable.

In less than an hour, we heard the blaring of horns, the flash of the jeep lights, the roar of a hungry tigress and in its wake followed, a huge open truck, with an enormous cage perched on the back of the truck. Large high voltage lights flooded the entire area in front of it. Amidst the confusion of reverberation of a badly maintained engine, that vibrated in resounding spurts, flashing headlights and the loud voices of more than a dozen men, came Terry jumping over the jeep, running towards us he was shouting "Listen chaps I've done it. The tigress is here and bloody hungry at that." I sat silenced by my disapproval and rising annoyance at this cold-blooded denial of ethics.

Hari followed in his wake laughing hilariously and others followed in fast succession. Hari announced "Our lady tiger, I mean the one in the cage has to drink brandy – we had to buy three bottles of brandy, as was the ring-master cum trainer, required brandy to make her ladyship roar." Roaring with laughter he said "I bought three bottles of brandy – I mean Indian Brandy, but her trainer tells me she refused to drink any brandy except the famous French brandy Eggshaw No.1 so I had to buy three more bottles."

By this time I was really indignant and then flashed back "What nonsense – it appears that both of you are drunk."

Ash now entered the fray "All this shouting and high excitement should be brought under control, we are yet to hear what arrangements have been made and what other requirements are in our court, so we may proceed with our shooting plans.

Rupert who had been silent up till this moment, was trying to piece together a very confused delivery between Terry and Hari, now called everyone to attention, "In case none of you noticed, dusk has fled and the night is moving in swiftly, if this circus pantomime has to be launched, we had better be quick with our plans and get a move on, to find an appropriate place where, more than one tiger is likely to be interested. There was complete silence, then the ring-master made his speech, "Sir we have starved the beast, obtained four legs of calf meat and we have already given her brandy to drink several times almost directly from the brandy bottles. We must hurry to find a place for setting her cage in the right position if she has to act as bait for the tigers."

Rupert's mind was already at work so he divulged the plan he had in mind, "There is a pretty wide and deep "gully" covered with heavy undergrowth that would shield the location of our jeeps, while we drive the truck and tigress to higher ground. We would then wait until the tigress calls, all the tigers would hear her calling and move closer and then closer. As the brandy heats up her blood, her brain would be overcome due to her hungry stomach. As she gets more and more excited, the tigers would be making their way to get nearer and nearer, till they too could smell the blooded calf legs tied to the corners of the truck. Once we know exactly where one of them places himself, the jeep nearest to it will have their "shakari" switch on the search light and the one holding the double barrel gun will put two clean shots into him. If he does not fall, his partner will use his riffle to finish the animal".

After receiving our instructions, we boarded the four jeeps and proceeded into the night jungle. Since Rupert knew every inch of the terrain, he and I left in the first jeep, the rest were to follow. We made it to the "gully" in good time, allowing us to choose the most appropriate places to place the jeeps. The truck driver and ring-master moved to higher ground, but made sure the truck could be seen by all four jeeps ensuring that all had full visibility of the truck and the tigress in the cage.

The ring master poured more brandy into slits made in small pieces of beef covered with blood. Her hunger was evident as she devoured, the brandy dripping pieces in small morsels that vanished in quick succession. After only a few small morsels he left her to her own devices and went to sit in the front of the truck with two more shakaris holding riffles and a terrified driver at the wheel.

As her annoyance grew the tigress's calls became louder, longer, aggressive and more frenzied. It was not long after that, we began to hear the tigers "mating call" in answer to the calls coming from the caged tigress herself. After a short interval we began to hear responses to her calls from three to four different directions. This meant that there was more than one male interested in her demands. The call and replies went on, but only one male stalwart pushed his suite much faster and his call came nearer and nearer. Now he was pretty close and moving towards the truck where there was both a blooded meal and a mating tigress.

On each of the jeeps we stood up, guns at our shoulders ready to fire when the time was right. The tiger came in through the side corner facing our jeep. It became Rupert's right to fire his gun and he stood ready to so do, waiting for a sure angle for a clean shot, when he was just about to fire Terry had his "Shikarie" turn on the great dazzling search light that almost blinded Rupert. In that moment that was lost the tiger bounded into the darkness of the bushes, out of range for any gun or light and so he was gone.

We all knew what had happened but if you are a good hunter, you have to be a good sportsman. All Rupert said was "Lets all get back to base, and Terry, you take charge of getting the truck and tigress back to the circus."

In the silence that followed the anti-climax, jeeps returned to the rest House and Rupert then said, "We should get a good night's rest, we start out at 7 o'clock in the morning to hunt down the 'Rogue'. Goodnight everyone" we all took our leave and returned to our sleeping arrangements for the night.

The usual drill was a bath at night so after rising at dawn we dressed, breakfasted and arranged the shooting gear onto the jeeps and left the base according to schedule.

After a couple of hours of reconnoitering we saw no trace of the "Rogue" which was another disappointment. Keeping tongue in check, no one spoke a single word out of place. The shadows of the night before had left its mark, so we took each step in a wary manner, so as to hold the "peace".

Unexpected and out of nowhere we were suddenly attracted to our "shikares" and our "mahavats" (elephant drivers) gesticulating with great excitement. We descended from our jeep that had been moving at a crawl and went through the high grass to where the beaters were in a cluster, jabbering away and in very good spirits. They showed us what they had found. There was no elephant to be seen but a mass of rather fresh elephant droppings which we usually say "The Rogue left his calling card". This was a clear indication that somewhere there in the vicinity, was where our "rogue" had set up his residency. It was here that we had to set up our shooting base. All the jeeps were now lined up in a single line and the equipment carried by our hunting boys, to the high trees that grew in small clumps with plenty of open space of grasslands. His first requirement was food. Here there were plenty of trees and long grass growing.

Rupert chose an area and supervised the erecting of the "machans". The trees he chose for each "machan" was allotted to three men. Two men on each cot were responsible for the use of the guns, while the "shakari" himself was responsible to watch out, and to deal with the unexpected and the security of the gunners. His duty included the visual survey of the area and the assessment of any danger.

When all the "machans" had been securely bound to the branches of the seven different trees, it began to form a wide semi circle. Rupert was quite satisfied with the strategy and placement, so he decided to find the last suitable tree for the erecting of our "machan". We walked through the long grass till we came to the last few trees on the left, but they were not matured enough and could hardly bear the weight of the three people who were to sit on it. Coming to the last tree, Rupert went ahead of me as he always did, then I saw him suddenly freeze, standing quite still with his hand behind his back, he moved me back and kept taking, one slow backward step after another. I had assessed that danger was afoot, without a word I too kept moving back, obviously he had a good reason for his silence. As soon as he caught up with me, he took my hand, turned me around and fled way down to the end of the line of trees, where the others were waiting for some action. He told us that just as he turned and rounded past the trees, he had seen the "Rogue" standing in the high grass, using his trunk to gather a larger trunkful of grass, twisting his trunk round it before yanking it out of the earth, he vigorously shook off the mud and was shoveling the morsel into his mouth. Because his head was facing away from where Rupert entered, he neither saw him nor smelt his presence because the breeze was moving in the opposite direction.

Once we knew where he was, we tied another "machan" for Rupert and myself and organized, that the beaters and the jeeps must come from way out in front, the men beating their drum, making their wild calls and the jeeps moving slowly forward reviving the engines again and again. After clear instructions had been given all round and Rupert was satisfied, the shakari, Rupert and myself climbed up the tree and waited sitting on the tressel seat. After some time we began to hear the beaters approaching – this was the sign for us, to get ready steady on our mark but no "Go" the base word was to "wait" for the signal from Rupert.

As the commotion and jeeps got closer and closer the Rogue turned and ran forward in our direction trumpeting loudly. An elephant does not possess a light foot nor is his body bulk, easy to move, this makes him into a slow runner. As we sat there alert, his approach was somewhat slow and lumbering, but his trumpting was crazed with hysteria and terror. When he had come into a sure and comfortable range, Rupert pressed the trigger of a heavy bore gun which is especially used for this purpose. Both his shots found their mark, but for the thick hide of the elephant more guns are needed. In this case the extra gun was not really needed, Rupert had got both shots in quick succession right between the eyes. The "rogue" fell to the ground and his loud crazed bellow ceased. It would have taken him more time to die, but that would have been cruel, so taking my riffle Rupert put in another couple of rounds to ensure that the elephant was actually dead and his life, not lingering threshed in painful spasms for several hours, which would have been the natural way.

Once the Rogue was shot our work was done and the government machinery took over. It now became the property of the state. It is customary that if a "Rogue" is shot by someone holding a permit to shoot it, after some time one tusk is delivered to the gunman as a reward for such a deed. When Rupert received his tusk he sent me a piece. I had my jeweler make me a double pendent, moulded in a gold frame set on a short golden chain and I had a pair of ear-rings made in the shape of elephant's tusks. I still have them after these many years and now my grand-daughter Natalia is the proud possessor, which I have bequeathed to be passed on to my great-grand daughter Noor-e-Fatima.

It would be interesting to mention here that once long ago when Tahira Nazira, my daughter had a slight altercation with a friend of mine, Kathleen who said to her "What do you think — you shot a tiger" Tahira's quick repartee was "No I didn't, but my Mother did". Everyone present had a good laugh, and we all appreciated her quick wit and her smiling face.

> *We are no other than a moving row*
> *Of Magic Shadow-shapes that come and go*
> *Round with the sun-illumined Lantern held*
> *In Midnight by the Master of the Show;*
>
> *The Moving Finger writes; and, having writ,*
> *Moves on, nor all your Piety nor Wit*
> *Shall lure it back to cancel half a Line,*
> *Nor all your Tears wash out one Word of it.*

~ Omer Khayyam

★ ★ ★ ★ ★

Truth Conquers the Universe

STRENGTH OF MR. JINNAH'S CHARACTER
The Cauldron of Independence Was Boiling

Mr. Jinnah had a tenacious strength of character and a set mind of his own, he was sure of the policies which he upheld with conviction. He was a savour-faire diplomat, in his own skilful way, he managed to maneuver his stratagems to meet the occasion, thus accomplishing his decisions. He was highly educated for the legal profession, but a self made diplomat with a self-possessed and immovable will when conviction was present, for which he was all too often criticized by the press, as a stern unyielding, uncompromising and an unshakable individual. This biased and imbalanced view was projected from a highly bigoted and dogmatic Indian press, much of which was written speculation, character assassination, with the intent to malign and dishonour his name. His private domestic tragedies were of such a nature, that the encumbrance of steel barriers were required to shield his personal life. It had become imperative to ensure a screen of protection to shield his family, with the young and beautiful daughter of Sir and Lady Pettit, who were members of a noble family, a highly esteemed couple, respected by the social hierarchy of Bombay. The marriage between the young couple was entirely the framework of their own making, even at the displeasure manifested by her parents, for they were not Muslims, but of the Parsi persuasion, with deep rooted adherence to their own religion. The newly wed couple were deeply in love, with the marriage-bond as a "fait-er-compli" situation. The written pages of their journal could not be re-written, nor the marriage annulled as the bride herself was a major with the legal right of consent for her own marriage.

Mrs. Jinnah was young with a husband who adorned her and their beautiful daughter, but this bliss was not granted to them for very long – tragedy struck Mr. Mohammad Ali Jinnah, when only after a few happy years of marriage he faced the unfortunate demise of his dearly beloved wife, who left him a very young daughter. After the death of her mother, his daughter was taken into the care of her maternal grandparents, leaving Mr. Jinnah bereft of both his wife and his daughter. The tragedy he suffered, the anguish for his lost wife, the separation from his daughter was too near the heart, to be left exposed to the media and viewing by the public, hence his withdrawal to a fortress of silence, submerging his sorrow in work, he was transformed into a man with a vision and a mission, all other doors and social friendships were shut out, making him a man of sound authority, and an unwavering statesman.

After such harrowing circumstances, Mr. Jinnah threw everything to the winds and attached himself to the arena of politics. Being an intelligent, astute, brilliant and a highly self-possessed man, he awakened, aroused and activated the Muslims of India to bravely march into the avenues of a separate homeland for Muslims, within the dominion of the Indian sub-continent.

It would appear to some that Pakistan came into being within the "twinkling of an eye", but that impression is completely erroneous. As early as 1896 at the turn of the century, Mr. Mohammad Ali Jinnah returned to India at the tender age of twenty, after completing his studies in England. He possessed a full-fledged law degree and a "Bar at law" from Lincoln's Inn in London. His family was from Sindh, but he resided in Bombay, where there were vast opportunities to feed a legal practice and the field that would enable him to build up sound political associations. He moved and mixed well and judiciously in the higher echelons of Bombay's society of the legal, judicial and political cadres, from where he received a sound welcome and was well respected. He had the inherent quality of a sagacious leader, and the intrinsic value of ethical morality, but most of all he recognized his own worth.

Unfortunately the family business had fallen off during his absence in England, thus his father desired him to enter the business to use his contact and ability to re-build it. This he gently but firmly demurred. With this determined posture he left in his wake a very provoked and irate father.

He was offered a number of well positioned jobs in Bombay, but he gracefully, and firmly refused all the offers that came. The best offer came from Mr. MacPherson, the then Advocate General of Bombay, who was highly impressed with Mr. Jinnah's work, his quick progress, the manner in which he carried and conducted himself as an upright and honourable gentleman. In view of this, he was recommended to Sir Charles Ollivant, the Head of the Judicial Department, who in a very short time appointed Mr. Jinnah as the temporary "Presidency Magistrate". Mr. Jinnah's superiors were full of praise and considered his work and presence, as exemplary. At that time years ago when the value of the Indian rupee, money-wise, was worth something, he was offered the appointment of a judicial nature, at the princely salary of Rs.1500/- per month. Mr. Mohammad Ali Jinnah declined this generous offer saying "Sir! No thank you sir, I will soon be able to earn that much money in a single day."

Mr. Jinnah was a stickler for good manners, decorous behaviour and the respect of formality. There was much negative propaganda against him in the Indian press regarding his stance of being a "pure gentleman". Perhaps some impure gentlemen may have been more acceptable. This side of his pure nature, displayed his pride, his moral ethics and his other western characteristics, but Mr. Jinnah was accused, yet he knew where to stop. With his polished manners and mannerisms, he knew exactly when to go on and how far to go. I shall reveal some episodes that indicate his "razor sharp" brain and "flashed-wit". The gentleman was blessed by God with a genius brain, adept at his subject and adroit in the carriage of justice.

On one such occasion it brought the highly biased Indian press nipping at his heels, accusing him of being arrogant, proud and demonstrating his vanity, at Mr. Gandhi's expense. The factual position was very different. Whenever there was a meeting to be held with Mr. Gandhi, Mr. Jinnah went to meet him, at his home residence for discussions regarding the political affairs and the development of India's Independence. There inevitably appeared a perpetual barrage of miscellaneous interruptions, forth coming from various members and individuals around Mr. Gandhi, this was to ensure that the meeting would be aborted. After several such occasions, Mr. Jinnah informed Mr. Gandhi of his inability to conduct a meeting at Mr. Gandhi's residence. This complaint to Mr. Gandhi, who took cognizance of it, brought the desired result.

Mr. Gandhi acquiesced to this and visited Mr. Jinnah's home, where the meetings were held. Of course this put a spanner in the wheels, blocking the press the opportunities and advantages they were seeking. One could imagine the "black fury" and lashing resentment, of a biased press, that had been circumvented and outwitted, as they had to wait for an announcement by either party or both parties together.

Another classic prototype episode regarding Mr. Jinnah, that was bandied and shuffled around by the dissatisfied opposition, deals with a meeting that Mr. Jinnah was to have with Mr. Allama Inayatullah Mashriqi at "Qarul Bagh", where Mr. Allama was staying at the "Khaksar Camp". The Allama received Mr. Jinnah in an ordinary simple tent, that had seen better days. The tent's floor was spread with a cotton "durrie" on the raw unbuilt floor and there were no seating arrangements. This was expected to create a problem for Mr. Jinnah, causing him an embarrassment, for it was reckoned, that as a "pure gentleman" he would display his inability to sit on the floor, this would show him up as a foreigner.

It was well known to all, that Mr. Jinnah was always dressed in formal light coloured suits, with appropriate neck ties. On this occasion he wore a white sharkskin suit, with a shirt and formal tie, and added to this his feet were encased in European laced shoes.

There were no chairs made available for him to sit on, and any formal seating present. Everyone stood around to watch Mr. Jinnah and the embarrassment that was about to follow. Unfortunately the plotted scheme back-fired, as Mr. Jinnah very neatly sat down cross-legged on the floor and greeted Mr. Allama Mashriqi. Silence was the boomerang that followed.

In a perfectly calm and affable manner, Mr. Jinnah took out his gold cigarette case and offered the Allama a cigarette from his case. After he had taken a cigarette from Mr. Jinnah, he too followed suit and took out one for himself. Before he could light it Mr. Allama took out two paisas (equal to a British penny farthing in those days) Mr. Jinnah queried his host regarding this very odd gesture of paying a price for the cigarette, the reply he received from the Allama "A Khaksar does not accept anything, without paying its price." When Mr. Jinnah heard this, in a very graceful and in a very cultured manner, he bent forward taking the cigarette back from Mr. Allama said "My cigarette is much more than two "paisas" and I don't think you can afford it."

Mr. Jinnah had an extremely sharp brain and a fleet mind with deft, astute reactions striking from his teeming brain, repartees were swift and decisions were crystalline perfectly sound. His unsurpassed "rapier" retorts were outstanding but daunting. On one occasion in 1941, when he was pleading a case before the Sindh Chief Court, the courtroom was over flowing with an overwhelming, mammoth crowd, that had emanated to hear him speak. The courtroom, the halls and the very corridors were overflowing beyond capacity. In view of this unprecedented influx the presiding judge, Chief Justice of Sindh – Mr. Justice Davis informed the court clerk, to have the doors of the Court room closed.

Mr. Jinnah rose in his cool sanguine manner and smiling, he said to 'his Lordship'. "The doors of justice should always be kept open" Hearing this, the Chief justice ordered the opening of the doors with immediate effect. The proceedings of the court, went on as usual and the crowded, courtroom and halls confirmed Mr. Jinnah's trust in them, there were no sounds, no "calling to order" no demonstrations from the audience. This faith in himself and his calm procedure in the court won him new laurels.

On July, the 26th, 1943 there had been an attempt on his life. He displayed presence of mind and exhibited his determination to continue to work, for a free and self-dependant Pakistan for the Muslims of India.

On one occasion when Mr. Jinnah was pleading a case before Mr. Justice Martin 'his Lordship' lost his temper and shouted "Mr. Jinnah you are not addressing a third class magistrate." The rapier tongue of Mr. Jinnah within seconds flashed back. "There isn't a third class counsel before your Lordship". There are countless such episodes regarding Mr. Jinnah, that made him an outstanding lawyer, the highly capable and dedicated leader, of the Muslims of India, thus he rose to be the "Quaid–e–Azam" of Pakistan.

The partition of India and Pakistan was signed on the 14th of August, 1947. From then on Mr.Jinnah became the "Quaid–e–Azam".With him, there were a great many other outstanding Muslims with the same ideology, but the seed planted in Mr.Jinnah, was well before the turn of the century.It took time to germinate, to sprout, to grow under the nurturing wills of men like Mr.Liaquat Ali Khan, Sir Abdullah Haroon, Pir Ali Mohammad Rashidi and there were many more to follow and from East Pakistan there was Sir Surrawadi and Mr. Nazam-ud-din.

Much was printed against his English approach to western clothes of suits and shirts, of ties and shoes, this very stance divulged the beauty of his honesty. His ethical, trustworthy and morally characteristic background with his own personal preference was never to be sold for the sake of gaining popularity. His ability was enough to make him a "leader of men."

Due to this, he was attacked as being, an inferior class of 'Muslim'. This was quite, absurd and the illegitimate birth through negative assertions and unscrupulous propaganda, hoping the Muslim backing that was escalating in his favour, would fall back in shock and withdraw their patronage. This would then tumble and weaken the Muslim League thus producing a "Divide and rule" political situation against the objectives of a Muslim Pakistan.

Mr. Jinnah's own Islamic identity can not be refuted. In 1939, ten years before the partition of India he firmly stated "So far, as I am concerned I am willing to be branded so, for doing my duty towards the Muslims. I was born a Muslim, I am a Muslim and shall die a Muslim." This was the "star of India" reporting his speech of the 6th of August. This was published on the 7th of August, 1939.

In his own words he stated that "I am not a learned Maulana or a Maulvi, nor do I claim to be a well versed theologian, but I am very much aware of my faith and I am humble enough to be proud to follow my faith as a Muslim within the dictates of the Holy Quran.

On the 30th of October, 1947 after the birth of Pakistan he said "We thank Providence for giving us courage and faith to fight the forces of evil. If we take our inspiration and guidance from the Holy Quran, the final victory is ours. It is necessary to build up Pakistan as a bulwark of Islam." Mr. Jinnah quoted the Quranic Sura Al-Maidah "Today I have perfected your Deen for you and completed My favours upon you and approved Islam as our Deen."

There are more than two hundred and fifty speeches in which Mr. Jinnah expressed his own Islamic devotion and as a servant of Islam, vowed to secure a separate state where the Muslims of India could live their lives beneath the umbrella of Islam, teaching, practicing their rituals and the injunctions from the Holy Quran as required by the "Divine Message". Fear of castigation and anti Muslim pressure, put restrictions on open and unconcealed projection of Islamic ritual. Islam teaches the Muslims through the words of the Holy Quran that "There is no compulsion to religion."

Does any of the anti propaganda against Mr. Jinnah suggest that he was not a Muslim at heart, nor did he conform to the rituals of the faith, therefore he could not be the leader of the Muslims, in a fair and free Islamic society. The whole theory is absurd and maleficent, to serve some under the surface intrigue.

The ideology of a free Muslim country was not the brain child of Mr. Jinnah, infact he was to be nurtured and propelled into the basic ideology by his seniors. He and his political group, were the flag bearers of the ideology, but the progenitors formed the basic tenets, developing a creed, a philosophy, and a mounting belief that produced the dogma of an exclusive "Islamic State" for the Muslims of the sub-continent. He was tutored during his stay in England while preparing for his "Bar at Law". His association with the cream of this political ideology, were the minds of the great men he looked up to, they inducted him into the ideology and instructed him well, grooming him without prejudice or single thought, regarding this young prodigy then aged twenty, turned out to be the leader of a state, created by their ideology.

Here I need to present a small summary of the individuals he worked with and learnt the true rudiment and nature of politics, that would be played out in the sub-continent to create a new Muslim state of Pakistan.

The first and the most important was Mr. Allama Mohammad Iqbal – 1877. Mr. Allama Iqbal was among the greatest thinkers, writers and poets in modern Islamic history. He was born in Sialkot in northern Punjab on 9th November, 1877. He received his Masters Degree from Government College, Lahore, then he taught philosophy at Government College and established himself, as a talented poet before leaving for England, to further his studies in philosophy at the Cambridge University. Mr. Iqbal also studied Law and was 'called to the Bar' at Lincoln's Inn. He went on to receive his doctorate in Philosophy from Germany.

On his return to Lahore, Mr. Iqbal could not remain aloof from the major political and religious scenario. Inspite of his praise for Sufism , he was concerned that the Sufism as practiced in the sub-continent, was not the true spirit or message of Islam. His conviction was, that nothing less than a separate homeland for the Muslims was essential. By 1926, Mr. Iqbal's brilliance, was noted by the Muslim League and in 1930, he chaired the Muslim League Conference in Allahabad. In his presidential address he formally stated that the requirement of the Muslims of the subcontinent, must work for an independent Muslim homeland.

It was ten years later in 1940 that Mohammad Ali Jinnah, as president of the Muslim League, formally made the same demand at the "Pakistan Resolution" meeting.

There were meetings and an exchange of letters between Mr. Iqbal and the Quaid, as Mr. Iqbal realized that Mr. Jinnah alone, could guide the Muslims of India. He was constantly exhorting Mr. Jinnah to declare a Muslim homeland to be the aim of the Muslim League. He managed to write till his death on 21st April, 1938. It was tragic that he did not live to see the Muslim homeland, for which he had given the Muslim debate a practical direction, providing an intellectual base as the demand for a separate homeland.

Another great leader was Mr. Rehmat Ali who was born on the 16th November, 1897. He was a member of a series of Round Table Conferences in London to discuss the political reform in British India. During his stay in London, he met the Muslim League leaders and urged them to press, for nothing less than an independent homeland for the Muslims. Mr. Rehmat Ali was dismayed by the general lack of support, so he wrote pamphlets and issued declarations. On 28th June, 1933, he circulated a pamphlet entitled "Now or Never". For these 30 million people, the land was to be called "Pakistan". The letter 'P' stood for the Punjab, 'A' for Afghan, and pathan, 'K' stood for the state of Kashmir, 'S' took the position for Sindh and 'tan' was for Balochistan. This spelt the word "Pakistan" which also means "Land of the Pure".

This gave Mr. Rehmat Ali the unique honour of being the originator of the name of the new country. Mr. Rehmat Ali has the distinction of coining the name, of this large Muslim country called Pakistan. Unfortunately he died in England on 3rd February, 1951. He envisaged his 'dream' in reality, but did not see it develop or constrained by political and material debacles.

Sir Syed Ahmed Khan was born in Delhi on the 17th October, 1817 to an old and prominent family of the city. His contributions to the community had been immense and his leadership ever present for the Muslims of India. He had brought the Muslims educationally, from the medieval age into the modern world.

He restored Muslim credibility in the eyes of the British Rulers. He advocated that the best progress, was to learn from western technology and education. His valuable contributions to the development of the Urdu Language that needed expression with a wide range of vocabulary became his passion.

Although Sir Syed Ahmed Khan has often been criticized for being too pro-British in his approach, his greatest gift to the Muslim community of the sub-continent was his realism to look to the future with confidence. A bright future could only be built, by a developed present. He helped restore Muslim self-confidence, he built bridges with the British administration and laid the foundation of a Muslim educational and political movement. Sir Syed knew that in the future, the Muslims could only rely upon themselves, so to this end he helped to equip them with a sound education, enabling them to crest the challenges of the future.

Along with Mr. Allama Iqbal, Mr. Rehmat Ali and Sir Syed Ahmed at this stage of planting the seed of the ideology, for a separate state for Muslims there were others. This ideology was not only for philosophers but a great deal of stalwart Muslims bringing with them their heavy contingent of political compatriots and followers.

Unfortunately, Mr. Jinnah did not live long enough, to develop the Islamic state of Pakistan, with a politically secular and democratic base. After his death on the 11th of September, 1948 stability fled, sliding down hill. Some must 'rise' to build a Dam to rescue the country, ensuring that Pakistan retains its sovereignty and is not washed away under a tidal wave.

Unless we read the 'writing on the wall' which is plain to see as it stands we cannot survive.

It is the sacred duty of the press to safeguard our very existence, if we are to survive the genocide, holocaust planned to subjugate the Muslims of the world.

Without those founder members with their Herculeous brains and the mammoth Muslim compatriots that stand behind as willing to sacrifice materialism and their personal ambitions for a separate Muslim homeland, and the ideology, cannot be free as a sovereign state, ensuring development. Dependence is as bad as non existence.

The problems in Pakistan today are the problems that touch, nearly all the developing countries of the world. The problems, are not the lack of ideology but the requirement of "power" of the "world" that is played out across the "International chessboard".

Materialism has been launched specifically to reduce, the underdeveloped countries to a state of poverty, so that the reins of Power remain under the gripping and iron hands of "International World Power", while weak impaired countries make their rounds, with a beggars bowl for survival.

★ ★ ★ ★ ★

Truth Conquers the Universe

TIME ABSORBS TRAGEDY
Gracious And Touching Memories

I reckon the time factor for my autobiography as I presented, it encompassed a span period of seven decades. For the initial decade of my life, I had almost no revealing individual identity, that is worth the mention, thus the following throbbing seventy years, cover the actual time-span of an active and meaningful life for me, as a result, I consciously laid the foundation and built awareness of myself, my surroundings, my social environment, my mistakes, and even my wasted efforts that surfaced at a later date. With appreciation, I have been the recipient of many honouring credits. Life has drawn its bow with arrows that wounded me, hammered and clobbered me, bats that walloped me, grief and tears that blinded me … but with His justice, and Mercy came bouquets, and awards in appreciable numbers with significant crowns of dignity. In these my octagon years, I gauge my life with a credit balance of tributes that out-weighed the tragedies that befell me. Time absorbs tragedy, becoming a great healer. One does not forget, but there are graciously and touching memories, that beautify life. There is loss, but no loneliness for the overbearing demands of life, goes on and living is the passing of time.

When I returned to India from London, the territory was beginning to be a powder keg of dynamite. There had been a devastating and sharp decline that registered the growing culmination of the Mughal Empire, through a series of internal wars of supremacy, or enmity instigated by Western diplomacy, creating friction between the princely states, added to this was the speedy advancement of foreign traders, such as the British, Portuguese and French trading companies, that originally sought to purchase spices, fine muslin and beautiful silks from India in the name of trade were welcomed. The Muslim Mughals and Hindu Marahatas, it was natural that they had their own differences – but to compound this common danger, began a resolute policy of "divide and rule", by setting up one prince against the other, by subtle friendship and assistance, friendly diplomacy, leaving both Mughals and Marahatas weak and unable to defend themselves against the powerful martial forces that were mustered against them. This eventually paved the way for advancement and the supremacy of power by the British East India Company. Large potent British trading posts were established and developed becoming substantial and stronger, until India was no longer an independent state but had become just a mere vassal territory of the British, Trading companies reducing the power of ruling princes, leaving the states with only limited powers within the domain of their own state. The British administration increased, becoming stauncher by the day, their power spread further and wider across the sub-continent, until they held the powerful reins of government in a tight iron clinch. Unfortunately, the weakened princes yielded one by one before the heavily armed British troops that had been originally created and trained, for the protection of the widely growing assets of the East India Company. Later these trained troops were converted into a force that became the Government's official army, with regiments placed all over India, and their cantonments sprung up everywhere. Their police force was empowered with the strength of local power behind the throne of the British Empire.

With these two conflicting cultures behind us, the scenario in later years changed, as the elite families of Indian were propelled into the higher stratum of learning, they were sent to Public Schools opened by the British in preparation to man the Indian Civil Service of the bureaucracy, the sons of Princes were sent to England to be groomed by British Public Schools. The result would be quite obvious. At such a tender age, when one was given an entirely English education, our native cultures began to recede, to be replaced by an English way of life. An established standard of decorum and culture, was monitored and the Indian gentry needed to receive a British Public School education for India. This called for a change in social behaviour, where officers displayed this, was most noticeable at the height of society, where even the members of the "Chamber of Princes" willingly donned the attire of the English, their mode of living was cultivated, they borrowed the style of almost all mannerism, exhibited by the British. The national image of Eastern culture was swiftly undergoing an innocuous, but well structured and a finely defined change in the annals of a time pace – it was to become the "lull before the storm". In later years this very change became the "eye of the storm."

The smouldering past acceptance was currently, as ice floating in warm water, or leaving the need to conform as a dying ember, for apparently it was no longer the need of the hour. As the maintaining resistance grew, so did the change of a western way of life. With allegiance to the despised crown no longer a prime factor, Princes and Potentates reverted to wearing the Indian "Prince's Jacket", leaving dinner-suits with their black bow ties hanging in their wardrobes. It was no longer considered the only correct mode of dinner dress. Gold encased emeralds, platinum clawed diamonds, pidgeon-blood rubies in over-sized buttons, were on perpetual display, holding together the 'princely jackets' they wore in every royal colour. An incessant reminder that foreign subjugation, had become unacceptable and inoperative. Wearing sparkling raiments, be-jewelled head-gear, swords in scabbards, ornately crafted precious stones dominating the weapons, that challenged the forceful, superbly cut suits, meticulously trimmed and finished by unrivalled tailoring houses of Europe, this display of opulence was displayed strictly to command the respect they demanded from the Rulers of the Empire. The turnstile of Indian social life had began to function spinning in reverse, turned and energized by the silent but demonstrated elite. Unfortunately, the underling or masses did not have the resources for this display of superiority, so they existed, just as silent inferior subordinates. A whole era was undergoing a change of direction, that was silent and subtle. There were no obvious announcements, no commanding or demanding orders to be followed, no glaring animosity, no apparent external changes, no gracious consultations, no anti-government organization – only a new discriminating finesse in the East of a rising Indian superiority, just the taciturn smiling disdain that cracks as easily as egg-shells. The invisible lines of division were conspicuous when notices began to appear, such as "dogs and Indians" not allowed, were printed on boards placed by indifferent Western rulers, totally oblivious to the resentment and insult to the feelings of the Indians. These crude orders hung outside clubs, restaurants, train compartments, public utilities and other places that were reserved exclusively for the Westerners. As these inimical indignities had been spluttered everywhere, an imperceptible retaliation movement now raised its flag, clubs began to open for, "Indian Nationals" only, some of the first class railway carriages and the Famous Kelners restaurants, dinning cars and restrooms became the exclusive domain of the Indians. The seeds of change had been well scattered, nurtured and apparently well sown, after maturing, now the long awaited harvest was to be reaped, while the emblem of Independence emerged couched on the national flag of green white and yellow.

Since I had been brought up in a multi-cultural society, and many Indians had embraced much of the Western mode of living, where a modern and western atmosphere surrounded me. With my education derived in a highly elevated classical English convent, I had imbibed an inordinately substantial content of western views. But with my background heritage of a cultural Persian Islamic family, my conflicting cultures clashed causing within me an emotional disturbance, as eventually, I had to come to change my mode of life. I required to make a choice, and decide my immense dilemma. I really must admit that perhaps occasionally I may have sometimes shown the obvious result, I fell short of being a cultural thoroughbred. Unfortunately I was oblivious and failed to discern who I was and what I needed to represent until I attained my early twenties. Being a product of pure unmixed Arab blood, was I an Arab? I displayed the colouring of a Westerner, but was I a westerner? In my dress code I was anglicized, leaning towards French elegance, so was I French? Even my early acquired British elegant manners were quite apparent, it manifested the influence of my English education, many other aspects reflected the years of residing abroad, it was evinced clearly in my voice and mode of speech, but was I English?

There was a time lapse before I could segregate the wheat from the chaff, I manifested a great desire to retain what I considered appropriate, for my self-respect from the time I was a teenager. In my religious beliefs, there could be no possible compromise, instead it forcefully deepened the guarded norms of my principles and my ethical conduct. Keeping in view the requirements that construed to present a gracious lady in her demeanour, conduct, genteel behaviour and modulation of speech. I processed my cultural equations, in the process of segregating my true values I encountered no difficulty with the placement of my ethics, integrity, principles, honesty and modes of decorum, all these moral values I had learnt at the feet of my parents, and taught by the media of my religious books. The Holy Books of all revealed religions, declare presenting the same norms, the code of principles, of responsibility, of modesty, of integrity, of honour and even humanity, which is accompanied by sympathetic benevolence. The older I grew the more advanced, and more evolved and more matured I became with the ever increasing knowledge. As the windows of my mind opened, the wider became my consciousness, it also began to open my vision. I was not to allow myself to become a cultural half breed. I realized more forcefully my obligation to retain my own cultural norms and even more important my religious beliefs, which I could never contemplate to split, nor apportion this sole quintessence's and singular apotheosis. To conceive my true roll, I beckoned the dawn of necessity, I needed to be steadfast, if I was to maintain my identity and for myself respect, I required courage, to face the mutation of several previous naïve decisions which at that time confronted me, I traced back in recall, my early adolescent convictions without adult vision and I could never have envisioned how infinitely far apart, distinctive with each its own individualistically isolated, these were the two cultures in which I was reared. As I opined, I began to validate the conducive truth that stood sentinel to my conscience, I set about to extricate myself from it, for my all Islamic knowledge and national cultural, rose to confront me, the vital key had been overshadowed, but I realized and was grateful that my subconscious mind had still been alive throughout those formative years.

Returning to a time long past, the armistice between Germany and the allied forces of Britain and America brought World War-II to it's final end. In India, the more the control aspect of the stringent emergency was evaporating, the greater grew the seed of independence ripening under a blazing sun, which became the unrelenting pressure of the copious Indian prosessionists, demanding independence from the Imperial Empire. A non violent, but highly active resistance came into force, challenging movements once again, reared its irrepressible head with defiance, giant size consistent processions and rallies blocked the roads, a multitude of robust but silent demonstrations were on a daily basis, hunger strikes, "disobedience" movements dauntless slogans of "Quit India", escalated into unsupressible daily and nightly performance, sprouting slogans of ideology and freedom, came from every street all over India.

The previous dormant political groups, now opened wide their doors to admit every Indian who desired to bestow his own support, joining the struggle like a tidal wave, gushing forward seeking its unrestricted freedom. Recruiting for the resistance of the masses was neither planned, nor did it impose a problem. The masses eagerly joined the political arena voluntarily. They were admitted to political groups, under the watchful and widespread wings of the brilliant and capable leaders under whose wisdom every move was carefully planned. There was one sole aim, the "restoration" of the Indian territory, still in the clutches of the British Empire. The Indians loved their homeland, assured the restoration of it as their motherland, with great men and politicians, who were determined to set up a state owned by a National Government, as the slogan went "of the people, by the people, for the people." This rapidly soaring movement was deeply motivated and established without a grain of selfishness, or for self-grandizment. The deep rooted resentment was extremely visible creating a successful opposition, due to the "stigma" by the "white" population, not only that but they treated Indians as second class citizens, degraded them by relegating them to a third class status, there upon their very own homeland.

The largest and the most powerful political party at that time was "The All India Congress" led by Mahatama Gandhi, Mr. Moti Lal Nehru, and his son Mr. Jewaharlal Nehru. The next strongest political party was the "Muslim League" led and developed by highly educated men such as Mr. Allama Iqbal our national philosopher and poet, Sir Syed Ahmed of Aligarh, Sir Syed Ali Imam, Sir Syed Hassan Imam of Bihar (my two grandfathers), Mr. Mohammad Ali Jinnah of Sindh, Mr. Liaquat Ali Khan from the United Province of India and Moulana Abdul Kalam Azad from Kashmir. These are only a few of the celebrated political giants of that time. The Sikhs had their own political party with Sardar Patel as their leader and other smaller political parties began to develop, with new up coming parties that were manned by highly educated men of status at the helm of affairs, – men such as Mahatama Gandhi, Nawab Chathari, Raja of Patiala, Nawab of Junaghar and Raja Sahib Mahmoodabad, an unending trail of legal Indian brains were to be found in every party, having the one common cause – the determination for self rule and an independent Indian identity.

The winds of change could be discerned and observed everywhere, consciously the mode of a national dress had begun to make an appearance, discarding Western suits, sport jackets and dinner suits were replaced by Eastern apparel such as the native dress of Achakan, Shervani, the Princes Jacket, dhoti and Gandhi caps.

For the Indian ladies sarees once more replaced the smart coats with fur, hand bags and gloves of expensive leather, hats with feathered adornments were cast aside, gloved hands began to evince uncovered manicured nails, decorated with arms encircled with coloured bangles. Along with this rapidly changing scenario the clubs, restaurants, and public places opened their doors to the Indian public without any prohibition or restraint, even the clubs permitted the entry of dogs without discrimination albeit that they were to be leashed or chained to the rails of posts for this purpose, but mainly as a precaution against rabies. The degrading wooden plaques on the front doors or gates displaying "Dogs and Indians not allowed" soon found their repose in the log fires. The time had arrived for the Indians to stand up and be counted.

There were so many diverse cultures through which I have passed, which at times left me confused. I was in the process of evolving my own life, facing the reality of maturity. I discerned that some groups displayed diagonally opposite cultural norms while others had baffling concepts between conservative structure and a fast developing modernism, which made discriminating and the cutting away from any particular sector confusing, making an assessment became extremely difficult. It is surprising that under such a mammoth conflicting criterion, I did not slip into a psychological or a socially mixed up personality, consuming my own scrambled brains. As I grew up, I continued to search, unearth and comprehend that a portion of what appeared to me was to be very misleading, creating conflicts, I required to deal with it and disentangled the knots and tangles by a process of elimination, but this discovery emerged only after I had acquired an early maturity, at the age of approximately twenty. My hazy concepts of the world's conflicting images assassinated my dreams, desecrated my loyalty, provoked the battling emotions that enveloped me. I observed that actions did not follow the philosophy that was being propounded, and much of what I heard was unbelievable. I became acquainted with the greed of man and it astounded me, I was stunned by the degradation of man's materialism, but my unspoken words were never heard, it was to remain asleep under the cover of a mutually agreed silence. This was the conflicting world in which I was about to embark.

★ ★ ★ ★ ★

GHANDI: 'FATHER OF THE NATION'

Mr. Mohan Das Ghandi became "Bapu"

I now dare to present and express my impressions of the "Father of the Indian Nation". Mr. Mohandas Karamchand Gandhi, later known as Gandhijee who affectionately bore the term of endearment as "Bapu". An Indian by virtue of his birth, but by a set of un-envisioned circumstances his family migrated to African settling in the East Coast, where he was brought up. His way of life was set in the family manner, that maintained their Indian and Hindu culture, with the norms of their own ideology and superiority. Gandhijee went on to college in South Africa, with the intention of completing his higher studies. During this transient period he had ample time, the verve and the vigour to observe, to dislike and to reject the arrogance of the European communities, towards the non-whites. Their obnoxious, racist and intolerant behaviour towards the natives, were degrading in conduct, infact towards "Blacks" as they called them. The local inhabitants were insulted and dismissed merely as "Blacks" because they were supposed to be without feelings, self-respect, and dignity – the "Whites" most certainly kept their horses, dogs and even their cats under better living conditions, with fully nourished bellies, they kept "blacks" for the grooming, of their horses and dogs with full medical support by white doctors for, their animals were superior to the "blacks".

I had the fortune to meet Mr. Gandhi, though only a few times, but I had read and imbibed a great deal about him, from the daily newspapers and magazines that expressed in detail the important features regarding his speeches, almost as a daily routine. To me in those far off days he was a complete "enigma" to my perhaps confused mind. Since my father knew him well, praised him for his bravery of open resistance, his exposure of the government's subjugation tactics, and his persistence in raising the anti-British slogans of "Quit India" against the foreign rulers.

As I have already stated that in my early formative years, to me he was an 'enigma'. While in Africa, before his outspoken protests and rebellion against the "degrading" treatment by Europeans metered out to the true owners of the land, the deep confounded prejudice against the local population of "Blacks", he took on his unmitigated fight for freedom, his protest against subjugation of slavery and his obeisance to Foreign Masters was not to be found amongst the virtues of Mr. Gandhi.

Mr. Mohandas Gandhi protested, demanding respect and equal rights for African Blacks and whites alike. As a young man he was very much aware of his self-respect and human rights. His clothes were well made, his presentation good, he was known to be a well dressed gentleman like any Englishman in a perfectly cut suit, finished with a formal shirt and a correctly knotted bow-tie, which was an art of its own kind, if it could be achieved, in fact at that time he was a "dandy" gentleman. While still in Africa he followed the fashion of the day, with polished patent-leather shoes, woollen scarves and to top it all an Englishman's felt hat. Despite his European dress code, he was an Indian at heart in every aspect of the word. Once when he boarded a train in Africa, a snobbish white European, brought in the railway guard of the train to remove Mr. Gandhi from the compartment, even though he had a first class ticket, he was informed that the compartment was meant for the European white community alone. This infuriated Mr. Gandhi (as divulged by him to my father and other members of the community when they sat together). In protest, Mr. Gandhi doffed his hats, burnt his already coveted English wardrobe, and returned to his motherland that was India, where he donned with pride, the local national dress of "Dhoti" made of white cotton and a local "Kurta" which is the Indian equivalent of a shirt.

Later when he was confronted by reality, where ideology has little space, as dire poverty reigned all over India, by the half starved people, and an almost a half-naked population, Mr. Gandhi was conscience stricken, then he actually embraced their poverty, wearing a small loin-cloth, no top shirt, just a "sacred thread" that all Hindu men are supposed to wear. Gandhijee wore his sacred thread cross-wise across his bare chest, while his feet were left unshod for in his book, shoes belonged to Englishmen and Europeans. His head was clean- shaven, no headgear donned his head, leaving him with complete exposure to the elements and inclement weather. What he saw was an appalling necessity, of living the stringent poverty and baneful, starving existence of the poor, he became the defiant, the defender, and uncompromising objector creating his march against the Masterful Rulers. It was a protest of non-violence, hunger strikes, silent marching and the call for freedom and independence. Mr. Gandhi took his protest formula of remonstration, agitation and defiance through every province, capital cities, towns and even small villages of India. He never stayed at the comfortable hotels, he resided in the "dharmshahlas" (religious house of the temples).

There was also a synonymous approach towards his food – as a Hindu he was a strict and pure vegetarian (many people practice the code of a vegetarian). His unchangeable and consistent diet, was several glasses of milk a day, a small quantity of fruit and a negligible portion of unleavened bread. Most of his days had become "fasting days" for some reason or the other. Hunger-strikes were not uncommon, but on many occasions the government authorities resorted to "force feeding" but "Bapu" as he was named by the doting public, continued his protests by fasting, when arrested he went to jail, and this happened quite frequently.

The victual provisions for the poor was hardly sustainable nourishment and fuel availability almost non-existent. Under such circumstances, meals consisted of a meagre helping of some grain products cooked in the simplest form. The powdered flour was made from grain mixed with water and a pinch of salt then kneaded into a dough, flattened with a rolling-pin then stone-baked and consumed. This was only a basic nourishment, which was highly insufficient in quantity, or quality of dietary needs. The poor subsisted on an irregular, insufficient and an unchangeable routine of a singular diet. At that time over eighty percent of the sub-continent of the Indian population, eked out their lives existing on malnutrition, it was an accepted verdict of, sleeping quite frequently on their empty bellies.

The devastating poverty and the degradation of begging pervaded the air, plus a great deal of inadmissible sad situation regarding the down-trodden masses, was voiced by the "Chamber of Princes". The consistently mounting arrogance, could no longer be tolerated, nor banished by diplomacy, it created distrust with a mounting aversion to the rulers of the Empire. The dams of hatred broke down, flooding the banks of endurance, rippling waters of disharmony that swelled into roaring waves, anti-government slogans, were heard and read everywhere, arson, torch light procession, disobedience and silent marches, became the powerful weapon of confrontation and the order of the day, resistance stormed on, brandishing anti government slogans on the walls, diverting the civil defence mechanism into a defensive and powerless corner.

Indians were at a silent war with their foreign rulers. War on the Indian sub-continent demanded independence, it was an irreversible march with legions of freedom fighters swelling in overpowering numbers that emerged to unite as a single bonded force, supporting what should have been variable battle-fronts, instead there were volatile political clashes, all followers accepted the form of resistance chosen by their leaders. Fear ceased to exist, dormant embers came alive with dauntless courage, welding a staunch defence of a civil population, their new exhilarated courage became harmonized, they marched in step with the drum-beats of war, asserting their claim for Independence and a free India.

There were freedom fighters without ammunition, there were untrained farmers with courage like soldiers, there were even women taking to the streets. Men were fighting on starving bellies, men who valued their honour not their lives, they faced without fear the unsheathed boynets of the Empire. Blind courage coursed through their veins, that drove them into courageous, but non-violent action. All they needed were leaders they could trust and depend on, leaders they could respect and believe in. The vast population eventually conceived this spirit of the resistance, they could understand it, because Mahathma Gandhi lived like them, he ate like them, he slept like them. He was a man who needed no worldly trappings, he was a man of deeds and of action, a man who needed no ammunition – mass resistance was his cannon, where a hundred men died for their country, two hundred stood up to replace them. There appeared an unending sea of volunteers, who were willing to die from a British regimental bullet, but still waving the flag of an independent India, in the dying hands of Hindus, Muslims, Christians, Sikhs and half a dozen of other religious creeds. Believers of all persuasions bonded themselves into a single identity, of "Indian" developing the force of resistance, defiant women joined to march with the men of resistance, as did my own maternal Aunt Al Syeda Mahmooda Imam. She was placed under arrest, time and time again, her incarcerations were not a few, but she wore them with pride, they were the medals of her resistance. Each time she was released, she promptly marched once more, leading the ever swelling processions. The ladies of the upper class, walked holding banners aloft, bare-footed, open flowing hair and wearing plain white cotton sarees under the sizzling and blazing sun – undaunted they carried plaques of "Quit India" voicing the resistance of the whole country as one unbeatable voice, they were the flag bearers of the insurrection, chanting the message of "Bapu" the father of the nation. The words "Quit India" were to be seen and heard everywhere, it appeared painted on walls, doors, posters, banners, railway compartments and even the cinema houses. It became an embarrassing slogan for the Ruling Empire.

My Aunt Al Sayida Mahmooda Begum was being arrested by the D.I.G himself. He said to her "do you realize that you are speaking to a D.I.G" she retorted with "I don't know about a D.I.G but I know I'm talking to a PIG. She was promptly arrested and put in jail. "Bapu" went on hunger strike till she was released.

The "Mahatma" was the name by which Mr.Gandhi was called, he did not believe in violence or ammunition, he believed in passive resistance of strife, so no arms were permitted, nor carried by the processionist. They projected their demands and refusal of enslavement through marches, strikes, and hunger fasts. Their sole intention was the claim of a free India. In an era of war and ruthless killing, freedom was to be achieved only by uncompromising resistance without violence, but also a move of non-cooperation. Amazingly enough this form of confrontation was indeed successful. Many of Gandhi's co-politicians of the time disagreed with his ideology and were adverse to his opinions and the persuasion of non-violence as a weapon, they believed it could not harness independence without the use of violence. Mr. Gandhi was a rabid Hindu and the public masses loved their "Bapu", they particularly waited for hours, oblivious to weather conditions, in the rain, in the blazing and blistering sun, or even standing for hours in thundering rain storms to catch a glimpse of him, when he made his way to attend some scheduled function, or procured his passage through streets and lanes to reach the temples. All too often, he just met people walking in their midst, for they were his followers, reposing total trust in him and faith in his ideology.

Here I feel that I must recount an exclusively interesting episode about Gandhijee, as re-told to us by my Father, Justice Syed Jafer Imam. A meeting had been arranged in Mussorie, the queen of the hill stations in India. Amongst the hierarchy of the political parties, who were there to discuss and comb out a number of unsettled issues on matters of resistance, where the political giants had clashed. When the meeting was almost over and about to conclude, my Father requested Mr.Gandhi's permission, to put to him a question this request was most graciously granted. I relate here the dialogue as recounted by my Father.

My Father, Syed Jafer Imam posed the question, "Mahatmajee what soap do you use? He inquired breezily.

Non plused Mahatama Gandhi observed, "Why Jafer? it is a very strange question", he remarked with a smile.

My Father turned to Sardar Patel asking, "Sardar-jee can you tell us what soap do you use"?

Father waited for an answer, but there was none forth coming, instead Sardar Patel gazed in wonder, regarding such a personal question as unbecoming.

Most baffled and impatient Mahatma Gandhi said, "Jafer you must be referring to something else with a depth of meaning. What is it?"

In a very serious manner my Father intoned, "Apparently we all use a different type of soap as is our personal desire, when we perform acts of ablution and cleanliness, for the exterior of our bodies. Is that not so Mahatma Jee?" He waited for an answer, Gandhi Jee remained silent.

A totally confused Sardar Petal inquired, "Jafer Bhai why is that so important? Surely it makes no difference to me or anyone else, who uses what soap, for their body cleanliness."

Mr. Jewharlal Nehru who had been amused at this exchange of conversation commented, "Of course it makes no difference and is a very personal matter. What are you aiming at Jafer Bhai? Your question cannot be without holding another meaning. Come share the answer with us."

Mahatma Gandhi was a very astute politician. He gave a small statement about himself, "As a matter of fact Jafer, cleansing is a very personal habit and the choice of cleanser is also very personal. For myself, I use only milk and water and some gram flower. I find it an excellent cleanser. Gram flower is full of Vitamin B and is much used by ladies for beautifying the skin – it has tremendous refreshing powers as well."

Looking straight at Mr. Gandhi, my Father clearly spoke for all to hear, "Then Ganjhijee, why does it make a difference to others if people use different religions for their inner spiritual cleansing? That too needs to be accepted as a personal choice. Don't you think so. There would be less communal clashes" Nawab Chattarie rose to the occasion, saying "well spoken Jafer Bhai – religion has to be accepted as an individual's personal choice, it should have no place or bearing on politics – it has turned out to be the basic reason for the great dessent that has split the nationalism of our country. In my opinion it is a treacherous form of politics."

Mahatma Gandhi's ideas appeared to differ with my Father so he gave his views, "If it serves the purpose of cleansing one's mind, there is no harm in adhering to one's own religious beliefs. Every country has a state law to which every national must conform – but religion is personal and has no part in state matters."

My Father had some very clear views on the subject. He requested, "Then Gandhijee would it not be wise to proclaim it in your mass meetings, where you have a massive audience, do proclaim, that religion must not be allowed to raise its head, especially in a country that has a multitude of religious persuasions. This could and would disrupt the harmony of a political government and civil rights, if it were allowed to become a part of our national politics. It must be contained now before it is too late."

Sardar Patel who had been a silent spectator was very pleased and addressed My Father, "Jafer Bhai you need to leave your legal profession in the Law Courts. Come and join us in our political arena, thus serving the nation with your clear headed deliveries. Men such as you are needed at the helm of national affairs."

My Father was thoroughly amused and replied, "Sardar Sahib thank you for your kind invitation – I am a dedicated lawyer and certainly do not have the makings of a politician. I have consistently left that to the elder members of our family – these master minds, such as my father Sir Syed Ali Imam , my Uncle Sir Syed Hasan Imam, and Sir Syed Sultan Ahmed, Mr. Mohammad Ali Jinnah and some others are brilliant nationalists and are the great men of their time". Even though several of them did not see the birth of Pakistan and India, they were amongst the founding fathers of the Indian resistance for independence, Sir Ali Imam and Mr. Hassan Imam were the founders of the Muslim League and All India Congress in Bihar. They were men of, both power and wisdom.

Then Gandhijee posed my father a question and the reason behind his query regarding soap, "what was meant by your question, for you must have had a reason". My Father spoke slowly but very clearly to Gandhijee, that if each person could use a different and individual means of cleansing for external cleansing, then there should be no problems or objections as to which spiritual cleanser anyone embraced. It is not a national issue. Internal purification should be left as a personal matter, with no cause of friction between the members of a community, or how men should practice their own religious persuasions. What they believe in, or are born into, different communities, should leave no cause for national disharmony.

Gandhijee was in total agreement as he himself had decided as to how his spirit and his body were shrived. He propounded that in his opinion there should be no dissension or confrontation between the multi-theologies of religious denominations. There was an important need to teach the doctrines of harmony, tolerance and non-violence, to all complex conflictions that divide the communities. Gandhijee projected himself as a portrait of passive resistance, in favour of independence for the ultimate Motherland. He eventually called for unity between Muslims and Hindus, bonded only by nationality, his non-violence against communism and disunity, finally resulted in his assassination during the inter-communal prayer meeting he had called, to remove the incompatibility and strife that reigned between the clashing Muslim and Hindu communities. His effort to promote harmony with the cause of non-violence cost him his life, at Birla House New Delhi, he became the target for assassination and the bullet found its mark, taking "Bapu's" life and spirit with it, surrounded by the tranquil garden, where the prayer meeting was being held. The crowds had come to unite the dissenting communities under Bapu's call to cease Hindu Muslim bigotry.

In later years, when I had seen one national flag of a nation divided into two, each with a different colour and emblem, I saw the birth of a new country namely Pakistan and the birth of a precious homeland for Muslims. This came as the result of the "Partition of the sub-continent", where existed a gross and unbridgeable abyss of difference of belief and cultures. Thus there emerged, an antagonism with the poison of a serpent's venom that reared its head, spilling the poison of enmity, using culture as an excuse for the separation, between the once happy and harmonious masses. This changed violently into shameless hatred, the slaughter of innocent people, the destitution of the masses, the split up of families and an enmity that still exists to-day after more than half a century has lapsed.

Politically times had changed, these same conflicting people, had previously lived together in simple harmony as brothers, enjoying each other's festivals with grace, suffering together their tragedies, mitigating erroneous acts with indulgence, but now the sifting began for a single righteous religion, the jaundiced judgements regarding purity, the inimical and antagonistic stance towards untouchables, the unsympathetic treatment of widows and many more fanatical injunctions, eventually it built an all consuming barrier of hatred, that led further into severance, dividing an amicable and congenial society with an enmity that rushed in and grew beyond all proportions, nurturing deep-rooted hate, corrupting good will, into ill-will and prosperity, into devastation, the evidence of the suffering has already lasted for over sixty years, with unhealed wounds. There is an enormous chasm, that is unlikely to be bridged if religious fanaticism continues to prevail. The past could never be retrieved, but the past respect for the future is not unattainable. There have been countless times, that the worthy efforts and hopeful aspirations that were made, were once again washed away due to this unnatural barrier. Numerous genuine attempts have been made to close the breaches, but all genuine effort has been in vain, each attempt has been sabotaged, others subverted, in favour of prejudice or self-interest. Severance abetted by treachery has been rampant, total disregard of emotional and physical needs for human identity and also its security. Thus decades of time that is fleet of foot, has lapsed as new stratagems emerged only to be jeopardized, confused, confounded leaving perplexity, as to why and how the hazards of an already smouldering situation is consistently refuelled.

Looking closely at the picture created by world maps of the sub-continent, was something to which Mr.Gandhi must have paid his keen attention, his assessments would have noted the areas blatantly marked in green on those maps, where Muslims were in the majority covering that area. The maps coloured in yellow, where the Hindu populations resided were in the majority, thus he embarked upon his last effort to keep the sub-continent together as one undivided block. To bridge the gap, that was the correct moment of time. The time was ripe but the war of hate followed, as a vast multiple of the public stood for him, but found his "uniting" policy unacceptable. Their mistrust became the very foundation of the enmity, that cleft the sub-continent as a sword cleaving the homeland apart. Those who were firmly entrenched against his policy soon conspired to do away with Mr.Gandhi himself, so they could burn his policies on his funeral pier – thus at that last "Inter-Communal" prayer meeting for bonding, his body stopped an assassin's bullet. Indians as a nation were devastated and he is mourned. Even today he stands as the eternal "Father of the Indian nation".

I was somewhat young to have been a witness to the proceedings, but much of the political activity held for me sufficient interest, so I read enough in the papers of what could be termed as a vibrant, oscillating drama, played by political acrobats, trapeze artists and between the government forces of authority and the unbreakable resistance for an independence. Indian news came from the unending stream of political speeches published by the "national press." There were streams of news, limitless denials flowed out eagerly awaiting the palpable news items, that varied in even tangible substance, wildly jostling for attention with the intangible, all vying for supremacy – only to be contradicted on the following morning, by a favour-seeking emissary, or a condemnation against the "Raj".

At that period of time there was no concept of television, the radio, newspapers and magazines were the main source of public information, so I had to depend entirely on these to derive and glean the news, of the up to date issues and political situations. There were a variable number of newspapers such as "The Indian Nation", the "Amrit Bazar Patrica" and "The Statesman" with more than a dozen other Indian papers blasting out, a tidal wave was being created by the fighters for freedom and independence. It received the most space on the sheets of the daily newspapers. Gradually, most of the government and pro government papers dropped out from pro government propaganda, which left the well read, but solitary English paper "The Statesman" to print its pro government imperial news that expressed their pro British Empire stance, bulletins and multifarious articles, pronouncing that their power control was not weakened. They lost the public interest due to their dubious and flagrant propaganda and assertions.

The main media of information was the radio news bulletins, as education for the basic population had been completely neglected, the grassroot public were unable to read – but basically, as all radio transmissions were, an arm of the Government, so it was indeed difficult to assess the truth, incorrect or unbiased political scenarios, which was obviously inspired with a typically one sided presentation, delivering bare and minimum facts as controlled and revealed by the "Imperial" government organ.

As one could deduct, that under these conditions there emerged a third media of information, it came from the various groups from budding politicians, intellectuals, lawyers and the great leaders who forgathered in diverse meeting places, convening to start a formation for their own politics, they discussed the state of current affairs, then began to discuss and formulate plans. This subversive movement was diligently spread from groups through groups, through cities, to towns, and even far off villages, inciting and strengthening the overgrowing forces of resistance, from the non-political cadre, but for the authentically honourable men, who joined the swelling tide of worthy leadership, without prejudice or self interest, he attracted innumerable followers, who could be trusted and could be relied upon. The political giants increased and the list kept growing with a never ending commitment.

These were the great men who gave birth to an independent India and Pakistan. After them there came an ever increasing younger generation, to take the reins of independence into their own hands. It was headed by the newly founded Government of Mr. Jawaharlal Nehru, of India Mr. Mohammad Ali Jinnah of Pakistan, Sardar Patel, Mr. Liaquat Ali Khan, and a host of others who pledged their lives for the stability and the establishment of their newly formed countries which to-day is India and Pakistan.

★ ★ ★ ★ ★

Truth Conquers the Universe

FIRST SIX YEARS OF
MARRIED LIFE
The Years I Would Prefer
To Forget

The first six years of my married life, was one of a nomadic traveller, but without a clan or leader. For a home or house responsibility I had none, for company I had my small growing daughter Tahira and a pair of devoted Alsatian dogs. I acquired them on one of my trips to Germany, they had been bred from Champion stock – they were in fact the genuine German Shepherds, not the inter-bred as we see today. While I ceaselessly wandered through different countries and civilizations, my parents looked after my daughter, and my dogs. When Tahira was two years old she accompanied me, travelling everywhere I went. I find it amazing that in later years, she didn't imbibe the passion of "Wander Lust". As Tahira grew up she won a French scholarship spending four years of her College life in France at the University of Beaseace, on the 'French Swiss' border. When she was in university it was the era of "hippies" "flower children" and "drugs", yet by God's grace, she tread through that period without 'falling'. She excelled in her academic studies, obtaining double Master Degrees, before returning home. Not long after, she contracted a marriage of her own choice to a major of the Pakistan army. She taught French at the American school but performed her duties as a good wife, an excellent mother, and a responsible housewife. Tahira gave birth to two daughters, maintaining her career as a professional educator, administrator, and teacher at Esena Foundation.

My wanderings, were not the product of my own choice, but rather my own weakness as an undemanding wife, I sometimes travelled with my husband, staying at expensive hotels, or high class apartments for small durations of only weeks. Even when I went to the hills for the summer, his choice had been Nanital Tal at 8,000 feet, up in the mountains, with a splendid lake that lay like blue green jell at the base of a mountain cup, where the two rounded spurs met, leaving a diminutive passage for the lake water to gush down the mountains, through a wide gorge, as steep as a canyon, creating a spill gushing down as water tumbled over rock slabs, that were more extensive and the width broader, it could be credited as an impressive waterfall, of course nothing like the Niagara Falls in Canada or the Victorian Falls in Africa.

On the hillsides surrounding the lake on both sides, small and large cottages had been constructed by various owners, for the sole purpose of renting them out to the yearly summer visitors, for a duration of two to three months, who leave the plains to avoid the blistering summer heat. Once, I had been a resident in one of these cottages, where I lived alone with only an occasional visit from my much travelled husband. Even winning the India Derby, with his great stud "Beaucephlous", it was still placed under the flag of a "business trip".

My financial circumstances had been catered for, all that I needed to buy, had been well attended and taken care of. I was gifted with a yacht of my own, that was called Molly and I enjoyed the innumerial challenges that the lake proffered. Along with the yacht came, two through-bred Arabian stallions manning the stables which came with the rented cottage. I spent many hours sailing on the lake, I rode the horses, like there would be no tomorrows and in hindsight, I recognize this as the manifestations of a neglected wife. The play for my hand in marriage came just after I had been chosen as a beauty queen in Mussorie in 1947. Later in 1948, I was married becoming the wife of a businessman. I suppose I was just another added trophy to the many racing and bridge trophies he had acquired. A few months later I found myself in a rented apartment in a prestigious locality in Calcutta. I was then presented with a car that was an Oldsmobile Thunder Bird, this too proclaimed his social elevated status. I'm of the opinion, that the Thunder Bird and myself shared the same level of status. I had no plausible explanation, but I was aware that I could not compete with "Bucephulas" as he was the one and only Indian National Derby winner.

I lingered and dwelt in this homeless wandering state for several years. At first it was one town to another, then it crystallized from one city to another, then with some progress it became one country to another. By then I had the concept of travel arrangements at my finger-tips, using my capability, I stumbled through trying to make a home in one country after another, I even coped with a choppy two and a half years residency, in East Pakistan. I passed those days living in four small rooms, a bathroom and a bare kitchen. There was no running water. I had to pump water from a tubewell and carry the buckets of water to the kitchen and bathrooms, this so called luxurious building was in a jungle area, seventeen miles away from Decca. I was supposed to be grateful that I did not live in a "Basha hut" which is a room or two built with bamboo and dried leaves that was built up, plus a thatched roof.

We made a trip to England that summer, starting with London, then on to the lake district, We spent a short time in Edinburgh, Paris and on to Geneva. By the time I arrived in Rome I was travelling alone. I traversed a number of European Countries, sight seeing the ancient treasures of Europe, and the art and architectural delights, it was too boring, and a waste of time, for the hard core business man, who was supposed to be my life's partner. His preferences were a life of clubs, bridge tables, the glitter coins that went with poker, roulette and other spiced card games.

To my discredit the social lives of Princes and hard core gamblers were not present in my cup of "tea leaves". We prudently agreed that to disagree and produce skirmishes was valueless, and as I had heard and seen the couples I knew belabouring and berating each other with stinging words and the complete loss of dignity, only to share the same bed at night. I was neither prepared to lose my self respect, nor the dignity I demanded as my birth right, nor was I prepared to share the same bed with a man, who often made an attempt to insult me. We developed the best solution for our mental and social incompatibility. We each went our own way. He was the provider of a home for my daughter and I carried out my duties as a proficient house-keeper, a competent Mother of my daughter and as a polished hostess, thus I earned the reputation of being "the hostess with the mostess".

The next step to provide me with a regular home was when he flew me to London, spent a month of a lively vacation, but at the same time he also made the arrangements to buy a house in Richmond where Tahira and I were to reside. He drove me down to see it and it was indeed a lovely period house with large gardens. I realized that he wanted to leave me there in England and he himself would "come and go" when it pleased him, or wished to do so. Our multiple trips to England in those days had no problems as both of us were British nationals and no visas were required.

At this stage I put my resistance into action and booked my seat on B.O.A.C. on its scheduled flight to the East going via Calcutta. I and my daughter were to make our way home and we would stay with my parents. Sense prevailed and instead of letting Tahira and me go to Calcutta on our own, my husband, my daughter and myself were re-booked on a B.O.A.C. flight to Karachi. After ten days in Karachi where he and his father had bought an over large-sized marble-floored spacious building, I was not allowed to take up my residence in Karachi. I was flown to Lahore with my five year old daughter and went to the haven home of a cousin for a few weeks until a small two-bed-room house was rented for me. Later as the town developed he continued to rent another bungalow for me. By this time my daughter was eight years old and I had moved four times from one rented house to another. I was convinced that he would never construct a permanent home for us. In view of this in 1958 my parents transferred the finances from London which enabled me to buy land in Lahore. From my husband there was no assistance and I never requested for any collaboration or support.

Building materials were in low supply in Pakistan and constructions were roaring ahead, because Pakistan was a new and budding country. I had to get permits for almost everything needed for construction, from cement to steel, from conduit pipes to heavy duty cables. I wove my way through one office after another, from factory to factory in my effort to procure permits. Despite the pressure, I succeeded in building a home for Tahira. I had hardly finished the basic construction, only three rooms had flooring, there were no doors or windows completed, just a bare skeleton. Almost immediately I found myself holding a packet of divorce papers. The rest is now history that I prefer to forget.

I found myself without family in an alien country, with a British nationality, a daughter, but no plans for survival. But Allah provided for me a contingent of families that were father figures, brothers, uncles and sisters who were not of my blood, but who rallied round me to give me the love, the support, the succour and the emotional bank, that I was so badly in need of. To these friends I cannot give them enough praise or thanks – all I have been able to do is to always be there for them, despite the hardest of circumstances.

I was a non Pakistani who had come to live in Pakistan where all manner of opportunities came my way, doors opened like an "Open Sesame" with the treasures that have been my life's fulfilment, awaited me. I have tried to serve my adopted country and serve it well and if the honours that have been bestowed on me speak, then, perhaps I have served it well.

When I came to Pakistan in August of 1952, I once again found myself moving mixing and trying to relate to a totally new social pattern. The colours were bright yet conversely sombre and the pattern of life completely diagonally opposite to what I had experienced. It appeared to be like the "Two faces of Eve". This was both at the work level and the social level.

Everybody who considered somebody made a desperate effort to become a member of the "Gymkhana Club" where a large number of the social elite were given printed memberships. There were occasional some "Black Ball" casualties, but more or less well controlled and social climbers recognized for what they were after. There was another high brow club named "The Punjab Club" but it was basically the Englishmen's club. In 1952 there were still a large number of British and Foreigners still working in Government departments, the law courts, and also the Armed Forces. This was almost their exclusive club coming down from past decades. The shadow left by the non Pakistani social segregation, coming down from the Imperial Rule exhibited itself particularly at a club level.

The new Pakistani nationals wore their nationality with pride and rarely gave a thought to apply to a foreigner's club for membership. On occasions one heard on the grape vine, that someone had mistakenly applied and found there were too many "Black balls" in the voting box.

Gradually the foreign membership sank until there was a need to have enough members to maintain the club financially.

The building was Imperious and the grounds, spread over scores of acres, so there was no lack of facilities for the members. Swimming-pools, tennis-courts, squash courts, open air dance-floors, and walking tracks skirted the perimeters of the club estate. The club had residential buildings for suitable accommodation as it was also a Residential Club. The presentation and way of club life was totally English. Every comfort was draped in English elegance.

The indoor, facilities were as luxurious as those to be found on the outdoor grounds. Several large lounges, bridge rooms, smoking rooms, billiard rooms, reading rooms and half a dozen other rooms for various uses that were desired by the members, were catered for. The public rooms were built creating enormous floor shape with high vaulted roofs. Life-size, gilt framed paintings of Queen Victoria, George the Vth, George the VIth, Lord Cornwallis, Lloyd George, Lord Mountbatten and other great personalities covered the wall expanses that were left between huge heavy gilded mirrors.

The dining rooms were well appointed for daily formal and informal meals by members, their families and acceptable friends. The large banquet hall seated 300 guests. Buffet suppers had begun to make an entry for large festive occasions after the declaration of World War II in 1944.

The immense ballroom sparkled with highly polished "Parquet" wood flooring. Groups of cushioned chairs ringed the hall for ease and comfort yet the entire hall never lost its touch of beauty, elegance or aristocratic aura.

From the ceiling hung monumental scintillating rainbow fired crystal peardrop pendants from the chandeliers, with a central rotating sphere of light creating an orbit of dancing moonbeams, that silently and slowly waltzed past, melding emotions into a mist mistaken for love.

There were no live bands at that time, and the use of a gramophone with records were unthinkable at a club. So to fill the gap, of an absent orchestra, to beguile dancers to perform some new ideas and arrangements had to produce a formulation, so someone had presented the club with a "brain wave", that there were ready made bands under the Police, there were Regimental bands of various units that could be taught to play dance music in waltz timing, foxtrot timing, tango timing, the quick step and Rumba timing. No sooner the suggestion was made, the bands went into action and in double quick time, they were double timing the up to date dance requirements. The "cha cha cha" had not yet been introduced and the "jitterbug" and "Charleston "were still in its infancy. The clubs could do without them.

At the far end of the ballroom was a high stage for the members of the band to sit complete with their Pakistani service uniforms and decorative trappings. The balls and dance nights were still a formal function with a formal dress code for the members as well.

As the membership fell and the foreigners were returning "home" it was decided to open up and encourage the local gentry, to seek membership without the fear of "black ball" results. Some of the newly promoted officers of the Government who were almost holding the reins of Government, became members and encouraged others to apply, but since most of the members were content with the provision and facilities of the Gymkhana Club, the inflow of applications were slow. Eventually the highly prestigious Punjab Club had to move its location to new but much smaller premises. Thereafter it became a highly elite club for Pakistanies but under some very strict, vigilante and elevated social rules. Even today it is not easy to become a member of the Punjab Club. Majid and myself became members as soon as we were married in 1965.

In 1952 when I arrived in Lahore, Pakistan was a newly born state. Rehabilitation in every way was being given top priority to re-settle the people, the administration, the accommodation, the rationing of food and all the essential services that man needs for not only survival but to re-establish the wheels of Government. The days were full of work and pressure for everyone from bureaucrat, business men, and departments of utilities were ceaselessly involved almost seven days a week, with long hours of duty without any real source of recreation. Apart from the clubs, the Railway Institute, and regimental messes plus two decent hotels, there were no dance halls, no high grade restaurants, theatres or developed parks – There was no place to relax after a hard day's work. The best recreation that Lahore offered were a few cinema houses with English Pictures.

For the new breed of Pakistanis they had to make the most of the situation by having private dinners in their own homes. The wives came up to the mark in their effort to produce the food for the dinners, or the finger food that were presented at the cocktail parties, but this too was all within certain limitations.

There was no television to fill in as entertainment, there was no record producing companies to provide music for the record-players. The only entertainment that could be provided was perhaps bridge or just plain chatting and passing on gossip. This didn't do very much for the men as for as entertainment was concerned.

But like all things necessity is the "mother" of invention, so a suitable substitution had to be found. The recently opened "Radio Pakistan" had a score of both male and female singers and the newly opened "film studios" had inducted professional singers and dancers from the famous back streets of Lahore to perform at the studious, for creating films that were being hastily produced. These entertainers were not classical performers, just dancers and singers with good voices of any quality, but out of necessity they were engaged, as they served the dire purpose of the producers by providing some action and scenic footage for the desperate need of the studio requirements. Actresses were scares, as the film world was at Bombay and the studios in Lahore were at only an introductory stage and their occupation was in it's infancy, as it was not yet an industry. There were quality limitations, due to the fact that there was very little experience, almost zero technology, craftsmanship nil and films lacked authenticity due to limited research. Much of the presentation was done by singers and dancers as the backdrop to "romantic" films.

The management of Radio Pakistan and the newly open film world, were indeed very co-operative to fill in the lack of social entertainment for the elite so they provided the otherwise unavailable need by sending their singers, dance entertainers and also poetical renderers to entertain with their renditions the special groups of cliental that were the new elite. These entertainers were far from rich infact they were lacking enough finances for themselves, but the new means of this unexpected earning financial advancement with elevated induction that was in growing demand pleased them very much so they provided the best of their limited abilities that gave a great deal of pleasure by playing almost for the exclusive enjoyment of the male audiences that attended these special "entertainment" dinners, from where they received much appreciation and some liberal finances.

At that period of time the "upper class" circle of the elite who were not yet club minded, were graciously invited to each other's homes as a husband and wife couple. No sooner the dinner was over several of the less enduring wives would bid their hostess a thankful "adieu" and retreat to the purity of their own homes. The hostess always had to be present but she needed some female company, so personal friends and a few reluctant relatives would remain to keep her company, the hostess appreciated this as she needed a back up team of her own level and social status. Like it or not, their duties had become obligatory, despite the lack of good taste and their aversion to the circumstances, by which this "new" trend was a way to be accepted under the heading of it being only a "relaxing diversion". In those early years, in a new established country without many facilities perhaps it was some type of solution.

As the evening progressed and the atmosphere got under way, with laughter, praise-worthy comments and verbal appreciations, the businessmen possessing more financial intake had more than enough money, would start to split a wads of notes and encircle the heads of the singer's head, tuck it into her blouse, and others would send a shower of fluttering notes around her where she, her partner and her "caretaker" would pick them up from the floor. It brought on another round of singing from the group of four to five entertainers with more appreciation from the audience with louder and free speech accompanied the gaiety and some hilarity with gleeful exuberance and high spirits.

Syeda Anese Majid Khan

Oblivion

While night still ruled the world with stars
Dawn awoke from a death like sleep
Shattered the gilded arrows from her Orient bow
To kill the star like subjects of the night.
The golden chariot mounts the Eastern sky
The sun god's stallions rear their fiery heads
Enshrining both the mansion and the shanty
Of master and his bondsman in morns liquid glow of light.

Still hazy from the cups of last night's pleasures
He heard the call for prayer from some distant Mosque
To where, the devout hastened for the early morning prayer
But all he heard were the voices of his late night's dreams
As though an angel summoned him to the cellar door.
Could he dare to enter the temple of the Infidel
That only knows the worship of some ruby juice
Quaffing the nectar as though it was the Chalice of the gods
Partaking unholy communion from that wassail of denial
Till all the past sank into obscure oblivion.

~ Esena

When I went to such a dinner for the first time, I could not comprehend this type of entertainment. As a matter of fact I did not even know that there were these types of parties. I had moved with my husband through a society of High Clubs, race horse owner, high playing gambles, elite balls and high class banquets, but was totally ignorant regarding personal entertainers coming into one's own private homes. I was unable to place this within the bounds of my way of life. After I had attended the third such party where some mild and sexy undulations were added to the singing. I knew that I could not accept to be a party to such low grade entertainment, so for the next couple of invitations I refused to go. My husband suggested, that I go but could leave after dinner like some of the other ladies. I declined his suggestion saying "I don't intend to be your ticket to these parties". He went without me.

A week later he told me that he would be giving a dinner of about forty people and that I should make the dinner arrangements for the Saturday, two weeks hence. At first it was no problem as I was the formal "hostess" of his house and was accustomed to making these arrangements. After the invitations went out and I had begun to create an appropriate menu, I received two strange phone calls. My friend Gereldine and her husband Majidulla were very close friends and our club type of people, so I had also sent them an invitation.

When Gereldine phoned me she asked me "Are you really going to have this after dinner entertainment in your home?"

I inquired from her saying, "What entertainment are you talking about Gereldine?"

She was flabbergasted and said, "You mean you really don't know"?

It became my turn to be curious, for I had no idea what she was referring to, so I said to her, "Gereldine I don't know so please tell me."

She said "that's what we thought – your husband has asked the bureaucrats and film world people to dinner, with some enjoyable singing and dancing after dinner. But as you know we don't go to these type of dinners, so Majidulla and myself couldn't understand why you of all people would be giving such a low grade party".

I said to her "don't worry Gereldine there will be no dinner, therefore there will be no entertainment. I can assure you that I have no intention of turning my clean and moral home into a public entertaining hall."

Gerelline said to me, "You mean that don't you? Good for you. You'll have all the support we can give you and work up quite a few of our social friends to crush the stories that are about to be circulated, we will stand by you."

I thanked her by saying "I always knew that I could make the right friends – I love you both."

I spent the rest of the day drafting out a written note saying I regret that for some unforeseen circumstances I was unable to have the dinner and I hoped that my inability would be regarded gracefully. I had the regret cards printed. While I was having it printed I bought air tickets to Delhi, packed Tahira's and my suitcases, ready for departure I addressed all the envelopes and sent the driver to deliver them to all the guests invited by me. Since I had not invited the film world or Radio Pakistan, I left him to do it himself.

The next day I told him that I was going to Delhi and he wanted to know when I would be back, as there was a dinner to be arranged.

I handed him the "regret" note and waited for his reaction. He told me that he would not let me go, so I informed him was that if I didn't go, there would be no dinner arrangements in my home – so it might be embarrassing for him to have me in town but no party at my house. If I left for Delhi he had some semblance of "face saving which I suggest that it would be wiser."

His temper and frustration knew no bounds, there were shouts, threats and persuasion in turn. I receded to my den, took out my paints and proceeded to prime my canvas. He walked in and out of the rooms, up and down the corridor, tried to talk to me, to irritate me, accuse me, cajole me and once again threaten me with a divorce. None of this had any effect on me, so he got into the car and left the house. Three hours later he came back very gentle, very pleasant and said he wanted to talk to me. He said he really wanted me to stay, the dinner was for some important people and he was sorry for threatening me. He took out of his pocket a sizeable velvet box and gave it to me. I did not open it. Then he opened it and there were a beautiful pair of gold bracelets in the box. I did not touch them, so he tried to put one on my hand. I picked up the pair and walked over to Becky my Alsatian and put them near her paws and said to him, "I think you have confused the identity, perhaps she will serve you better" He was struck dumb.

I left and went to my room and took Tahira with me. I closed the door and started to read her a story. I didn't see him again as the next morning, I caught the flight to Delhi. Two weeks later he came to Delhi and asked me to return to Lahore assuring me that I would not be the one to hostess his parties. I insisted that unless there was decorum, decent people of a well behaved society, there would be no entertainment in my home.

We returned to Lahore and he continued to go to the homes of others, but I also heard that he gave quite a few parties at various other places. It was not my concern, we already had separate rooms. I continued to perform all my social and official duties but I made my own circle of friends.

★ ★ ★ ★ ★

REHABILITATION OF
THE DISABLED

1. A disused Army Barrack
   A dilapidated discarded building in a high state of dis-repair.
2. The new gardens and pathway for free movement and enjoyment of nature.
   A wonderful diversion from barren sterile wards and dreary bedsteads.
3. Monthly dinner nights akin to the monthly Regimental Mess Dinner.
   A colourful evening dinning in comradeship and special meals.
4. Intense restructuring and re-modeling of disused and unkempt land space.
   Remodeled to cater to the growing needs of the patients netball field and game courts.
5. The Wheelchair March past at a formal function.
   The reforming of an army unit even under handicapped conditions.
6. The Netball success – winning goals on wheel chairs.
   Not the easiest task to manipulate a wheel-chair and score a goal.
7. Putting the short from a distant wheelchair.
   It needs stamina and physical power to cast the heavy ball.
8. Mrs. Anese Rashid (Majid) Commander of the Unit.
   My life dedicated to the disabled men of the unit it became my pride and joy.
9. A Javelin thrower enjoying the ability to launch his Javelin through space.
   It sails through the air to a distant target.
10. Receiving the Commanding General for the first Asian games a "Sports Day" at the Disabled Centre.
    Foreign delegates attended, praised and gave an uplift to the games
11. Pakistan's disabled a "success story" in Paris featured on the cover of the World Veteran's Magazine in Paris.
    Pakistan the proud possessor of International marksmanship.

★ ★

★

PHYSIOTHERAPY FOR RECOVERING

At the Paraplegic Disabled Centre.

1. Sir Ludwich Gutman, Chairman Director "Stokemandville" Rehabilitation Centre in Britain. The world's famous "Master Performer" in the care of the Disabled.
2. Visiting Team of Army Officers.
   Reviewing the facilities for the rehabilitation of the Disabled.
3. Sir Norman Acton for Britain - Director of the "World Veteran's Association".
   Bestowed tremendous encouragement to the work at the centre.
4. Therapist Miss Taylor, Nursing Sister, Mrs.Kathleen Waymark and welfare worker, Welfare Officer Miss R.Rukhsana.
   A dependable team dedicated to their work.
5. Multiple types of physical recovering therapy available for rehabilitation.
   Vast damage needs vast equipment for Rehabilitation.
6. "Indoor Swimming Pool".- the generous contribution of Mr. Butt
   Patients and Visiting Team from Ghana exchange words with the paroplegies.
7. Foreign Delegates enjoy an evening at Dinner with the officers of the establishment.
   Informality is a great "bond" for working together.
8. Physiotherapy for muscular development.
9. The Core Commander Visiting to view the new established working of the unit. The unit became my personal "offspring"

★ ★

★

SPORTS REHABILIATION
(MULTIPLE SPORTS ACTIVITIES)

1. Archery performed from Wheelchairs – successful aim at Target.
   Recognition of self ability and precision delivery.
2. Sports for free movement and flexibility of limbs.
   A basic exercise performed several times a day to enhance dexterity.
3. Throwing the Javelin was a well-liked sport.
   Participation in games has a mental and emotional uplift.
4. Mrs. Anese Majid and an officer busy with administrative instructions.
   Constant vigilance and endeavour is required to move forward in performance.
5. Relay on Wheelchairs – the participation was exhilarating.
   The ever ready challenge to team work with successful results.
6. Netball on wheelchairs - a demanding sport of dexterous ability.
   Movement on wheelchairs is a stage by stage development of co-ordination.
7. Table Tennis on wheelchairs -
   To meet a bouncing ball and return it is a self indulged moment.
8. Badminton on crutches - a difficult but a challenging game.
   Balance and eye contact is indeed difficult but the challenge is met.
9. Out to meet the world.
   Going out into town performing personal errands using specially designed wheel chairs brought patients the self-respect they looked for.

★ ★

★

DISABLED SPORTS DAY (FIRST ASIAN GAMES)

1. General and Military Commander – from Australia
   An esteemed visitor of the Australian Armed Forces was full of praise.
2. Commander-in-Chief Lt. General Musa of the Pakistan Army.
   An interested Commander-in-Chief giving encouragement and participation.
3. Delegates from Ghana - Nigeria, Ceylon, Malaysia, Indonesia, and Britain who graced the function in 1961.
   They were impressed and gave due encouragement to the players.
4. Delegates being entertained at dinner.
5. Sir Norman Acton of the World Veterans Association Inspecting a Wheel Chair March Past.

★ ★

★

Truth Conquers the Universe

ARMY DISABLED CENTRE
My Involvement with Rehabilitation of the Disabled

We often ask a question, for which there really is no answer – we stop to think and then move on, to do the best we can without the answer. That is life.

The disabled too, ask the same question with "why me" they too move on to do the best they can.

But, there is "an answer" as you may read by Rudyard Kipling. The philosophy is perfect for our emotional survival.

The Answer

A Rose, in tatters on the garden path,
A cried out to God and murmured against His Wrath,
Because a Sudden wind at twilight's hush
Had snapped her stem alone of all the bush.
And God, Who hears both sun-dried dust and sun,
Had pity, whispering to that luckless one.
"Sister, in that thou sayest We did not well –
"What voices heardst thou when thy petals fell?"
And the Rose answered, "In that evil hour
"A voice said, 'Father, wherefore falls the flower?

" 'For lo, the very gossamers are still'.
"And a voice answered, 'Son, by Allah's Will!' "

Then softly as a rain-mist on the sward,
Came to the Rose the Answer of the Lord:
"Sister, before We smote the Dark in twain,
"Ere yet the Stars saw one another plain,
"Time, Tide, and Space, We bound unto the task
"That thou shouldst fall, and such a one should ask."
Whereat the withered flower, all content,
Died as they die whose days are innocent;
While he who questioned why the flower fell
Caught hold of God and saved his soul from Hell.

~ *Rudyard Kipling*

I had seen many disabled, as I moved through life and probably accepted it, but I was never confronted by the trauma that it enfolds. But now, I was torn between the heart-rendering disability I was witnessing and the broken spirits of valiant men, as I saw them at the Army Disabled Centre in Lahore. My heart leapt forward in some uncontrollable desperation, to bring them some little succour, to befriend them, to minister in some unknown way even some type of relief, to elevate them out of their sense of worthlessness. I searched for words to bring them hope, but I found no words to make this unrealistic commitment, I could not promise them any consolation, but could I possibly look them in the eyes with platitudes and false promises that are voiced, knowing that perhaps there could be no fulfilment. Yet I knew in my inner being I could not forsake them and walk away. I could not forsake my dreams, return to earth, where relevant and plausible thinking took me on my own journey of life.

I immediately realized that if I had to live with my scruples, it was with these disabled men my life must find fulfilment. Unasked I was confronted with a colossal and stupendous task, for could I provide some succour. I faced the fact that throbbed, because I had no formal training, a leader to guide me, nor a teacher to develop me, how far could I go, what could I achieve. My superior at the Combined Military Hospital was a colonel from the Pakistan Army, doing his duty as an orthopaedic surgeon at the hospital. He also did his job as the doctor of the centre, he was an orthopaedic surgeon, but was not always available, nor was he a rehabilitation specialist, which at this point, was the potent and most fundamental need required by the disabled, infact it was an ultimate and paramount requirement. A bed to sleep on, food to eat and clothes to wear did not constitute the intrinsically human state of "living".

I was discouraged in my aspirations from all sides, the people around me, the unusual circumstances of, a lady of my class did not work and that too in an all male unit. The clash of cultural norms, became my enemy, the lack of formal medical training, mocked my aspirations, the dearth of experience made my desire indecorous, the absence of physiotherapy and vocational training, was questionable, last but not the least my youth had become my adversary, as I had just turned twenty-seven and also a Muslim girl from a conservative community I was a well educated Muslim, from the society, a little bit of "easy on the eye" for I had been a "beauty queen" twice over, before reaching as I considered this matured and advanced age, but the world looked at me differently. But disregarding the face of all opposition, I duly found myself driving my car through the blocks of Army barracks in the Lahore Cantonment. As my convertible Chevrolet car nosed its way down a rough bumpy roadway, made by the constant use of cycles, motor-bikes, and delivery vans, I had a chance to view the army buildings, they were long barracks, designed for utility and Spartan living. They were clean, bare, simple ochre washed walls, huge pent shaped roofs, covering the enormous barracks. Many acres of land lay between each barrack, but not a single flower-bed or flowering shrubs broke the stringent and barren perimeters.

I parked my car in the shade under a mulberry tree, then entered the building where the Colonel awaited my arrival. He greeted and guided me to the official office of the Army Disabled Centre where I took a seat. The office was sparsely furnished with the minimum of maintenance which was in evidence. The Colonel offered me a cup of tea while we talked regarding the areas of work that needed to be improved. The dismal conditions that were obviously present did not appear to worry him.

After a cup of tea that I hardly drank, we proceeded to take a tour around the entire establishment, that was to become the domain of my charge, or rather it would be more appropriate for me to use the word "challenge". As we advanced through those silent wards, I saw beds filled with haunted men, whose limbs were imprisoned, whose hopes had fled, whose memories of a home had faded into a far and distant past, whose desires had dissolved into a nothingness, whose hopes had vanished like the morning mist. There was only the memories of the past, there was no present and they could not think of any future. I was appalled to see barracks full of the "living dead". They ate, and they slept like the living, but their dead eyes were devoid of emotion. As I walked past my eyes fell for I could not look at them, I fell not only silent, but my high and lofty hopes of yesterday were shaken and hope receded at a very fast pace, leaving me to face nature's conspiracy to accomplish my abandonment, in the face of the impossible. I reconstructed what I had seen, creating a scenario of mortification and degradation within myself. The presence of a roof over their heads, simple garments to cover the body and a sound medically prescribed diet of the basic provision, indifferently cooked and doled out to silent broken men, did nothing to compensate for the lack of human uplift, or respect that I had just witnessed.

What I saw that morning, as I traversed the wards and premises left me shocked into silence. I felt myself sliding into the depths of morbidity, I could not envisage any elevation of the complexed situation before me, because no starting point existed from where my ideals and effort could be generated into practice. I departed the unit that morning as a disillusioned, depressed and despondent woman. I had previously been witness, to the tragedy of ravaged bodies, sacrilegious abuse of women and the massacre of innocent children, at the time of the partition before and after Independence of India and Pakistan, but this was not the indifferent killing as in a war, but here these valiant, disciplined, obedient soldiers of our nation, were men emotionally dead, physically maimed, living with a nameless future. I spent the night in prayer – beseeching my Benefactor for help and guidance. He came to aid me, He has never failed me.

I spent the next several sleepless nights in meditation seeking, searching, exploring and sifting the random thoughts that gushed through my head. I dressed and went to work each day finding something that I could do. For a time I could find no deep practical answer to light my way, or embolden my hopes, then I would spend another night in prayer, beseeching and entreating my "Great Benefactor" to raise my almost comatose, stunned spirit, to enlighten my dying vision, to infuse into me the spirit I had lost on that first day, when I came face to face with the true disabled.

I had become a visionary with soaring hopes of happier and better times with a constructive rehabilitation programme, but my days at the unit were spent simply making acquaintances with the staff and patients, retreating to my office to draw up plans and schedules that perhaps would not be given birth, delving into the unit's administration files to learn what I did not know, but all that appeared to be on paper, was extremely far from the actual human care which was their basic requirement, and what I was aiming for. I was making no real progress in the working responsibilities I had taken on. For the record of my service it did not matter, as I was on "honorary service". I had volunteered to take on a rehabilitation program with a trial of three months. I was losing faith in my ability to achieve some better conditions for the patients. But more than that, the more I looked into the eyes of my men, they took my desire and intention to work for them, in a variation of forms. Some were sceptical, some perhaps saw me as immature, others perhaps a social butterfly playing Florence Nightingale. What stung most was, the facial expressions of the men who scoffed at my intentions, men who were indignant that a woman and that too a young untrained one, who left their male ego offended, they gazed at me in pity, in desolate condemnation, last but not the least their eyes challenged me in disrespect. My humiliations was complete, thus driving me to leave the unit. I was torn between my hurt, my pride, and their suffering. I knew that my honour and my respect had to be maintained, for I myself had volunteered to undertake the task of recovering their human dignity. It was I who needed the courage, the empathy was not enough. I was required to humble myself for I was no better than them. We were born alike, we came empty-handed and all would go back empty handed. My religious Doctrine of Islam taught me that "all men are equal" I endeavoured to maintain this code of life.

In my despondence I needed visions. I made another tour of the premises, alone this time on my own, even though the Colonel had instructed me never to leave my office without the escort of a male office member. Most often, it was the units Quarter Master who accompanied me. That day I needed to be alone, I had to come to terms with myself,

I was on trial with my official status behind me – I was on my own strength. Now this situation had been challenged by one of my most crippled patients, as he sat on the bed, legless up to his knees, his hands too were crippled, and his fingers extended only to the base of the fingers, where they ended as small amputated stubs. Fortunately by some minor blessing or miracle his left hand still had a thumb and a part of his index finger. As a result of these multiple disability, he had almost become an introvert as each day was spent sitting on his bed, unable to communicate with anyone except a few who passed his way. Even in this, there were limitations, as in such a hospital most patients are bed-bound and hardly anyone is actually passing by. Being a brotherhood of patients some friendly visiting does take place. This type of introverted emotion often leads to bitterness and morbidity. This must be elevated at all cost, before rehabilitation can be achieved.

On that particular day, it was I who happened to be in the ward of twenty-eight men, checking out the service of the mid-day meal, but I wasn't at a great distance from Saeed Ali's bed, so I went forward and enquired after his condition. Gazing up at me, with his cynical, but widely open eyes…within the next moment he had challenged me by offering me the plate from which he was eating. The following is a very interesting dialogue between us. It had a great bearing on my decision to take up my duties as an officer and their welfare status.

Saeed Ali looked up at me smiling with a smug look on his face he asked, "Sir! Will you share my lunch with me." He smirked and his eyes challenged the commander in me.

In a very genial way I approached his bed saying, "Whatever you wish Saeed Ali, if that is what you desire, yes I shall be glad to eat with you."

With a bitter – sweet smile he still challengingly declared, "Yes I'd want you to – will you eat with me from my plate as I have no other. Do you mean it …Sir?" he queried in disbelief.

He appeared to be waiting for my dam of indignation to burst open with a curt censure. He failed to get it.

My reply was prompt and clear as I told him, "I most certainly will, if that is what will make you happy."

He still did not believe me – he had faith in no one's word. He pronounced himself "defiled" so that is how he saw himself.

Saeed taunted me in disbelief, "No you wouldn't …Sir – I've defiled the food on my plate. I have eaten from this plate, as you can see, after all I am a cripple and unclean."

Though he was trying to bait me, I could still hear the "pathos" that churned his self degraded emotion. I had to stifle my unbidden tears.

I was stunned with shock, at such a cruel comment about his disability, my anger rose as I commanded him to stop, "Saeed Ali stop – don't say that! …. You are as clean as I am and it would be my pleasure to eat with you and even to feed you myself. What makes you think that you are defiled." Taking a piece of bread I mixed it in the curry, placed a piece of chicken within the folds of the bread and extended my hand, putting the morsel to his mouth. He deliberately took my fingers on to his lip, but I did not flinch, instead I picked up a piece of bread dipped it in the gravy and lifted my hand to put the morsel into my own mouth. I had been aware, that I was on trial at the unit, even more threatening than a court room.

Saeed Ali would not give up – perhaps he could not because of his crippling psychology, "Sir! Stop my mouth is dirty my spit is on your finger, I am a diseased man."

This was an undreamed of challenge that I could not have visualized in any far off dream. I had been convinced that the men would rally, once they knew I was working for them.

It was time to establish my real worth, or position in the unit, I gently took his hand and said, "Saeed don't say another word. I am your sister, sent here in Allah's mercy to create a new life for all of you. He has placed you in my charge, and it is a charge that I will not dishonour. Now all of you are my sons, my brothers, my friends. I am also the mother of this Unit."

Bowing his head … taking my fingers to his forehead he looked up and saying, "Allah! Be praised – sister place your hand upon my head, I never ate a more tasteful and satisfying morsel in my life, we acclaim you as our sister and the mother of this unit". A miracle had happened and

I prayed that God would lead me into the right path as my intentions and desire was not for myself.

I would have liked to answer him with a "thank you" but I could not, I did not dare to trust myself or the tumult of my emotions, I could not risk the breaking of my voice, as there was a consolidated clapping of hands, and words that called me "Sister" and "Mother". In grateful silence I fled from that wonderful ward of wounded men and retreated into my office where I closed the door. Uncontrollable tears were rolling down my cheeks, as I put my head down on the desk. I broke down sobbing in gratitude, for in that miracle I had just witnessed. I saw the hand of Allah working for my men.

It was such a deep emotion, that I experienced then, five decades ago. Today I share this with you, as I believe that the Lord is ever at our side. We need the faith to "believe" it.

A short time later there was a knock on my door and a request to enter, Mr. Mubarik, the Quarter Master of the unit, who was a Subadar Major (Junior commissioned officer) but a man of deep perception, wisdom and courage, sought permission to enter. His manner was gentle, his speech very decorous and his religion "submission" to the will of Allah. My stressed out heart, had to be reined in and brought under control. I used no make up, my eyes were not blotched, so I needed no repair job. My back and spine were badly in need of stiffening, I needed command over my emotions and it required to be done with urgency. I immediately did so, before giving permission to enter. When he was seated he requested to speak to me openly, so I informed him, I would welcome any advice pertaining to the rehabilitation programme and any progress of my unit was my paramount and dedicated desire.

After about an hour of explaining to me the dire consequences of their disabled condition, there were family responsibilities and financial family needs. They all were recruits from the villages far away, as the change of unit posting did not look to individuals, as all the men were a part of the Pakistan army. They could not attend to their lands, pay and develop better conditions for their children and a number of wives had only one child or no children at all. The entire picture was bleak.

I thanked Mr. Mubarik for the time and understanding he had given me and his advice had opened new doors that I needed to open for finances and he left my office.

It was then, at that very moment I realized I must move through the wards and the premises alone, this was my unit, these were my men, and I was their sister. It was for me to find the answers to many basic problems. Leaving the office I traversed the premises of the barracks, I visited the kitchens, and scanned the store rooms. I traversed the grounds amazed as how I now saw everything in a new light. If this was my unit it needed to be looked upon as a home for normal people with only one exception, they had two wheels replacing two legs. As I walked and viewed the grounds, new ideas, flooded my brain, diverse thoughts, flashed through my mind, a new approach was obvious, progressive plans with manageable rehabilitation came tumbling into my head. With the expansion of various departments such as physiotherapy, swimming activities, Olympic games, libraries and vocational training sectors were all possible for paralyzed men. These flashed within my inner eye, opening new avenues of advancement and earning power needed to be introduced. As I re-entered the building, I stopped short at the rear end of one of the very long verandas, that surrounded the entire perimeter of each barrack. What I looked at now, were broken down arches, large unidentifiable maps made by unplastered walls of broken plaster which had fallen off and there was no concern to have the wall redone. As I stood gazing at it, I envisaged hope, to find a solution, with the walls as a starting point. It was not complicated at all, but because of my overwhelming anxiety to their in human conditions of living, their emotional trauma and death, their future expectancy, I had missed what was in front of me. It had eluded me all this time. I suddenly became aware as to where I should concentrate my paramount efforts, in a practical and materialistic manner. My unshakeable faith in Allah had granted me my request, these walls were where I had to establish the starting point.

I returned almost striding swiftly to my office, but suddenly I needed to slow down my pace, to a mere quick-step rhythm. I knew that I would be under surveillance by the patients. I took my place at the desk, requested my secretarial officer to have me connected by phone to the military Divisional Garrison Engineer of the Cantonment. He wanted to know why, as we had nothing to do with him. I just said "phone him,

I want to talk to him." Shaking his head in bewilderment he left my office, soon after I had him on the phone, I requested to see him as soon as possible. He was completely taken aback, he questioned as to who I was and I told him who I was. Perhaps it even amused him to know, that a lady had the army disabled centre under her charge, none the less he promised to come over some time, when he could make the time. A couple of hours later, I had my head down making duty schedules, and other plans when Mr. Butt was announced and he entered my office briskly without any preamble. He briskly introduced himself, as I welcomed him, but the minute the formalities were concluded neither of us wore velvet gloves. And I sensed his great disapproval, to be sitting in a lady's office and that too an army unit. His "all business" attitude left me little hope of gaining any co-operation. I held my mounting irritation in check to pre-empt his negative attitude.

Mr. Butt did not approve of a lady in command that he made quite obvious. "Firstly young lady, tell me what is a girl like you, doing here in this all male unit?" he asked very briskly and in a disapproving manner.

I kept my irritation under control, as I really had an important axe to grind, so I used a smooth tone saying, "Before I answer that question Mr. Butt, I'd first like to show you around – if you see it, I may be more able to answer your questions currently that blind words would not convey. My requirement, or my dire requirements would be without doubt obvious to you if you saw the place, therefore I would have a better chance of obtaining your generous co-operation to help my men to live in decent conditions and a better life."

I had still not caught Mr. Butt's attention. He scathingly said, "Miss or is it Mrs … You certainly have a way with words, but perhaps if I see it, we could cut short the time of explanations. Let's go and survey what you have in mind to show me."

His words were clipped, his tone brusque and his manner condescending. I kept myself under control and spoke of my aims, "It is not what I desire to show you Mr. Butt, but it is what I intend for us to see today, thereby you may judge for yourself what is the minimum need, for the decent living of human beings. Come, for this walk with me and I'll let you decide what you can do for me and my men."

Mr. Butt stopped short in amazement as he shot out the words "Your men!"

Our walk was interrupted as I stopped walking and stood still. I gave him a long look and a half enigmatic smile. I think he caught the trend of my thoughts.

Very gently but very positively I proclaimed, "Yes Mr. Butt my men. When I took charge of this unit, these patients, living in an unnamed hell, became my men, they became my commitment. I'm not here because I need the job I'm here on Honorary service. I'm not here to kill my time because I'm bored at home, or my desire to pass time, on wasted coffee parties, nor am I rampaging around your cantonment area to lasso an unsuspecting officer for a suitable match for my spinsterhood. I'm not here to entrap one of the many young officers who man the twenty or more army units that surround this one, because I'm already very comfortably married, well educated and the respected mother of one daughter." Mr. Butt raised his eyebrows so high that the coming questions he may have had, had no need to be conveyed.

Mr. Butt remained silent for quite a while. His head was down, his eyes gazing into his lap. He sat there with his shoulders slumped, his hands together and his fingers winding around each other, thoughts battling for an answer, officialdom fought for curt, uncompromising decisions. The air hung heavy with the emotional tussle, that was beginning to overwhelming him in a whirlwind of human empathies.

There was a distinct change of mood in Mr. Butt, "Are you really serious about this mission? How did you get embroiled in a situation like this? I would have imagined, that someone like you could be more comfortable, at the social balls and of course the morning coffee parties, that swirl around the city from Monday to Friday. I would have thought, that your natural habitat would be a merry-go-round of fashionable social events – I observe that I am mistaken and this surprises me. Well, lets go back to your office and talk about your requirements and the dire needs as you put it, for your men."

My heart went soaring like blue birds over a rainbow. I was convinced that I had touched a human sprig. Anything could lie beyond that door. I said a silent prayer of thanks once more.

Then very graciously I invited him to have a cup of coffee. He found the offer tempting and I smiled, "I'll serve you some special coffee – beware it might be the "Spide and the Fly", my office and its needs could be the web you'll get hooked to, anyway I hope, so." So saying I asked Sister Waymark to arrange for our "special coffee" curtsy of Madam Anesea herself.

Now a smiling and affable Mr. Butt cheerfully agreed saying, "Perhaps, I will. I am myself amazed at the suffering and degradation of humanity as I see it here. How did it come about? I knew we had two or three barracks for the disable men but no one ever spoke or mentioned its existence. I'm glad my curiosity brought me here, for I couldn't for the life of me, conceive of a lady running this unit. We may be able to do something here. Infact I think a great deal can be done. I'll do my best, and that is a promise. You tell me what you have in mind and if it is possible I shall do it for you."

We continued to walk down the veranda which led to my office, and as we went we spoke of the many possibilities for the rehabilitation of these patients. When we sat down and awaited the arrival of our coffee, Mr. Butt enquired about my training, my experience, and my interest in medicine. When I told him I had done Literature and Psychology as my subject at University, he appeared to be even more baffled than before.

I explained to Mr. Butt, that I badly needed the barracks to be renovated for a start and in many ways actually re-molded, so it could be more suitable, for easy movements of crippled men with crutches and paraplegic patients in wheelchairs. It would provide mobility, free them from the confinement of their beds, which had become for many, a prison cell of confinement. Unless one sees their dead eyes, sunken lips without a smile, pride shot out of their damaged spines and acceptance in submission and silence, one has not seen the real degradation of human beings, wounds heal but emotional destruction is really dead. Wheelchairs needed ramps for easy coming and going between the various barracks within the grounds and they would also have the opportunity to once more enjoy the day basking in the sun, or sit together in the cool evening breezes, appreciating the very spacious and well – kept gardens.

Apart from these personal pleasures I needed the high rafter ceiling to be totally converted, as they currently provide the nesting homes, of over two thousands pigeons that leave their droppings and calling cards across all the wards, even on the beds and heads of these defenseless patients. The men are so demoralized they cease to complain, more often than desired, the cleaning is left undone till the regular routine cleaning of the next day. I oft wished I had a camera with me. Mr. Butt's eyebrows rose by inches in disbelief, he almost had me laughing. I said, "Yes Mr. Butt this is the actual way in which our broken army stalwarts have lived for a long time." All he said was "I can't believe what I am hearing. Young lady I am both touched and convinced at your emotional dedication. You'll get every bit of co-operation that I can extend for them and I salute you for your commitment and perseverance."

I had been most unrealistic in my dreams for the men, I envisaged a great big swimming pool where our large number of paraplegics could swim, for it is the only place where their disability disappears and they function like normal people feeling totally free – the joy that accompanies this particular type of freedom is unimaginable. But dare I ask for this - - - I reckoned the cost would be too high at this period of time, so I thought it better to make this demand at a more feasible moment.

Mr. Butt and myself discussed the many possibilities of the remodelling of the barrack, starting with the immediate requirements, to lower the ceiling of all the wards, and other barrack rooms, halls and passage-way. The extermination of pigeons, re-erected arches, scaped walls that would then be replastered, proper ventilated windows to be inducted and also the instillation of a suitable heating system. While Mr. Butt and his engineering teams were to tackle the imperative building requisites, several of his teams were to attack the premises, to conduct the re-wiring, adding a more modernised electrical system, bathrooms were to be torn down and new appropriate one created. These yawning dismal barrack rooms were to be converted into bright, healthy and cheerful wards, with false ceilings and concealed lighting introduced. Dispensaries were to be re-designed for multiple uses under the care of special nurses. We needed recreational rooms earmarked for indoor games, such as cards, chess and caramboards, a music room and a library were also added to the list of changes. Two educational classrooms that would emerge with a teaching staff to prepare some of the patients to take up educational Board exams and obtain a degree. These vast and multiple developments would change the face and structure of the entire premises. It could become a unit to be proud of.

On completion of the outside, one side of each barrack was to have long gradient ramps that had to be built, enabling the wheel-chair patient's access to come and go easily with total freedom all over the premises. When we got around to build the basket-ball court, we added a badminton court also for quick construction. The patients consistently made rounds, curious to know how they could use the courts sitting in their wheelchairs. They were extremely sceptical of putting any credence in my repeated assurances, that it was possible and it was being done in other rehabilitation centers all over the world.

While the whole complex of the premises had undergone vast structural changes, the use and style of everything I had envisaged had been carefully defined and created by Mr. Butt and his beehive squads, for there had been a constant drone of shuffling workmen and fleeting feet, that scurried along with all types of building materials. During the months it had taken for reconstructing the buildings, I had used the time to make contact with the representatives of the world Organization of CARE, they in turn prevailed upon a Swedish firm to donate wheelchairs to the disabled hospital. In due course I received 24 beautiful and graceful wheelchairs, products of steel and chromium with grey leatherette seats, with backs of the same colour. This had been an unexpected boon in the right direction and the moment I had so eagerly waited for. Apart from this, CARE sent us six knitting machines and I put them to use starting a vocational earning avenue.

I entered the wards at about four o'clock as it was early evening and I requested the men to accompany me, to the basketball court where we could start to practices passing the ball, before we attempted to play a game of netball. At first no one moved, others rejected the possibility to manage, or to propel a wheelchair and catch a ball at the same time. Realizing at once what needed to be done, I had to accept their unwhispered challenge, I responded and stepped aside, moving to an empty wheelchair standing nearby I sat on it saying to them "move - - lets go". I propelled my chair in the direction of the ramp and proceeded to go down, only two or three men moved to follow me, but from the corner of my eye, I could see the rest of them huddled together at the top of the ramp, some in stern rejection, others mulling over the possibilities, but several were making their way down the ramp. I told one of the male nurses to get a chair sit on it and follow me, so I kept moving slowly down the ramp, a few of the patients moved forward then followed, making it into a procession of wheelchairs. When I reached the centre of the court they surrounded the court with a frame of wheelchairs, watching with deep interest my next move. My head male nurse Pyaara Massey joined me on the court passing and catching the ball, as we wheeled our chairs nearer to the goal post, with a large circular iron ring painted red attached to the post. With my heart in my mouth and more than a wee prayer on my lips I beseeched my Benefactor. I raised my right arm, balanced the large ball resting within the circle of my finger tips, my eyes assessed the distance, gauged the angle, then gave an upward thrust that sent the ball up into the air. I closed my eyes tightly expecting to face the humiliation of "No Score". I bent my head, but my ears were assailed with the words of "Bravo", "wonderful","Congratulation" and clapping of hands. My heart stood still my "Lord" had claimed a goal for me. Curbing my tears of gratitude, I turned to them and said "you too can do it – who will join me on the court." There were a flurry of wheelchairs and an excited mass of men including the male nursing staff, the building teams of workers, and the newly appointed gardeners made up quite an audience. I made the players ring their chairs around me at a distance, then I kept throwing the ball to each man on the court for him to catch. At first it was almost into the lap that the balls fell, but as they became more adept, I aimed the ball higher to approximately shoulder level, soon they became dexterous and we began to practice throwing the ball while moving the chairs forward or back, following the path of the ball. Then came days and days of "shoot" practice, they had learnt to pass, to defend, to propel their wheels, to stop short when needed and now many of them were good "shooters". The men gave me their co-operation, which really made me proud of them. Some patients managed to gain from the games but some did not, that is also a part of any natural game. Once we had scored a victory on the courts after a real game, they began to believe that living again could provide some joy. They had enjoyed some pleasures of sportsmanship which instilled in them new life. Life had become meaningful and it could offer a future, if they summoned their courage, and projected sincere effort in the act of co-operation. Netball played on wheels gave the sports programme the backbone to forge ahead.

The sports list of activities grew rapidly advancing to archery, javelin throwing, putting the shot and it all worked out well till in July 1961 when the first "Asian Games" were held on the courts of the Army Disabled Hospital situated at Lahore Cantonment and was well attended by the members of the World Veterans Association. The delegations came from Paris, Denmark, Ghana, Nigeria, Canada and Stoke Mandevill in Britain, others were from Indonesia, and Sri Lanka. The occasion turned out to be an unusual but impressive function. With a great deal of appreciation and tributes paid towards the well developed centre and the extremely good sports presentation, by the disabled and paralyzed participants. With it came the publicity of the Asian Games bringing a wide spectrum of interest on the world circuit, it also aroused curiosity, initiating respect for the disabled in the minds of a once indifferent public. My deep thanks, my respect and my prayers of gratitude, still go out from me, for Mr. Butt. Whatever work I have performed, or I managed to achieve, the credit goes entirely to Mr. Butt who gave my men an honourable home, a decent living and helped me to draw worldwide attention to project the perception that "Disability is not inability".

The Wheel

Prayer has held its place through time
Its very essence springs from Truth
Its form varies with place, with time and race,
But honest prayer clings only to the truth.
The time has gone for folded hands in prayer
Joined to match the angelic stance of reverence
With lowered lids and murmuring lips
All tributes to an actors grace.
Prayer springs with automatic form
To lips profane from wordily vice
And broken beings crushed upon life's wheel
Till naught but genuine prayer falls from the lips
Till none but God can lift them up.

~ ESENA (1971)

★ ★ ★ ★ ★

Truth Conquers the Universe

SWIMMING POOLS FOR
THE DISABLED
Contriving for Water Therapy
for Rehabilitation

As one reads on, the story of the Disabled one begins to recognize the "Spiritual Courage" given by the Divine Benefactor.

There is loss of mobility, but it is replaced by the generous ability to "live" once again and life becomes meaningful.

Each prayer brings with it the "Hand" to cover the physical disability and the spiritual needs once more emerge.

This is the answer to our daily prayer.

The Morning Prayer

By the grey silent hours of the morning.
By the night that lies in the stillness of dark
My Lord hath not forsaken me.
My Lord doth not hate me
Though I am a sinner,
For my Lord is Merciful,
And my Benefactor.

My Lord hath given me all that I need,
In humility I now crave the grace of contentment
He found me an orphan and gave me protection,
He found me a wanderer and directed my steps,
He found me destitute and enriched me with love,
I have drunk of His Bounty
For my Lord is Bountiful
And my Benefactor.

I am an orphan, a beggar and destitute,
I must never oppress, chastise or enslave,
I crave His Blessing and Light of His Word,
For my Lord is Merciful
And my Benefactor.
(Sura Al Dhuha – XCIII)
In prayer I bow my head.

~ *ESENA*

The opening of the swimming pool would become their ultimate joy. On the premises there was a dump barrack of an enormous size, which came in handy for my new project, it would be perfect for a covered swimming pool with plenty of place to accommodate wheelchairs and the male nurses in attendance. I made my plans, found answers to all the objections and barriers that were sure to arise to block my schemes. With some persuasion and more sympathetic cajoling I might even be able to inveigle a valid and cogent motive to my dream plan. Warranting that the expenses of such a structure and programme would incur a vast sum of finances I decided to "bell the cat". Only this time it was not a cat that needed the belling, so once more I phoned Mr. Butt requesting his presence over a cup of coffee. Usually one cup was never enough, once I embarked on the lists that would initiate the inception of my new projects.

Mr. Butt duly arrived breezing in with his usual jaunty and carefree style. He sat down resting his elbows on the desk, brought his fingers together joining the tips like a Church steeple point. He asked "So young lady what can I do for you now?" I talked to him about the need of a swimming pool – he leaned far back into the chair, threw his head up looked up at the ceiling and guffawed loudly. I found his merriment out of place, and I was about to make a caustic comment, but I lent against my chair and waited. I suddenly realized that Mr. Butt was not here only as the Divisional Engineer, but also was now working with me for our common ideology, hence he had become a friend.

My rising mercurial indignation started to fall, once again I was regaining my composure. Smiling he said, "Madam Anesea you amaze me. Do you really think that such an elevated luxury is possible to obtain. Your concepts for your men are laudable, but your courage to imagine that such a heavy expenditure can be incurred, must be extolled. You really do believe we can do it! Don't you. Every time I see you I get more curious about what makes you "tick".

Dismissing his remark, without hesitation I was back to extract the best for my men, so I answered his question. I said, "No Mr. Butt! I'm not asking for the luxury of an elegant swimming pool as you call it, or a luxury for the ladies of leisure of the club or members of our "high society". This pool, that I require makes you raise your eye-brow. Well listen to this. I need the pool for the physical-therapy of my patients. What is more, but you fail to comprehend, that it is actually a genuine physical necessity, it is the freedom of movement, and movement of unconfined limbs that is absolutely essential for a paraplegic. In fact it also helps, to change the whole psychology and concept of an invalid dependant on others. With the buoyancy of the water, the useless limbs are freed, they are no longer crippled, so that if there is no water space made available, they are never going to experience again the pleasure of freedom, a man is then bound for all time, to a wheelchair and that's if he possesses one. Most invalids don't have the benefit of such a luxury. Unless one lives with them, one cannot ever contemplate or comprehend the emotional burden paralysis imposes on them, due to their unfortunate confined circumstances. They recede into themselves becoming introverts and the victims of a negative psychology, which haunts them as poor degraded specimens of men, as you would have or should have by now observed for yourself. I would expect it to be natural for you after all these long months of observing and rebuilding a new place to improve their living conditions. Don't tell me that you don't see it or feel it. You may not be able to comply with my need but I trust that you know me enough, not to ask for what I can do without."

Holding both his hands to his head in disbelief he said, "My God! You really are serious, and also very seriously involved. You gave me to understand that you had no training for this job. I'd say that you are more than adequate for the mission you have undertaken. I do see the need and your touching concern for your patients and it touches me when you say "my men" they really are and fortunate to have you."

Looking at him straight in the eyes I hesitantly asked, "Then you will help me! Could you say "No" after knowing how important the swimming pool is in the programme that lies ahead of me? I have no formal training or degrees for such work, but in the seven months that I have been here, I have consulted many, many relevant books, infact consumed them like a book-worm, swallowing the pages of every book or material that I could lay may hands on. So I do understand the complications of their medical and emotional, infact their psychological needs, I keep reading the seventh edition of Grey's Anatomy and it lies as my bedside companion. I have delved deep into the requirements of their medical disabilities, how far medical and physiotherapy can take them. Now I have to assess where their future lies, and how far I can take them. I have raided the Asian Foundation to acquire books on rehabilitation and also scrounged a large quantity of books from the Foundation to boost my newly set-up library at the centre. I have learnt a great deal, but it is infinitesimal in comparison to what I need to learn, which is a great deal more. I'm still a novice with much to learn . . . I have no one to learn from and I am aware of that. I have a long way to go but I depend on Allah to guide my steps.

When Mr. Butt spoke to me he was a different man – he had felt the misery of the disabled and walked as a friend beside me to help. His comment was, "Anesea I do believe you have a mission and a very creditable one at that. Yes I shall give you all the assistance that I can. We shall start by cleaning out that barrack, moving out what is not wanted there, then we shall embark on the project of making an indoor swimming pool. Shall we be needing any shower-rooms as they will be on wheel-chairs?"

I was so pleased that I had won him over so I said, "Oh' yes! Mr. Butt we shall need several shower-rooms as we have patients who can walk with crutches, some with artificial limbs, some have mental disabilities and also quite a number who were, and even now some are still drug addicts. They will need the showers."

Mr. Butt's eyes flew wide open enlarged with horror and consternation, his eye-brows were about to reach the ceiling. He gasped in a horrified and unbelievable tone, "Are you telling me you have drug addicts here in this hospital? That does not make it safe for you to be here, it is positively dangerous for you to work here – there is no protection here for your safety – these men cannot be depended on they are not normal."

I wanted to change the subject that so displeased him, so I replied saying, "Mr. Butt I'll tell you all about that later, lets go on to talk about the plan for the swimming pool ... It is a dream that I have envisaged for a long while, so please help me make it a reality." He could feel the deep down emotional net in which I was bound.

Glory be to Allah! We were back on safe ground of the centre, talking about the swimming-pool.

Mr. Butt said, "Well ... about the pool, it is not simply a matter of the pool. The pool will need a constant supply of water requiring to be changed approximately once a week."

I was disconcerted to answer this as I knew the real problem was yet to come. So I took the bull by the horns saying, "Indeed! But let me inform you it needs not once or even twice a week, the change of water. In their substandard state of health and low medical conditions the water would need to be changed on a daily bases, but I'll compromise for three to four times a week."

I knew that I had to brazen this out, but once again, "Nothing ventured, nothing gained" came to my rescue.

A stunned Mr. Butt commented, "God be praised! (looking up to the Heavens) we have our inflexible lady using a word that I presumed must be totally alien to her, or did not exist in her dictionary, that has been specially printed for her with only positive words."

Now it was my turn to query, "What exactly do you mean?"

In a very slow and patient tone Mr. Butt delivered his explanation, "The alien but operative word here is "compromise" apparently it does not exist in your dictionary, as I have learnt to my unbelievable but dire cost. So now we have an added project of a tubewell for your means of survival. I must confess that I do admire the gumption, the acumen and the conviction that underscores the mission for your precious men. Yes indeed you'll get your swimming pool, designed totally according to your wishes, with a deep sunk tubewell to ensure that there is no contaminated water to jeopardize the health of your tender patients. What else may I do for you my lady?"

I took this in good humour as it was meant to be laughing, I said, "Oh No! nothing for me Mr. Butt. Perhaps you could build me some fountains, pathways for the wheel chairs in the colourful gardens I intend to plant, for which the beds are already being prepared – maybe an orchard or two and even a mini zoo." I burst into laughter and he joined me too.

Still in a mirthful tone he promised, "You will get all that, but not the zoo I must draw a line there, for if I do I can see you sending me into Timbukto for camels, to the Congo forest for a monkey and apes and even into Siberia for polo bears, you'll have me and my team rounding up the animals for you. That is where I really must bow out. I better leave now, as I have a busy time ahead of me, drawing up plans for your projects, getting on with the great works of a Art you have ordered. May I ask by when do you desire that we finish all this."

I could not resist that moment for a quip, "By yesterday – if that is possible."

Flinging up his head in the air he had a great laugh, turning one complete circle till he faced me once again saying, "What in the name of Heaven have I got myself into? If I had, had the slightest warning that first day you spoke to me on the phone, I wonder why I did not miss your unit by a long mile."

Smiling once again I intoned, "Curiosity killed the cat Mr. Butt. But I'll thank you a million times for all the help, tolerance and patience you have so generously exercised in fulfilling the needs we were urgently in need of. I'll never forget you in my prayers and that's a sincere promise."

Very seriously Mr. Butt spoke before his departure, "May God continue to fold you in His mantle and infuse in you more of the outstanding courage and dedication you extend to the handicapped. I salute you my lady."

Saying this Mr. Butt left my office. I closed the door, sat down, thinking for a while then said a prayer for him and beseeched Allah to guide me in my mission.

Three and a half years later a small team of my paraplegics were prepared to go to Rome for an International Contest of the Disabled. It was a year and a half later that my archers in wheelchairs did a superb job at the Paraplegic Games so they were featured on the top cover of the World Veterans Association Sports Magazine. I was proud of the men, and I do believe they cared about me more, showing me every step of the way, as they co-operated with me, we became a large family.

I set up a vast and varied vocational training department, using sewing machines, knitting machines, sock making machines, all donated by a number of companies and best of all we went into the assembling of tube lights. After making contact with Philips, the worldwide famous light and bulb company, we got a contract to assemble their tube-lights. To make the assembling possible a contractor was to be engaged for the setting up of long tables a, score of long steel and wood trestle-tables, to form four assembly lines. (this help was arranged once again by Mr. Butt through a contract company). Patients sat in their wheel-chairs on either side of the assembly line with small component parts and tools, thus laid out in rows or piles in the correct order required for assembly. Each section was completed and passed on to the next group, so that by the time it reached the end of the preparation line "Vola" we had a complete and fully fitted tube-light. The first time it was successfully completed, the production of an operative tube-light, complete chaos broke loose – there were "whoops" of calls, hysterical cheering, back slapping and even some patient's eyes veiled, that boarded on tears. I myself had the need to retreat to the privacy of my office, take my wildly beating heart under control and I had to stiffen my spine before I could go back to the assembly room where the men were waiting to cheer for me. I put my hand, face up and they responded with silence. I praised them for the fantastic and the amazing job they had accomplished, but first of all we needed to say a wee prayer of thanksgiving to "Allah" for this great day. When all the men of this unit could stand shoulder to shoulder with other working men of the community it was almost the rebirth for each man. "Allah be praised."

I had originally explained to them when I first came to the unit, that "disability is not inability". The only difference between them and the workers of the world, was that they possessed two wheels, while others were endowed with two feet, and I had proved it possible that first day of play on the basket-ball court, sitting in a wheelchair – they had performed with me that day what even healthy men cannot on two feet.

Another challenge of this great saga that faced me, was the removal of drugs of long standing, to which so many patients had become addicted. The fault was not of their own making, nor was it the drug-mania round the world, they were the unfortunate victims of some dire circumstances. All the patients were the results of war, military exercises, some mishaps at their work-site or plain vehicle accidents. On being admitted to the hospital for immediate attention, to stem the agony of the excruciating, harrowing and insufferable pain that has to be sealed off by injections of morphine, which is later weaned off, replaced by pethidence or a milder pain killer so when this is withdrawn some other strong analgesic is prescribed. Most individuals, have no problems with this method of returning to the normal threshold of endurance for pain, but there are unfortunately sometimes others who suffer the dreadful reaction of severe "withdrawal" symptoms so morphine is extended, which after sometime becomes synonymous with addiction. Such patients suffer a type of hysteria due to a low threshold of pain. Originally the morphine dosage in any hospital is continued for a short time to keep the patient comfortable. There comes a time, when they are physically well but drug dependant, yet ready to be discharged from a normal hospital – so where do they go? who knows? - no one takes responsibility for them, but to the credit of the armed forces there is always a place where they are able to go and be received for rehabilitation.

It would be inappropriate to call the barrack existence a home, but it certainly provides a roof over their heads, beds to sleep on, clothes to wear and food to eat, these were always available. Thus under those burdensome conditions, I had on my list a fairly large number of drug addicts to cope with, I managed to handle them as best as I could make it. It was not easy, nor were they co-operative. It took me months of study and research to comprehend the psychology of drug addicts. As I learnt, my headway was more than I had hoped for. At the end of one year there were no drug addicts residing in the unit.

At the time, I proceeded to embark on, the withdrawal of drugs from the patients of my unit, I knew that I was treading on dangerous ground. Looking back on all that I had learnt from my subject of psychology at the time of graduation, I could find no real constructive guidance, to co-ordinate the psychology of addiction that made me secure, in my efforts to plan or to envisage success for me it was sheer blindness. I bought books on drug addiction, on their psychology dependence, the dangers of hallucination, destruction of the blood balance, but the toughest of all was, what I learnt about the withdrawal symptoms, with the deadly consequences, the dangers of going under, and the latent responsibility that lay upon my shoulders. If by any unforeseen imbalance, there emerged a negative reaction, which I could not handle, the burden of a lost life would be the burden that I would have to carry for the rest of my life. Were my nerves sufficiently strong to absorb the tragedy and yet keep on working, or even worse my own imbalance of guilt could unbalance me in time. I had prayed to Allah for His mercy and His hand to strengthen my mission.

I read and re-read book after book, I planned and I replanned, then planned again and I prayed consistently to be shown the way, I prayed for light to discern an active path that I could follow to overcome the "Morphine" drug situation that had mentally disturbed some patients, others also who were almost crippled in their physical body.

I bought or obtained whatever material I found available regarding drugs, that could increase and enhance my knowledge on the subject.

Thanks be to "Allah" that I appeared to have comprehended and absorbed the fatal causes of "withdrawal" and the traumas that appear to accompany it. My recently acquired knowledge became my most useful weapon of defence, which in turn gave me the courage and confidence I desperately needed for my status as their superior office. Under those current circumstances, it was just as well that I had gleaned so much understanding of the subject, making it unoppressive and easier for me to grasp their disturbed psychology, because it was not before long, that I encountered my first and most serious conflict, or rather unfortunately my authority being gravely challenged by one of my patients.

That first time, it was imperative and the point at which I had to maintain my position of command or accept defeat, succumb to male domination, or decline the most difficult challenge of my career. I surveyed it with a clear head, the negative points of my position at that time. Firstly my age was drastically against me, I was well under thirty years of age, secondly I was a woman and the only one in a male unit, later I inducted ladies, a nurse, a physiotherapist, and two vocational training girls and a teacher. Added to these disadvantages that I had I attempted to ignore the unjust, inferior and the subservient attitude imposed upon women, by a majority of men garbed in chauvinism. Thirdly I did not come from a working class sector, the elite did not waste a second thought regarding the problems of the "have nots", so with the flip of their finger they dismissed the upper classes "high society". The men at the unit, had a silent but broad and meaningful smile when one talked of the "Islamic Brotherhood". With all these disadvantages working consistently up front against me, I had little chance to survive. Despite knowing that the dice was loaded against me, I made my decision to stay on the job, hold my command and beard the lion that threatened me. When my ordeal was over, I am gratified to proclaim that it was one of the most outstanding decision, not only of my career but my life as well. It carried me on the winds of change to heights of emotional satisfaction and the knowledge that the trust laid on me, by my men had been a worthy achievement.

I was working in my office after having made my morning rounds of the wards, the patients and the premises, which included, a number of army barracks that were the unit's kitchens, the large store-rooms for bulk supplies of medicines, cloths, linen provision, the coal and wood house, required for cooking and the barrack that housed our physiotherapy unit. It had apparently been an easy morning as everything appeared to be well under control and it was all quiet on the "Western Front", but that morning full of sunshine and blue skies amidst green lawns of sprouting newly planted turf, I could have sworn it was quiet on all the fronts. But I was sadly mistaken, as thunder struck the nearest ward to my office, It was infact the lull before the storm. All hell broke loose from the ward of normally controlled patients, which made me jump and move quickly to the door. As I got to the hall the Quarter Master and Chief accountant blocked my way and I was surrounded by male nursing orderlies, peons and a number of other office staff.

I asked Mr. Mubarik what had happened, but he requested me to go back to my office where I would be safe. When I heard him say the word "safe" I knew at once where I had to go and that certainly was not to my office. Instead I fled down the hall corridor in the opposite direction, with a trail of male staff beseeching me not to expose myself or proceed any further. Of course I certainly had no intention to conform to their protective counsel.

When I reached the centre of the ward, I took in at a swift glance the threatening scenario. One of my addicted patients Saeed Khan, who stood six feet four inches tall, broad shouldered with eyes as black as his hair and his thick moustache, was holding his arm aloft in which he held a large threatening kitchen knife many inches high above his head. His eyes burned like live coal flashing red signals and his dilated black pupils challenged me in cold infuriated silence. I didn't dare to flinch, for in that moment, I recognized that it was to become the battle of wills. As is my way, I spoke softly, but very clearly in subdued tones and my stance totally free of fear. Our conversation at that ominous time projected my position of command.

With authority in my voice I quietly spoke saying, "What is the problem Saeed Khan?"

Saeed Khan standing six feet and four inches tall, drew himself up to what appeared to be over seven feet, so he could intimidate me. Raising his voice to me, "Who are you to take my drugs away? You are a nobody."

Mildly I retorted without fear, "No Saeed Khan I have not taken your drugs away. You must be mistaken, but I do need to start you on a course of nominated doses, so give me the morphy that you carry on you." I put my hand out as I said this.

In high dudgeon, flamingly he spat at me, "No I

won't and I'll kill you." I still stood there unafraid of his threats, while he raised the knife even higher.

He lowered the knife above my head at a distance of about two and a half feet ... I did not flinch – some of the patients were dumfounded, mesmerized, while the all male nursing staff began to panic – the Quarter Master Mr. Mubarik stepped forward to guard me. I put my hand on his arm and held him back.

My ever ready courage came to the forefront and I spoke with authority, "No Mubarik! This is my ward, my patient and my responsibility." Turning to Saeed Khan, I spoke with calm dignity," "Just give me your drugs. If you give them to me you shall have what you need – but under my care."

Still his aggression almost out of control, he roared, "No, I wont – get away from me. I'll kill you! I'll kill you! I swear by God I'll kill you." I did not flinch and he saw my calm dignified authority.

The ward was hushed into silence, patients holding their breath, male nurses were ready for my protection, moving closer to him, still with my head raised and my arm stretched out, I slowly but loudly delivered my answer to him, "Saeed Khan if you have the courage to kill me .... I too have the courage to die – hear me clearly when I say I have the courage to die, if one of my men can be saved. Do you have the courage to kill me. Look into my face, meet my eyes and say that you have that courage then you may kill me ... I'm ready to die. If you don't kill me then give me the morphine you have on you".

I kept my arm out stretched, that was still extended and waited. Then after awhile when we both had challenged each other, each eye boring our own determination, our eyes challenging each other, conveying our individual wills, until his eyes fell looking at the floor. My hand remained extended and waiting for him to surrender the drugs.

Saeed Khan proceeded to take one vial of morphine out of his pocket. I waited for another, then another and then another till he had emptied his pockets as he said he had six vials. When he stopped, I knew he had not surrendered all that was in his possession.

I looked straight into his eyes with a gentle and understanding look saying, "Saeed Khan I thank you for your respect, but you also have to trust me. I shall give you the morphine, but it must be given by our nurses and under your drug programme, that has been chalked out and balanced by me. You will not have to waste your pension money, to buy what is given to you, it shall be supplied by this unit. Your needs shall be met through our hospital dispensary. You have to believe me and trust me."

A man on drugs will always be a "doubting Thomas" Saeed Khan was no different. Once again he spoke, "How do I know that you will keep your promise and give me morphine?" No one has ever prescribed drugs for us before. If I don't get it, I'll not survive, it is better this way – go way …. go way. I'd rather die than live this way."

Smiling I said, "No Saeed Khan I won't go, it is better my way. You may need help for moths, but perhaps for only a few weeks, but you have to let me try. If you co-operate, you may be lucky to re-act the same way that some of the other patients who have succeeded to free themselves of it – you have to trust me and I'll trust Allah to help us . . . Saeed Khan please give me the drugs. The vials that are in your pocket, I need for you to give them all to me . . . all that are in your possession . . . so that I can plan for you a balanced intake of morphine on a plan based on intermittent reduction."

One and two vials at a time were handed over to me in very slow succession and with a great deal of hesitation. I thanked Saeed Khan for his trust in my honour and his gesture of co-operation. I left the ward, but not before arranging for a nursing orderly to conduct him to my office, which he had never visited before. I had to leave the ward abruptly, as I had a lump in my throat, with my unsplit tears needing the privacy of my office. Once there, I bowed my head to the floor in a humble and heartfelt thanksgiving. This could never have occurred except by the intervention of my "Master Most Merciful". I had seen disaster saved by His Mercy. I had another man with hopes of regaining a normal way of life.

An hour later, Saeed Khan entered my office with a nursing staff member, the head nurse of my wards and dispensary, under the watchful and protective eyes of our Quarter Master. With due planning and Saeed Khan's own co-operation, the reduction of morphine was to be diminished fraction by fraction and the time space increased by fifteen minutes every fourth day. Replacing some of the problematic symptoms of "withdrawal" with anti-depression tablets Saeed Khan returned to be a normal person after seven to eight months. He attended the educational class and passed the Intermediate Board Exam. He was keen to advance his education, so I enrolled him in our teaching programme to obtain for himself a Maths Degree. Later he went on to become an accountant in the office of a semi-military industry. Allah be praised.

Already there has been too much written regarding only one aspect of my working career. I need to go further afield in the narration of my life. I need to wind up each section divulging less than what I desired to convey, but before I do so I must confess that the rehabilitation centre was the most difficult and challenging assignment of my life, But it left me a newly born person, perhaps I became more aware, more caring, and I became more perceptive. I revelled in the pleasure of satisfaction with each experience, with each victory over challenges and I acquired humility which was encumberate as I had learnt from my Holy Quran. It was consummate with my religious and spiritual beliefs. I look up and say "Thy will be done".

The World Veterans Association in Paris held an Exhibition of paintings done by World Artists, which was held at the L'oeuvre in Paris in 1962. Since several of the members of the committee had come for our Paraplegic Asian Games held in Lahore in 1961 they had, had the opportunity to view some of my paintings, when I had entertained the delegates at a reception at my home.

My artistic quality must have made some impression I presume, as I received from Paris the information with an invitation to participate in the exhibition under the patronage of the World Organization of UNESCO.

Paintings from around the world came for selection and only 140 were selected for the Exhibition. I found it difficult to believe, that the painting I had reluctantly sent on to Paris was amongst the 140 nominated paintings, that were to be hung at the Exhibition at the

L'oeuvre in Paris. My painting entitled "The Heritage" was amongst the selected paintings chosen for hanging. Approximately a year later I received a letter from the World Veterans Association, informing me that all those who desired their paintings to be returned would receive them back in due course but those who chose to donate them for the "Auction" to raise funds for the DISABLED should give their personal written consent, for the pictures to be put up for sale and the funds to be reverted back to the World Veterans Association.

Of course, I sent my official written consent for the sale but in my personal capacity, I was stunned beyond belief. This was not for real, so when I read the list of names of painters and top artists who had also their entries for the original and final selection I could never have innagued that my unprofessional presentation could hang along side such professional artists. The more I thought about it the more humble and silent I became. Not many people are aware of this singular honour bestowed upon me. But I could not think for any better way for the funds to be used, the disabled were my own special breed of men. A copy of the painting I am endeavouring to publish in this my biography.

Before I close this subject I bless and thank Allah for gifting me such a Mother as I had, for it was she who had undertaken to have me trained by some very able teachers of art. This was my personal reward for her efforts and her blessings.

★ ★ ★ ★ ★

ESENA FOUNDATION
HIGH SCHOOL

1. My Mother Asma Jafer Imam, Tahira and myself at the inauguration in 1964.
   Mother was a "gem" of purest ray serene – a "Star of Stars".
2. Begum Asma Jafer Imam, Patron of Esena Foundation
   Anese Majid Khan daughter – Tahira Nazira Qizilbash - grand-daughter.
3. Three generations of daughters stand together.
4. The Esena Foundation School Building - Location stability and space is the need for all students for freedom and play.
5. Myself in school where I still work and teach.
   My students are precious to me, and my life is dedicated to them.
6. Director Anese Majid Khan – 1st Principal Mrs. Shabnam Zafar
   Apparently we made a good team - a half century ago.
7. Mother Asma Jafer Imam and daughter Tahira Nazira.
   There was deep love and a bonding between them.
8. My "Merit Scholarship" students
   Their results are most rewarding for my work – I stand tall and proud.
9. Our enthusiastic " student audience" at a school function
   Their interest and participation is outstanding ensuring their development.
10. Our special group of singers the "Esena Chorus".
    They participate at every function – and are trained by the teachers.
11. Tahira offering Mother the scissor to cut the "inaugural" ribbon.
12. The original faculty of 1964.

★ ★

★

ESENA FOUNDATION FACULTY
2010

1. Chairman Begum Anese Majid Khan
   Director Mrs. Natalia Qizilbash and Directive Staff members at a meeting in the Administrative Office.
2. Group Captain Abdul Majid Khan – Late Executive Director
3. Director Mrs. Natalia Qizilbash with senior staff members.
4. Valuable Officers of the Directive Staff
5. Chairman Director Esena Foundation 2010
6. Senior Vice Principals, Heads of various departments – Each a Master of her own subject.
7. The Secretarial Staff of my office – without them I would be a legless individual.
8. Mrs. Natalia Qizilbash enjoying a "School Function".
9. Dedicated loyalty by the young men who trained as my Secretarial Staff are now valued men serving with devotion and love.
10. Cups and Prizes.
    These are the ultimate awards for consistent and elevated work by students.
11. Chairperson and Director appreciating the performance of capable students.
12. Members of the Directive Staff with the Head girl and House Captain 2010.

★ ★

★

DEVELOPMENT THROUGH THE AGES

1. Chief Guest and Begum Majid at the Silver Jubilee of Esena Foundation
   25 years the programme has been an excellent development one.
2. Miss Nur-e-Fathma Raza Qizilbash opening the occasion with "Qirat" a prayer of thanksgiving for the Silver Jubilee.
3. Our Merit and school Scholarships,
   Excellent work needs recognition and praise.
4. Mr. Raza Gillani, Minister of Welfare with other special guests
5. Fatima Raza Qizilbash with Mr. Gillani the Chief Guest.
6. Competitions are a necessary part of every student's educational life.

★ ★

★

ESENA FOUNDATION EDUCATIONAL PLATFORM

1. Mrs. Anese Majid Khan directs the programmes.
2. Debate, Poetry Recitation, Drama, and Quiz competitions.
   These are an essential for development through exposure to the media of "Public Speaking."
3. This is a competitive avenue which builds up "self confidence" and teaches a student to face challenges.
4. The Esena Lab.
   It is always busy with deeply interested students participating in experiments.
5. Biology plays an important role for students to know the function of their own bodies.
6. Junior students enjoying their "break time"
   Interlude – Milk, Juices and dry finger food is supplied by the school at no extra cost.
7. Instruction in the classroom becomes a personal matter between teacher and students.
8. A Prep Class in session.
   Verbal questions and answers develops a child faster than exclusive written tuition.
9. Class I in the classroom.
   Here the camera at work has distracted a teacher's session – it does not happen all the time

★ ★

★

ESENA FOUNDATION
OUTSIDE THE CLASSROOM

1. The Audience
   These students are very much "partisan" as they cheer at the Annual Netball Match a very coveted Trophy.
2. Shooters scoring a goal.
   The match is on and the scoring perfect.
3. Esena Percussion Band
   Our under seven year olds perform for the "Percussion" display at a Junior School "Sports Day".
4. A Fun fair Food Counter.
   Hamburgers and other specially cooked food is available at these counters on "fun fair" days.
5. "The Doll House".
   Students of Prep aged four years play with the "Doll's house" and other games of their age development.
6. A Special Party
   Students bring some cakes and other edibles to celebrate their own birthday with classmates.
7. Esena Baking and Food Competitions.
   Senior students compete for baking, Middle School children prepare salads, open sandwiches, and Prep School present sandwiches, boiled egg variations and simple fruit Salads.
8. The Annual Netball in progress.
   Students watch and cheer as goals are scored.

★ ★

★

THE DRAMATIC
WORLD OF ESENA

1. The King and I
   All participants are under the age of 15 years.
2. Queen Cleopatra, Queen of Egypt
   An undefeated Queen excellently characterized by a young student
3. The "King and I"
   The king has succumbed to the charm that lies beneath Anna's selfless care.
4. Extracts from the "King and I"
   Confrontation of the King with Anna.
5. Anna's arrival in Thailand
   The ship that brings Anna to an unknown future.
6. The Mikado
   The haughty grace of Katisha and the powers of the King of Japan.

★ ★

★

ESENA FOUNDATION DRAMA PLATFORM

1. Anthony and Cleopatra
   The Queen of Egypt with her ladies in waiting and security guards.
2. The Kalash Folklore dancers of Chitral.
   The world's Cultural Folklore. Cultural Folklore is a part of world knowledge and practical participation.
3. Fathoms under the sea is a fascination for all ages
   Sixty fathoms deep is a world of undiscovered richness.
4. "The Mermaid"
   A young Prince falls in love with a mermaid so he sails out to sea to "woo" her.
5. The Drama "Esena Galactic Venture"
   This is a saga of the "moon launch", the meeting with Martians and the arrival of multiple inhibitions from out of space. A comedy with a serious message.
6. The love story of "Heer Ranjha".
   A story of love into death as in Romeo and Juliet.
   The lovers die but their story lives on.
7. The Manipuri Brides
   A folklore presentation of graceful movement and body control accompanied by the wedding story of two young village breeds.

★ ★

★

Truth Conquers the Universe

TRIBUTE TO BEGUM MAJID

The Dedicated Tribute of Esena Teachers and Students

Tribute to

Begum Anese Majid Khan

By Mrs. Natalia Qizalbash and

The Esena Administrative Staff

"Beauty lies in the eye of the beholder"

We the office and staff members who behold your beauty, have arranged to bestow on you some titles pertaining to how we see you in the various fields of your work and personal life.

1. For us, you are a refreshing presence and therefore we award you the title *"Sweet Fragrance of Esena"*

2. You are the ever-present Mother figure for all of us, always loving and affectionate. You are the *"Mother of Generations"*

3. You are like a Candle in the dark, lighting the way for all of us. We give you the title of our *"Lady with the Light"*

4. You shield us from harm and are always there behind us giving us the support we need at adverse times. You are our *"Guardian Angel"*

5. We learn from those we love. You have taught us the true meaning of love and forgiveness. You are a *Messenger of Love"* for us.

6. You seem to radiate light around you and we bask in this light. The shimmering rays you emit touch the very core of our hearts. You are for us *"The Ultimate Beam of Light"*

7. You have the healing touch to mend our broken hearts, when we are feeling sad and hurt. You are our *"Faith Healer"*

8. Your clean and pure heart with its simplicity and spiritualism, makes you an *"Emblem of Sufism"*

9. The pen is mightier than the sword. You have always proved this point in the use of your pen, be it poetry or prose. For us you are *"The Sword of Penmanship"*

10. Your sound literary knowledge earns you the title of *"Master of Literature"*

11. You are the pioneer, the vanguard of private schools in Pakistan which makes you the *"Renowned Educationist"*

12. Your vast and accurate knowledge and experience makes you a "Human Encyclopaedia", which is always there when

we wish to delve into it. You are presented with the title
"Anesa Britannica"

13. You are a brave and daring fighter for the oppressed. We give you the title of **"Freedom Fighter"**

14. Being a great protector and advocate of human rights, we have decided to name you **"The Champion of Human Rights"**

15. Your caring touch healed thousands during the war and bandaged many a wound with your deft fingers. You are the **"Florence Nightingale of the Armed Forces"**

16. Your high quality stage productions at school have been appreciated both nationally and internationally for their perfection and elaborate style. This makes you, in our eyes, **"The Dramatist of the Millennium"**

17. You have a very impressive style of painting which is totally your own. It's a magic mix of colours and strokes which makes you a **"Unique Painter"**

18. Your Melodious and Sweet Voice reminds us of a bird's sweet song. You are our **"Sweet Nightingale"**

19. Your untiring efforts for the uplift of the needy and downtrodden, earns you the title of **"The Philanthropist"**

20. You have an impeccable style of dressing; Dressed always in the pink of perfection. You are the **"Essence of Grace"**

21. Your natural talent for graceful expression in action has never failed to impress us. You steal our hearts with your

performance and are the life of every party. You are the **"Rhythm Divine"**

22. Arabian Delight or Pasta Italians, it is always perfectly prepared and served which we have enjoyed. You are the **"Haute Cuisine Expert"**

23. Most of all, you reign forever over our hearts and souls. You are **"The Queen of our Heart"** and the **"Queen of Esena"**

The combined expression and thoughts of the Esena Administrative office staff.

★ ★ ★ ★ ★

Truth Conquers the Universe

ESENA FOUNDATION
An Education System for half a Century is a Key Success

It is strange to comprehend how the wheels of "Fate" move, conveying one into uncharted fields of abundance, then, just as suddenly one is confronted and engulfed in terrorizing dark forests, or swept away, carried on an unexpected tidal wave in total astonishment, only to be washed ashore on some alien beach, battered by rocks or some beautiful tropical island full of musical waves and balmy zephered sunshine.

1952, when I had to migrate to Pakistan, I desired to send my four year old daughter Tahira to some 'play school', as she was an only child and lonely at home, inspite of the animals and zoo I had acquired for her. There was no dearth of toys, books, art material and handwork projects. I taught her to read, to write and work with numerals. She learnt to sing and to dance, but it was inadequate as there was no competition or challenges for her.

I tried in vain to find a Nursery for her to attend, but my efforts were furtile, as I discovered that there was no such facility available in Lahore, so I had to undertake her informal education into my own hands. As time passed, I inducted a formal educational programme into her daily regime, but she still lacked companionship and friends at a class level. Personal friends came to play, but they had nothing in common to work together.

By the time she was eight years old, I was obliged to send her away to a boarding school. I had to register her at the Convent of Jesus and Mary in Murree. I was unable to fathom the reason for her inability to adjust to her surroundings at the Convent, but there is a great possibility, that in her eighth year, when her father divorced me in a most abrupt and unceremonious manner, it may have affected Tahira's security, creating a maladjustment at school which was the outcome of her "broken home", undulating her with a sense of insecurity. The following year, she would not accept, or even bear the thought to leave me, with the result that I refrained from taking her back to Murree. She stayed with me at home and I continued to conduct the program of her studies under my own tutelage. I was thoroughly able and capable of conducting and preparing her for the local Matric Exam.

Tahira was a clever girl and keen to do her Matric Exam. It would enable her to achieve foot space into college. I was not happy but acquiesced even though I realized that she was far too young to enter college, but if she could get in it had its compensations. It would provide for her a suitable opportunity to meet other girls, make friends and chat about the insignificant, but important topics of a modern world, that is the life blood of a teenager.

Both Tahira and I worked very hard and she was able to do her Matric Exam even though she was two years younger than the average age of a Matric student. This in itself brought its own dilemma, so getting her into college was going to pose a problem, but my appeal to Miss Mangat Rai, Principal of Kinnaird College, was one requesting it on compassionate grounds and I was ultimately able, to have her admitted to the best girls college in Pakistan, that is Kinnaird College for Women in Lahore.

Tahira was a good student and a loveable one, she was very happy in college despite my fears of insecurity. During the next four years she scored her triumphs by consistent attendance, active participation in all the college events and sound discipline. When she had completed four years working for her Bachelors degree which she passed with honours. Tahira won a French Scholarship to study for her Master's Degree in France at the University of Beseance. Tahira completed her

Baccalaureates, won another scholarship to continue her studies in France for her Ph.D in Education.

But can anyone hold back "Love" I doubt it – even if it is the wrong choice, the heart knows no boundaries. Tahira did not return to complete her Ph.D. She joined the teaching profession as a French Teacher.

By the time Tahira was to do her Matric Exam, I realized the trauma of the educational situation of no proper schools for young children. There were no planned and well conducted elevated modern schools for the children to attend, that could give all the facilities of an English Public School. It was at this stage I realized the dilemma of parents and the predicament for our upper and social class of girls.

In Lahore, there were only two convents with limited seating and a deep rooted and very strong religious outlook. This was now Pakistan, a Muslim country with a very aware Muslim society, where the Islamic ideology was essential and had to come into force with a new educational policy, when the administration was to be set up after the Independence of the sub-continent.

The only other girl's school, was a school and combined college for a highly conscience "elite class", under the care and direction of a very conservative Muslim Trust Fund. It was a conservative institution without the development of a modern public school programme. It was an elitist institution.

Both these situations with their limitations could not suit the up and coming educational requirements of a new developing society. I gave this a great deal of thought, even though Tahira had no need for it, but our female society most certainly was in desperate need of this elusive element of human advancement, to meet the challenges of the fast advancing future of the western world.

I owned a very large building in the newly developing residential area of Gulberg. I did not need the building for my own use as Tahira and myself had our own comfortable residential accommodation. My building would be ideal for all the amenities that a good public school would require.

Unhesitatingly I made an instantaneous decision to convert my building into a much needed school. I planned, worked out initial costs, calculated supportive finances for six months. Planned the courses of education, starting from Nursery to Class V to be the initial plan. I was confident that my perception would render the relevant positive results that I envisaged. In less than three months in 1963, the school was ready to be registered and inaugurated to open for the autumn session. By April, 1964 the school had over one hundred students from Prep Class to Class III. There was a rapid response to this new public school and admissions rolled in at an overwhelming speed. By April, 1965 of a new academic year, over one hundred and fifty students had been inducted into Class IV to Class VII. The development was rapid and the extra curricular programme very well applauded. Later in 1965, the classes for VIII and Class IX were inducted. At this stage full attention and preparation was underway for our senior students to take their Matric Exam in 1967.

As early as 1965 when the school was conducting classes of over hundred students, we were required to be registered as a Middle school with the Board of Education. The school applied for registration in 1965 and was fully registered. Then in 1966 our registration was upgraded as a full High School and in due course the school acquired the registered affiliation with the Board of Secondary Education in 1967

The years passed with a student roll racing ahead till now in 2009, the latest student Roll Number is T 657. Each letter of the alphabet is equal to 1000 students. The single Main School has had 22,000 students that went through this Main institution. Our two branch schools had their own set of student roll numbers that also ran into thousands, apart from the main school.

By 1995, we had prepared and as we had already been registered with Cambridge for our students to take their "O" and "A" Level Exams from the University of Cambridge, our first group of O' Level Students.

Esena Foundation was the first "private" school for girls to be opened in Lahore. It was ten years later that other groups found it to be a sound professional avenue, particularly for ladies.

Esena Foundation is not an institution only about education, every child needs to be educated, but what is education? Is it the learning of text books, the preparation of exam papers for particular subjects for an exam, I am unable to accept this as the foundation of education. For me, education means something much more elevated. It is for developing a child to discover themselves, to learn to live in a community, to recognize the law of equality, to tread the roads of harmony, to honour one's commitments, to harmonize in a society, to curb one's tongue, to learn the art of sharing, and above all the responsibility of honesty and truth. All of this is contained in the vessel of "character" where honour, integrity and ethics form a pyramid of a worthy human being. This is real education and this is what Esena aims to inculcate in every child, that is entrusted to the care of the institution.

This is what I have not only taught, but have made the effort to ingrain into thousands and thousands of students and teachers who passed through my hands for the past five decades. I pray that what I have taught them, has made them worthy members of the community wherever they may be.

This struggle was hard, time never my own, my nights spent in planning and writing, my days fleeting in instruction and example, but the results have been wonderful, as I see my students working in the United Nations, UNESCO, the WHO, and a host of other prestigious jobs. Eseneans, as we are known are professors and lecturers at nearly all the universities in the U.S.A, Canada, Oxford Cambridge, and Medical Colleges, as they carry the code we taught them here at Esena.

We are approaching our "Golden Jubilee" with never a single Second Division in either the local Matric Exam or the O' Level Exams that are governed by the University of Cambridge.

There is reams and reams that I could go on writing about Esena, but this is my biography so all I can do is to touch upon Esena as only a part of my Life.

The Science department of Esena is dedicated to my beloved daughter TAHIRA NAZIRA.

Dedication (1987)

She spent her life in fair pursuit
Teaching children to learn and grow,
Strew their path with knowledge blooms
Like brilliant stars on the milky-way.
Herself a blossom with fragrance rare
A flawless gem of purest ray
Left in her wake sweet memories
Then flew to God on Angel's wings.

~ Esena

Seasons in the Sun
Students Farewell Gift

Good bye to you our trusted friend
We've known each other since we were nine or ten.
Together with you we've climbed the hills and tress
You've taught us love our sums and ABC's
You've stirred our hearts when we've skinned our knees
Good bye dear friend its pain to leave
When all the birds are singing in the sky
But parting's in the air with us you cannot fly.
Perhaps like your girls we're everywhere
You'll think of us and we'll be there
You gave us love, you gave us care,
You gave us fun we had our seasons in your sun,
Yet there were the hills you made us climb
You prepared us for the seasons of our time.
To meet a world we thought sublime.

Good bye Madam our Mother, please pray for us
Perhaps we were black-sheep but you never saw us thus.
You strived to reach us, you taught us right from wrong
You gave us time to play and yet not too much song
You loved us so you helped us get along
Good bye dear Mother, it's hard to leave, but for now adieu.
For when all the birds are singing in the sky
When you feel that spring is in the air and hear us call
Remember us your children who are everywhere
Just think of us and say a prayer, when you call we'll all be there
You gave us joy, you gave us fun,
We had festive seasons in your sun
You gave us play filled with joyous song
Yet your reasons and your seasons were never ever wrong
You gave us love you fed us pride with trust.
You gave us joy, you gave us hope, we had fun,
We had all our joyous seasons in your sun
You let us laugh and play with song and dance
You guided us you made us strong
We believe our seasons with you have not left and gone
Because you enriched our seasons in your sun

Good-bye Esena our dear dear one
That gave us love and helped us find the sun.
Every time we slipped and we were down
You appeared your arms outstretched without a frown
You always found us and stayed around
To get our feet back on the ground
Good bye Esena, it pains to leave you
When all the birds are singing in the sky.
You tell us that spring is in the air and we must fly
You say like all your flowers, are everywhere
We wish you could always be with us somewhere
We had your love, we trusted you, we won
our prizes in your brilliant sun
We climbed to stars you made us rise and seek
You said they were not just starfish on the beach.
We had joy, we had fun, you gave us blessed seasons in your sun.
The stars you made us aim for and to reach
Will not be for us just starfish on the beach
You gave us hope, we fear from none,
We learnt our courage from the seasons in your sun
And the stars that we must try to reach
Are way up high above the beach
All our days, you gave us fun, we had our seasons in your sun
And the hills you made us climb
Groomed us for the seasons of our time.
We had joy, we had your love you blessed our seasons in your sun
And the hills you prepared for us to climb
Will make us reach the seasons in our time.
Because you made us see the stars
We were not blinded by other seasons of the sun.
Your children now leave without a fear
Thank you Esena, madam and mother dear.

O' level Students of ESENA FOUNDATION, 2000

★ ★ ★ ★ ★

Truth Conquers the Universe

ESENA'S MULTI-FACETED EDUCATION
First Private School offers Golden Knowledge and Opportunities

Through these fast moving decades, the teaching planning and guidance has been the exclusive projection of my "Blueprint" of the educational programme envisaged to be the benchmark of the Esena Foundation. At the very inception, my mind gave birth with a very clear vision, of what I would have desired for Tahira, but I was unable to give her, in her earlier years – because there were no facilities, but there was still time to give the girls of the growing generation of Pakistan a more desirable and a more progressive type of education, befitting the twentieth century developing world. For this progress to stand on a world platform was the need of the time.

By opening Esena Foundation in Gulberg, I was able to capture the desire of young college girls, to use their degrees with some purpose making the teaching platform an outlet for the young daughters of the elite class, inducting them into a dignified professional service. Esena was the first and only private school that opened in 1963 and 1964. Young ladies having just left college had no clear idea what they could do, to use their well earned degrees, so I opened a new avenue of practical teaching of the subjects in which they had achieved their degrees. They had degrees but did not have knowledge of the art of teaching. Esena became their training ground.

At the office level I inducted Mrs. Shabnam Zafar an excellent educationist having received her Master's Degree from the University of Beruit in Lebnan. She was a devoted Principal and an excellent teacher. Within a couple of years I had engaged Miss Tina Thomas with a Master's Degree in English and Mrs. Fakhra Hussain with a Masters Degree in Geography. As the school grew and acquired a very exalted reputation, our progress was elevated and I went further afield publishing our own text books.

Our education gained by vast reading and a number of extra curricular subjects, that had been introduced at the incept, after we had established our base. Such activity as library, debate, drama, games, general knowledge, art, practical sciences, book reviews, healthy games, competitions, computer science and other topics have been consistent as the rising sun. Our students developed fast and progress was at a rapid speed.

Here at the Esena, we lay emphasis on the participation of all these subjects, as a part of the students educational projects. Television shows from cartoons for the younger children and historical films for senior classes, take them to view worlds beyond the orbit of their homes.

Due to this fundamental process of education all our students pass every year with First Division or Distinctions. We are proud of our students and our students are proud to be Eseneans.

There has been nearly five decades of sending up students for the Matric and the 'O' and 'A' Level exams for Cambridge. Esena has not yet had a single failure and hardly a Second Division in their results.

By 1975, we had been recognized even abroad. It was at this stage that the opening of schools, could be a project of a new profession for ladies, so slowly one school and another school put up their boards and opened their gates. This became the foundation of private schools with their branches that are to be found in every street, having turned a residential building into a school. The trend is to have four to six rooms for classes and as the students move up another class a veranda is converted into a classroom or a room or two is added at the first floor level. Thus the school moves up into a middle school or a school with a Matric Class. They are purely academic with negligible ground activity.

Today a very high percentage of Private Schools exist in Pakistan. Their proficiency is to be questioned for only a mediocre percentage are able to pass a board exam. It appears that quantity is the aim of the time and quality is allowed to slip out of the running for higher education.

Esena has a very different approach towards education. We believe that education is not rendered solely by textbooks. Text Books present the material for a subject. Even the quantum of seven subjects does not give an education. An education is one where a child learns to think, question, observe and answer a great deal that does not come from the pages of textbooks.

This is the Esena that brought up my two granddaughters Natalia and Majdoline and now my great grand daughter Fatima.

The school at its opening was dedicated to my Beloved Mother Begum Asma Jafer Imam.

Dedication

For thee a bouquet I have bound
With tender buds of woodland flowers
And in thy honour I have wound
The blossoms in this school of ours.
Take them my mother star of stars
Gem blossom of a virtuous root
And in thy image mould these flowers
To open, blossom and bear fruit.

~ Esena, November, 1964

To Natalia

The years have fled, your childhood gone
The years between has given you strength
I was always there to take your hand
To lead you on to the joys of life.
I took your hand and pointed to the stars above
Prayed to the Lord to bless your life.
Teach you to tread the path for greater knowledge
I held you secure through tears of sorrow and blissful joy
I unfolded for you the treasure of stars beyond ones reach
I taught you to drink at the fountain of His Mercy
Today you stand as a "star" for children to follow.

Your childhood toys were quickly put away
Books and learning filled your time and life
You took your place amongst adults beyond your years
Walked with colleagues in love and gentle harmony
Your life you dedicated to teaching and grooming
In all your efforts there was no place for self.
The dreams I dreamed became your pilgrimage
You fulfilled yourself and the dream you sought.

As you stand today where stars do stand
Myself, I bestowed on you selfless cherished love unbounded
I held you in trust and you never failed to fulfill my faith.
I taught you duty which unstinctly became your prayer.
I see you now as the brightest star upon the Heavens
Whose light must now be the beacon of your life.

As I must wane don't grieve, take my place on your onward journey
I exhort you to climb to heights far above your dreams
You have learnt the lessons well – but must continue to learn.
To reach the stars, the climb has not been easy to attain
But you have succeeded in your quest
Thank Him for His watchful care.
Life has been hard for you –
Responsibilities came to you too young
Ahead of you lay thorny paths for you to tread
Far too early for such youthful years as yours

Yet you met the daunting challenges
With open heart and sturdy determination
Enduring the pressure that engulfs all those who succeed,

Till now, today as you wear the "Star" I envisaged for you
It was sought by me — but well blessed by Allah
It was He who bent you to a greater service of mankind
As you consecrated your life to teaching and developing
As you now build the minds and hearts of the young
Children in your care are your special creed.
Daughter of a Mother who had her life in fair pursuit
Teaching flowers to grow, to bloom, to reach the stars that

Holds out the keys for those who make the effort to ascend.
Go thou my daughter, my "Star" of Stars.
You are the Gem blossom of a virtuous root
Take your place as the rarest star that is called.

~ ESENA

Esena has been dedicated to the young ones of Pakistan God Bless all that you may touch - stay humble and pure for the gifts He has bestowed on you

Now after almost fifty years I must wish them adieu. I leave my blessings to guard all my Eseneans that I have loved and devoted my life to.

In this my sunset I can honestly say I loved Esena and served it well.

★ ★ ★ ★ ★

Truth Conquers the Universe

PROSE INSPIRATION: AL-QADR
The Power and Beauty of "Light" is God's Gift to Man

PROSE INSPIRATION:

AL QADR – THE NIGHT OF POWER

A great night for a gift of the Holy Book:

Syeda Anese Majid Khan

The Holy Quran

What a night of Light....
What a night of Revelation .....
What a night of Power ....
What a night of Devotion ....
What a night of Prayer

A book to hold – and a book to cherish,
A book to revere – and a book to learn,
A book to guide – and a book to reveal,
A book to read – and a book to understand,
A book to honour – and a book to follow,

With Light comes devotion and prayer,
With Light comes generosity and help,
With Light comes understanding and purity,
With Light comes charity and benevolence,
With Light comes acceptance and submission.

Power, is to be steadfast in righteousness.
Power, is strength over temptation.
Power, is gentleness in adversity.
Power, is unity in a community.

A Beautiful Night is the Night of Power and Light.

~ Sura Al Qadr XCVII

The Graveyard of Falle Flowers
~ Mrs. Tahira Nazira, Oct, 1987

Eternal message with dedication to my Beloved daughter

In the hour of dawn when there was stillness
At the moment between slumber and awareness,
I told myself "I hear the sound of someone chanting".
The bird of sleep that slumbered in my eyes
Took sudden flight from its nest of lashes.
The clouds at dawn, so heavy and so grey
Reflected the bleakness of the world outside, upon my face
My veiled eyes mirrored the sorrow of the fog.
The unbidden words that sprung upon my lips
Recited "Verses of sorrow" like the verses of dirge.
I thought I heard it clear at break of day,
When half awake and half in slumber there I lay,
When skies were veiled in heavy clouds so grey.

The sky a battle-field of proud and warring storms.
There was no sign of spring, or petal pointed stars,
No sign of butterflies dancing in the flowers,
There was no sign of my garden's fragile daughters.
There was only dancing of the naked branches,
There was only heavy cloud and battling storm.
It is a tale of death of the garden's tender blossoms
It is a tale of plunder of palaces built on higher braches

From the height of higher branches,
The flowers are falling all around.
Instead of "life" the height of Creation
Death has fallen and covered the ground.
In me is the "swansong" like the falling of leaves
Ebbing away in a river of sorrow.
The heavens are open, and the clouds slowly weeping.
Upon the tombs of my fallen flowers
My garden's fragile daughters.

I think of the wind, the rain, and the storm
And the years of their lives lost to the "ages".

I think of the wind, and the rain and the storm
And the years of their lives lost to the "ages".

THE ETERNAL MESSAGE
~ *Esena, August, 1987*

It was in the strangest of ways that I set about to translate and interpret the Suras of the Holy Quran. I had always been a regular and keen reader of the Divine Revelation since the age of twelve, yet when I look back and recall my early years, I do believe that I was only a Microscopic Lilliputian being, of a living philosophy. But a strong and significant "seed" that had been sown in my fertile mind, left the unsatisfied heart within me from a much earlier period of my life.

While in England after the age of five, I was enamoured and greatly aroused, deeply fascinated and listened to the stories that were simplified and taken from the Bible. By the time I turned ten years old, I had already begun a smattering modicum of the Holy Quran in English. The wonderful stories beguiled me, the presentation of the ancient Prophets intrigued me, so I read them and re-read them, fascinated by the goodness and elevation enfolded in their spiritual acumen, their moral strength, their steadfast principles, their sacrifice and submission. "Could there really be such men in the world?" I queried, if so, they were giants in their spiritual elevation.

As the years passed, I began to associate in my mind such men, not only as men of worldly power, but in their basic present social standing, they were not mere sons of the soil, but were kings, wearing benevolent crowns, as spiritual halos resting upon their heads. They were elevated by Divine decree to become the leaders of men, they were the chosen messengers, revealing the words of a philosophy of good living as ordained by the "Master Creator". These were the men whose lives were dedicated to truth, empathy and purity. In later years the chosen Prophets of the Lord became symbolized and compatible with certain virtues. Abraham became synonymous with obedience and submission, Moses emerged as the courageous defender and law giver of the Faith, King Soloman the emblem of Wisdom and Justice and the builder of The Temple of worship, David prostrated himself as the Example of repentance, Queen of Sheba the model of obedience and modesty, Job the paragon of patience, Joseph was renowned for his foresight and judicious perception and his empathy. If I were to enumerate each of the Prophet, their special virtues and the Master Creator's beatitudes, that He bestowed upon them it would run into a multitude of pages warranting the presentation of volumes.

There are a score of outstanding divine men honoured as Prophets – these prophets are common to all the four Revealed Religions, as found in the Holy Books, Islam has the "Holy Quran", the Jews have the "Jewish Toras" of their ancient history, the Christians are the devotees of the Bible and the four Gospels of St. Luke, Matthew, Mark and John, these apostles preached what was taught to them by Jesus Christ and their books are called the "Acts of the Apostles". The last of the four revealed religions were the Sabians, who are now almost extinct. For myself, I accept that I am a simple Islamic based spiritualist. But I have read and I am aware of the Jewish "Toras" following the revelations of the Prophets of old and the teaching of the Prophet Moses. The Christians give their devotion, adherence and adoration of Jesus Christ following his teaching that spread through the pages of the four Gospels and their original seventy-two disciples who travelled West of Palestine, they carried the "Word" of Christ across Asia Minor, Turkey, Eastern Europe and eventually to Italy and Rome, where they came up against severe opposition, from the government and the people who were the dedicated followers of Roman mythology. The early Christians were persecuted, but survived extinction as they made their abode in the catacombs of Rome. To identify themselves under these hunted conditions, they used for identification the sign of the fish, ate food only when available and slept in the catacombs. The fourth of the Monolithic group of religions were the Sabians. They are a very small sect, that is to be found in Southern Arabian and Yemen, their religion is a blend of several religions that make up the code of their Doctrine. At a certain period they were stone worshippers, then blended some of the Zarathustrian teaching into their way of worship, combined with some of the Muslim and Christian doctrines that were inculcated into their religion. As in the Holy Quran they were identified and been mentioned as "Ahle Kitab" "people of the Book" they have been accepted as members of the four revealed religions.

The older I grew, the deeper I read into the real meaning of the Holy Quran, the greater was my affinity to the Doctrine of Islam. I read, I searched and even indulged in Sufism for two years. Wearing white cotton sarees, no make-up, no jewellery and almost depended on a vegetarian diet. In the process of finding my "Beloved" I had forgotten how to serve my fellowmen and my deprived brethren, who are infact the children of my Spiritual Lord. I withdrew step by step from Sufism, until I came to a threshold where I felt I could adjust my life and spiritual aspirations in a balanced mode of life and living. I used the Holy Quran as my sole guide, I read and consulted the second "Holy Book" of The Muslims called the 'Hadith' for, my search was arduous, my sifting intense, my desire for knowledge insatiable, my ploughing through boundless books and my commitment to Islam and the truth that is infinite. I gave up some of my Sufi ideals and bound myself to the philosophy of good living as revealed in the Holy Quran through the chosen and last Prophet Mohammad (peace be upon him) by the Divine decree.

With this spiritual perception of the existence of a Super Power, who controls the Existence of the Universe, I soon became aware of my own spiritual leanings. I had sung the Latin Mass with the Catholic Choir, I helped the nuns to dress the alter with heavily embroidered cloth and the glorified vestments worn by the priest serving the mass, and the placement on the alter of the three and five pronged candle-stands that needed precision placements. I found myself in the Church all too often ... there must have been some devotional urge palpitating within me, that took me to the alter steps succumbing to a dissatisfaction in regard to a religious misconception that was lurking within me. I changed tract and took up the Bible and the doctrine of the Protestant Church. I had a keen interest and tremendous pleasure reading the Bible and I learnt a great deal through the highly principled lives that had been led by the chosen characters, that constitutes the historical background of our revealed religions. Through them I learnt to separate materialism of the world, from the heavenly treasury that each man must create for himself.

Time moved on and my interest grew. I read a great many parts of the Jewish "Toras", gleaned what I could and moved on to the "Bhagwal Gita" of the Hindus. I addressed myself to the "Gita" as taught by Buddha, the spiritual leader of Buddhism. I delved deep into all the written material I could lay my hands on, from each, I learnt something, but above all, they lead their followers to lead a life based on the philosophy of good living. Each had a spiritual perception and a sound civic code of common human conduct, awareness and a message to cultivate empathy and benevolence within the community.

I was born into a highly elevated Muslim family with my unblemished blood-line descending directly from the Holy Prophet. (Peace Be Upon Him) I was taught Islam as a family religion, but me, being me, had to find the answer not for the sake of having an ancestral religion, I had to find what I could believe in, what I could do to advance my personal faith. I had to embrace religion of human philosophy that I could relate to. I chose Islam because it appeared to be more aware of human weaknesses, giving guide-lines of how to accomplish elevation, not by prayer alone but by action, deeds, empathy, selflessness and even sacrifice. I could not relate to the theories that bore a code for "angels". I knew I was no angel, but an earthly human being, a sinner, and as such I required direction to tread the road of reformation and the augmentation of my mediocre spiritual perception. There was need to enhance and elevate my human weaknesses, correct the defaults in my way of life that did my life no credit, Islam gave me the rope I needed to rise above personal desires, lent myself to performance of worthy acts, as required of a good human being. For me, the Doctrine of Islam became my philosophy of good civic living. It elucidated for me the approach and direction for my spiritual advancement. Thus I became a Muslim not by the decree of birth, but by my personal choice and in the process, I found my feet taking the path of truth and "submission".

You have read about my past religious history, that laid the foundation for my life as a Muslim, I shall proceed to unfold the special circumstances that surrounded me, before I vowed to commence the English interpretation and explanation of the Holy Quran, that I undertook when I first sat down to begin the manuscript.

My dearest, loving and beloved Mother had passed away the previous year, so I made a trip to India, to ensure the maintenance of her grave, and the polishing of her tombstone, I planted roses and lilies, to replace the ones that had perished. I returned to Delhi to spend a night at the hotel enabling me to board an early morning flight back to Lahore, Pakistan. The day was completing its daytime orbit and the sky fell into a mild grey that comes before twilight. I moved across the hotel sitting-room, to the immense and sweepingly large plate-glass picture window and drew back the regency stripped cream and maroon brocade drapes, that had kept the window swathed. As I drew the curtain back I perceived the naked branches of a leafless tree, entwined between the lacy twigs was a silver of a crescent moon, but this new moon was different, the entire Muslim World waited to view the new "Ramadan Moon" a special new moon that indicates, the commencement of a month of stringent fasting. I too like a million, billion other Muslims who lifted their hands in prayer at the sighting of this moon. I was overwhelmed with a desire that overtook my spirit. I raised my hands in prayer and unbidden tears flowed from my eyes.

Man receives another chance to strengthen his faith, with the coming of each fast, to atone for a year of indiscretion, man craves repentance, beseeches for another chance to curb and harness his self desires, once again he begins to read the Holy Quran as an offering to the Benevolent Creator and as a refresher course. While reading the Holy Quran, one needs to inculcate and absorb what the Revealed Book ordains as a salutary way of life, worship of practice, worship in deeds, worship in benevolence, worship in sharing and worship in submission. As I lifted my hands in prayer craving His Blessing to enable me to fast for the coming month, I gazed at that silver crescent and made a commitment to begin the translation of the "Suras" (Chapters) starting the next day. As I had vowed, I began my submission by fasting and prayer. I was hardly aware of what I was committing, myself to, the words slipped from my tongue unsummoned, I was totally unaware that such a thought could enter my brain, I was not a student of Arabic, I knew my Quran well, very well infact, as I had not only read the text but had sunk into my research deeply, studying the capacious captioned notes that Yusuf Ali provided while translating the Holy Quran into English. His work had been thoroughly and deeply researched from all historical angles that could relate to the ancient history and tradition of the religious books of the monolithic religions. I was bound and committed to a sacred pledge I had made, for me there was no turning back.

I boarded the plane at Delhi soon after dawn, my fast had begun before dawn as the shaft of sunlight came up over the horizon. During the one and a half hour flight, I was struck by the enormity of my new situation, I had no clear vision as how to begin, no concept as to how to deal with a writer's work of limitless problems, I was bound to encounter, from the first submission to the publisher's table. I was yet to learn all this and more. Each day I peeled away several new Suras, and each night I got even more deeply involved – the days and nights rolled into one long session of fasting, writing, praying, and long sessions of editing the script. The nights were donated to translating and the days to editing. I lost count of the days and nights.

To continue the subject of how I came to conceive and dare to execute this totally "out of bounds" action I shall never know. Such a plan to translate, interpret and explain the requirements of a Muslim, who desires to practice the norms of the Islamic Doctrine, is a grave responsibility. There were no mentally arranged thoughts, no draughts for planning and even no suitable arrangements for recording, printing or even publishing. I just took the Holy Quran assembled reams of paper, pens, Islamic reference books, again praying, then I began my writing. I scoured numerous books, I combed the pages, hunted through manuscripts, and authenticated my submissions through pinpointing the true meaning of Arabic words. When translated into a second language they are directly correct, but fail to carry the intended meaning of the original writer which results in a distorted translation rather than the meaning, of the words used in an original manuscript. This fundamental issue has become the birthplace of varying interpretations that gave the basic breach to the one doctrine and creed intended for Islam. The Holy Quran had already predicted this breakaway. In one passage of the Revealed "Sura", it states that there are to be seventy-two conflicting creeds, that war and fables make, thus conspiring to divide the one and only true faith of Islam, leaving thus a confused state of mind – it is only after the seventy-one creeds have been established, living in a state of religious wars, within their own homelands, and as Muslims confirming the Quranic verse of "conflicting creeds". Each sect has the singular opinion that, their particular sect is the only true one. There is a total blindness to other verses of the Quranic Doctrine "There is no compulsion to religion". The status of the other three religions of "The Book" is accepted in the capacity of a brotherhood. Yet there is complete lack of tolerance, even within the Islamic brotherhood itself, Sunnies against Sheas, Muslims against Ahmedies, the Muslim World against Judism, Judism against Christianity, Christianity within the many sects of Christianity. This is based on the objections of each other's performance of rites and rituals, even though the creed is the same and basic ideology of one Monolithic God. This is prevalent in all the Holy Books of all four discordant religions. When in fact there should be tolerance and respect.

As my pen touched the papers on that first night of Ramadan, a new spiritual aura flowed off my pen, the ambience of reality engulfing the world of materialism appeared to slip away from my unbidden thoughts. My thoughts came clear, my pen drove on at a rapid pace, my ideology never wavered, infact my vision manifested itself with a clarity as never before. The pages flew past, the suras peeled away, every sura revealed to me a new dimension of this text as the philosophy of good living. Time had no meaning, the dawn was approaching and still I was writing, I returned to the world of the living as the Muzzine of the Mosque sent out his call for prayer and the commencement of another fast.

As I rose from my prayer-mat after a night of vigil with the Quranic Verses, I realized I was to begin another day of fast without the sustenance of food, the time to partake of nourishment had fled, it was now time for the prayer at Dawn, requesting for mercy and beseeching His Benevolence, towards my new day of fasting. I did this like all Muslims who are about to fast, but I also sent in an application requesting my Divine Lord to aid me in my desire to deal with the true meaning of the "Holy Quran". This was the second morning in succession that I was to fast without nourishment for the day, there were no regrets, instead I cherished the idea that it might work towards more spiritual thoughts. This new experience of finding deeper meanings of the Quranic Message was a revelation that bespoke of a growing sensitivity in me, with each sheet that left my pen. I proceeded night after night, for ten days, for twenty days, then more, thus I completed my 30 days of fasting and exactly half of the Holy Quran which was 80 Suras. In the next month of Ramazan I completed the other half of the Quran. How I did it and how it happened I'll never know.

With a time lapse of 30 days I had been able to translate, interpret and give an explanation of more than half the Holy Quran. By the end of the second month I had completed the typing, editing and designing of "The Eternal Message", in the next year the manuscript for the remaining Suras were completed. I offered my deepest thanks to Allah for the inspiration He bestowed on me enabling me to complete my mission. Two years later EMI did a complete audio recording of the Eternal Message. The narrator's voice for the tape recording of the tapes was my own. There are eight cassettes in each box done by E.M.I. The package has been designed by me and has been delivered all round the World. Prime T.V. has recorded fifty-two episodes delivered by me on Video tape. These tapes are seen on T.V. in over a hundred and seventy-four countries. It is played and viewed on six to seven channels on the American Canadian circuit. In 2007, my new set of Video recordings in English are now produced on D.V.D. for distribution. Allah in His kind mercy enabled me to have a fairly worldwide distribution of "Eternal Message" in the form of books and accompanied by the "Insight into Islam" Volume I and Volume II. These volumes deal with the life of the Holy Prophet, the laws and several topics in Islam regarding the five fundamental pillars on which the Muslim religion stands, the laws of marriage, custody, divorce, inheritance and other family related laws. It expounds material related to the planetary system, it incorporates the mysticism of the Sufi philosophy, the interaction of scientific elements, there are laws of justice, commercial business, norms and even the personal law of marriage and commitment. The self need of humility, benevolence and truth: The protection and equality, rights of women, as instructed in Revelations of the Holy Quran. Much of what has been ordained in the laws of the Islamic religion, has been destroyed and discarded because it has not suited the requirements and demands of selfish leaders, interpreters, ruthless rulers, men of power and an ambitious materialistic society.

For me this experience of delving deep into the beautiful philosophy of good living, never let me deviate from the Revelation of the Divine Message. My perception cleared, my vision soared, my understanding grew, my growing sense of spiritualism was gaining momentum, penetrating spiritual barriers that had previously confounded me. Life began to take on a new meaning, my hands went out to help the helpless in ways that had evaded my attention, nurturing became a way of life for me, empathy was a natural creed that I embraced and the quest for spiritualism never ceased. The more I learnt the more I hungered after it, the more clearly I found a depth of meaning. An unmitigated and paramount aspiration engulfed me to write of other topics within the boundaries of Islam. As yet I have not received the total bondage of my spirit, but I feel that I have entered the stage of spiritual adoption, the journey has been long, but not arduous, my fast for righteousness has been ridged, but I have been submissive to the fate He bestowed on me.

Today I stand outside the bondage of materialism; I make an effort to gain His compassion, leading me into the avenues that would lead me into the orbit of total spirituality.

After the recording of the audio cassettes of "The Eternal Message" I laid my plans to move them into the Western Countries which was the imminent call at this period of time. People migrated to England, United States of America and Canada where a second and third generation of Muslims were growing up with their basic language as English. This comprised Arabs, Pakistanis, Indians, Bangladeshies, and several African States. Islam was their fundamental religion, but Bengali and Arabic were alien languages to these new breeds. The concept and the religious code of life needed the basic understanding of the "Revealed Message" of the Holy Quran. Just performing the rituals of prayer, fasting, charity, not charity but the sharing with others and even performing the pilgrimage of Haj became a mere ritual, which is unacceptable to a genuine practicing Muslim. Apart from being a book, The Eternal Message are audio cassettes printed and boxed as one package. In the process of sending them around the world for the past twenty-six years, there are thousands of sets now all round the world.

> *Can storied urn or animated bust*
> *Back to its mansion call the fleeting breath?*
> *Can Honour's voice provoke the silent dust,*
> *Or Flattery soothe the dull cold ear of Death?*
> ~ *Thomas Gray*

★ ★ ★ ★ ★

Truth Conquers the Universe

CALLED TO THE
WORLD PLATFORM
My Work Accepted by
World Platforms

For some unknown reason "Fate" decided to catapult me like a ballistic missile, into an orbit, that was a world platform. I found myself in a perplexing situation where I was about to enter and embark onto a new world order and a consummately unfamiliar, redesigned phase of my life, that was comprehensively alien. I had had no premonition that my life was to take on such a dramatic twist, that anything, so strange, so drastic, so engulfing and so elevating was to happen to me. My whole world of relationships would change, not only my world, but my life of dedication would be propelled into an "International World Setting".

I had translated with interpretation and explanation of the Holy Quran into the English where the Islamic explanation of life and living was completely unfolded. This I undertook in the summer of 1987, just a few months before my beloved daughter Tahira went to her heavenly home.

By 1991 my name was entered and fed down the pipeline in Japan as the Sufi Ambassador. I became aware of this only when I received the intimation from Tokyo that I was now the Sufi Ambassador on a World Platform. This knocked me between the eyes so I was left dumb founded, as it made no sense to me, for I could hardly realize what had struck me. I found the situation gratifying, but also both startling and alarming, then completely overwhelming. I was torn between belief and disbelief, dreams and reality, worthy and unworthy, capability and spiritual disability. I questioned myself again and again, could I meet this monumental challenge, could I stand side by side on a platform of the genius, could I hold my own amongst, monstrous and brilliant International orators. I had very grave doubts.

I soon after received from Revd. Dr. Don Conroy the Bishop at Washington, a letter of such graciousness and the invitation to attend and participate at the decade meeting of the "Parliament of World Religions" that was to be held in San Francisco in August of 1992. I found that week by week I was getting propelled and further propelled into a Religious World Order. This did not confuse me, but I realized that if I was to hold my place with prestige, I had to do a great deal of work to enable me to present Islam in its true form on a World Platform. The responsibility rested too heavily on my emotional weighing scale.

A while later, I received a letter from the "Parliament of World Religions" incorporating me as a delegate amongst 7000 other delegates who were to attend the meeting. As all correspondence appeared to be concertinaed into a very short space of time, I thereafter received the information that I was to be, not only a delegate, but I was to be one of the two hundred world speakers. I had been elevated to the position of a world speaker, so the speed of my preparation raced on, I knew no time, no bounds, no rest, "Preparation" was the singular word of my life and existence for two to three months.

I was emotionally dazed, insecure, and somewhat disoriented. There was no one I could turn to for assistance. Before I left on the trip, I fasted and devoutly prayed to Allah to guide my unsure capability, I begged Him to infuse into me the right delivery, the correct concept of Islam with every true Light of the Holy Quran. I beseeched Him to cast his veil over me, to be my Benevolent Lord, to endow me with the words of clarity, I needed to project Islam on a world platform. Truth to tell I was scared, for I was only a midget for the responsibility I now held. I searched for signs to indicate if I was worthy, I prayed for His indulgence and the removal of my insecurity, Then on the 9th of Muharram, two weeks before I left for London on my way to America, I envisaged a sign and with it my insecurity left me. I was no longer afraid, I was free and I was a spiritualist reborn and ready to face "Parliament" with the Light of Islam.

Allah my Benevolent Lord had not forsaken me.

Once more I held my head erect, my vision cleared and my steps were firm and the Light of the Eternal Message became my sacred trust. There was no other inner life for me.

My love, my duties and my responsibilities in my personal world never changed, infact I had better vision hence a greater love and sense of duty.

I arrived in San Francisco in August to attend the eighteen days of the "Parliament of World Religions". By the end of the intense session, I was so overwhelmed by my experience of varied religious persuasions, even though there were the top representatives of one hundred and seventy-four World Religions. I met with them, listened to their deliveries and found that I was once again reborn. If I had known what I was about to encounter, I would have most willingly given up ten years of my life for the unrivalled experience through which I passed. Today after over twenty-five years I still feel the same, it is still true regarding the projection of my feelings. The experience was not one that was mind boggling, but a rare spiritual experience in a hugh and manifold coliseum of true worship under a sound moral code.

I had been invited to speak, to give lectures and presentations in many Universities of Canada, and America, right from Montreal in the north of Canada travelling down twenty seven cities that took me right down to Mexico and South America. I was proud but humble to be able to present the true light of Islam across the globe.

I was invited and had taken my lectures and service at the first church built in the U.S.A. where the British landed at James Town and the first Protestant Church was built in America. I was grateful to be able to take Islam to the pulpit of a Christian Church, to be not only welcomed, but my presentation on Islam extolled. It was not me for, I am nothing, it was my Lord and Benefactor who covered me with His mantle, to deliver His Message of Light and righteous living found in the Doctrine of Islam through the pages of the Holy Quran.

At the World Parliament in San Francisco I met, spoke, dined and parleyed with the Dali Lama of Nepal, The Arch Bishop of Cantburry from London, the President Ruddy Lubber of the Netherlands and many other Presidents from several countries. I had the privilege to sit and confer with the Red Indian Chiefs, who also conferred on me the title of "sister" with the special blessing done by an ancient "Spiritual Feather". I was blessed to listen to a most beautifully rendered "Azan" delivered by the Head Allama of Sudan that in itself was an experience. The lists of Scientists Dr. Rustum Roy of Penn State University, Dr. Don Conroy Bishop at Washington, Mr. David Granfield and many others became my friends. The lists can go on forever for, they cover a wide spectrum of religious speakers from 174 World Religions across the Universe.

I shall be presenting my speech at the Parliament of World Religions so one may have a glimpse of my thoughts at a World Platform level.

Soon after I returned from the World Parliament

in 1992, I received a personal letter from Mr. Mikhail Gorbachev of Russia inviting me to join the new founding forum of Mr. Gorbachev covering a new World Order.

I went to Washington for the meeting and after the second meeting, was graciously elected to the Board of the New World Order. I was delighted as I was the only Muslim woman on that board.

After I returned to Pakistan, I was once again to go to New York. Dr. Don Conroy wrote to me asking if I would care to be the Vice-President for the Global Stewardship of the North American Environment.

Once more I found myself in New York at the "Parliament of the World Religions" in September, 2000. I attended the Conference of Mikhail Gorbachev at about the same time in New York, and I attended the U.N.O. Conference of Millennium 2000. I spent five to six weeks in New York covering all the three conferences which all had agendas that involved twelve, sixteen and twenty days each.

The days were rushed from one conference hall to another and the night dinners were also centered around "special speakers" and cultural entertainment. They were outstanding and memorable days for, each night the evening dinner and speeches took care of four hours.

Now due to my ill health and advanced age I have been unable to continue with the travelling conditions. This is to my regret but I thank Allah for showing me a whole new world confirming my own philosophy of life. The world is a "Brotherhood" waiting for our care.

In 1996 the boxes of the Eternal Message audio-cassettes and books began to move into various homes, students references at the college level and other religious groups, one such box found its way into Libya with an employee of an oil company who had a friend visiting from America, together they listened to the tapes and when the friend returned to America she talked about it at a university convocation, where many people arrived from all over America and Canada. While talking, Dr. Roy heard the lady expounding on this new presentation about Islam. Dr. Roy desired to learn more, so he requested her to give him the address and phone number of the gentleman in Libya. A young girl who had come from Canada to be present for her brother's convocation, stood listening and when the author's name was mentioned, Sandy said she knew the author. All attention was now focused on her, questions of how she knew the writer. She told them that I visited Canada regularly and stayed for three to four weeks at a time with the Director of her company Ms. Peggy Dean of Dean Associates. Dr. Roy wanted her to procure my phone number. Sandy got on the phone and requested my phone number from Mrs. Peggy Dean. At that period of time I was in London and Peggy knew I was there, as we are in regular touch, infact from a very young age I took her under my wing and almost brought her up and also her brother Christopher. We have never lost touch with each other, and have always been as if we were a blood-bonded family, no family tie could be closer. Sandy passed on my phone number to Dr. Roy at the Pennsylvania University.

My telephone in London rang and I picked it up to answer it, a lady from across the Atlantic identified herself as Professor Roy's Secretary and asked if I was Mrs. Anese Majid Khan. She wished to know where Dr. Roy could purchase a box of the cassettes of the Eternal Message, I told her they were not on sale, but I send thousands of boxes all round the world. If she gave me an address I would send her the boxes by

Urgent Post Delivery. After taking down the Penn State Research Centre Laboratory address we wished each other a cordial adieu and hung up.

I took out six boxes of the tapes, prepared them for delivery along with the Book "Eternal Message" and went down to the post office. I dispatched the tapes and books to Dr. Roy in Pennsylvania where he was the Director of the Material Research Laboratory of the Penn State University. As a young student from India, he won the President Eisenhower Gold Medal for his research on Mica. He ranks amongst the top six scientists of the World and his interest in the subject of spiritualism baffled and astounded me, but the first time when I did go as a Speaker and a delegate to the "Parliament of World Religions" I rediscovered that my childhood friend was not only one of the top scientists of the world, but to my amazement I came to understand that he was a man of great Faith, expressing his ecumenicity in deeds, not just as a religion of rituals, but a man of great belief in the subject of theology, endeavouring to establish a rapprochement between Science and religion, also of the multiple platform of Churches and followers of the Revealed Religions. In his book called the "Passionate Realist" he wrote the following lines.

"An early childhood friend Anese Majid Khan of Lahore, Pakistan had emerged after an interval of decades to help Rustum Roy express his ecumenicity in collaborating with her interpretation of Islam to Americans and the Western World." In keeping with the above writing, he discovered that we had a great deal in common, but most of all we were spiritually bonded as "kindred souls" on the topic of the commonalities of Religions. We believed that religion was not served by the pronouncement of prayers and rituals alone and by mere vocal rendition, it is served by performance of conduct, as advised and commanded by the Religious Doctrines. In truth the actual form of prayer are deeds, for words without deeds have no meaning or value.

Dr. Roy and I both appear to possess the same interpretation of spirituality and the inter relationship between Science and the spiritualism. Both are the creation of nature, by a more powerful "Supreme Power" that controls the universe and the formation of nature. There is nothing that is new in the secrets of nature, but it is concealed by Divine Command to be opened and spread by the discovery of scientists, at a time ordained for its discovery, or the theory of evolution, which moves with a macro-ecumenism, radical pluralism, religious leaning in an effort to explore the deepest truths, and individuals aiming in their pursuit to "transcend reality", through multiple avenues of spirituality, that leaves space to focus on the bridge of human relationship, as a beacon of light integrating the materialism of the being, with the purity and perception of the spiritual, that manifests itself in both technology and true unbound – spiritual grace.

My life changed almost overnight. I was alone in my apartment in London that autumn of 1989, when just after dinner my telephone beeped several times, I went to retrieve that hand set, speaking gently I said "Hello! Who is speaking?" A gentle voice replied, "This is Kathleen Mourant of Pennsylvania University Dr. Roy would like to speak to Mrs. Anese Majid Khan", "Yes I am Anese Majid Khan" Kathleen said, "Would you please hold". A man's voice came on the phone, pronouncing no preliminaries, just a one line gun-shot projection "Are you Akbar's kid sister" I said "Yes indeed I am – who are you speaking", another swift undecorated sentence tumbled out of his mouth "you "bokaa" what the hell are you doing in London, it is me Rusty your childhood friend and Akbar's brother". Here I must explain what "bokaa" means. In English it is a very uncomplimentary word which plainly pronounces the recipient a "stupid fool" Thank God he dropped his delicate compliment pretty soon. Akbar was my brother and Rusty was his dearest friend from childhood until my brother died in 1967. We had been a threesome.

The last time Rusty had seen me, I was hailed as a Beauty Queen in 1947. My attributes were supposed to be many besides my so called beauty, for I never saw myself as a beauty, leave alone a "beauty Queen" I was supposed to have been amongst our younger generation, the most elegant, the most graceful, and the most sophisticated, thus combining elegance and grace, it made for a potent mixture. I used my talents to perform in many programmes raising money for the destitute famine victims, disaster struck individuals. I had been trained to ballet at the age of five, I learnt Indian Classical Dancing from the age of eleven, and ballroom-dancing was an important part of the social graces that was, at that time required to be a "lady" and the accepted form of social life in the higher echelon of the privileged class. To raise money for the victims of the degrading Bengal famine in Calcutta, I used my skills of Indian classical dancing, ballet presentations with drama, and theatrical presentations. Fashion shows were just beginning to emerge displaying the most beautiful saris coming from Benares on the banks and confluence of the river Ganges and the gorgeous unbeatable shot silk, woven in the South Indian region of Madras.

It was difficult for Rusty to even envisage me living in a world of personal spiritualism, or my retreat into Sufism even though it was for a short period of two years, after which I retraced my steps into a spiritualism of my own exclusive making, aligning it to what I had learnt from my fasting and the selfless duties as advised in the Holy Quran. Rusty wanted to know what had happened to all my vivaciousness, my elegance and my zest for living. To be a hermit was out of charter for me. All I told him was that the boxes of audio cassettes and the Books of the Eternal Message were not for sale, but books and audio-cassettes were sent all round the world free of cost. The reason for this was that a verse in the Holy Quran asks "What! Shall you sell the word of God for a miserable price?". My answer to this was "No!" Allah Himself will provide the means to spread the "Holy Word" if that is for what my presentation was intended. My personal finances flowed in with a reasonable flow enabling me to continue my mission of spreading "The Word" with a meaningful translation, projecting a worldly life encased in spiritual grace. The demand and out flow of the Eternal Message spread rapidly through a large number of countries, but it was evident that some visual form should now be on the anvil. Accordingly the Video tapes were produced for Prime T.V in London under the heading of the "Glorious Message". I received letters from all over the World posing questions for clarification in the Light of the Islamic requirement and the ever demanding social and professional requirements. These letters have been answered on Video tapes and DVDs. Both series of the Glorious Message and The Perception of Islam have been recorded by me as the narrator, and I hope that I have made my presentation well.

After going through The Eternal Message and the two volumes of Insight into Islam Dr. Roy apparently found the link that he had been searching for. It appeared that both Dr. Roy and myself operated on the same wave length and had a clear vision, that basically the four Revealed religions had in its base the commonalities and the same requirements projected through a presentation of varying rituals. In view of this, we worked together to unveil and proffer the commonalities and expound on the spiritual perception. We initiated our first debate of introducing the commonalities at a meeting held at Kirkridge, a retreat centre on a ridge of the Appalachian Mountains, a place where ecumenical spirituality is a comfortable abode and where the ethnic fabric of experience asserts itself loud and clear in the silence of the hills, that was once the path of a Red Indian trail. As a matter of fact the spot chosen for building this spiritual retreat is the very place where the Red Indians camped beside a beautiful silvery waterfall that murmured, its rippling waters were a soothing refrain floating upon the winds to settle and subdue emotional conflicts. The unharnessed and unbridled spirits of those hills make Kirkridge an ideal place to retreat and it encourages the state of meditation. By some mysterious Hand or perhaps by the will of my Beloved Master Allah I found myself standing in Kirkridge as the 'spiritual leader' that autumn morning in 1992. I always thought that I myself needed some type of emotional healing, but I could never have dared to conceive to be a "spiritual teacher" leave alone to be the Spiritual Leader at Kirkridge that year. I found myself a leader of the group for a period of two weeks. With every passing day I learnt something new, my arduous search was ever seeking advancement into the world of spiritual submission.

I must move on relating my position as a spiritualist but my experience at Kirkridge must be revealed as the Spiritual Leader. I must, inspite of the biased propagander regarding Muslims as fanatics, I was admitted, met and handled with tremendous respect, sensitivity and fore thought. My every requirement and far more, awaited my arrival. Before I left London Dr. Roy had phoned me several times, planning my itinerary for the lectures, my plane reservations, hotel accommodation, plus the topics I would be presenting at Kirkridge, as the singular position of Spiritual Leader for the duration of two weeks. A host of other details followed, and much was duly planned or re-adjusted by the many trans-Atlantic calls. I shall narrate, one such phone call I received as a single example of my preparation for the mission ahead of me.

My telephone bleeped and I picked it up after several bleeps. There were now long phone conversations that bridged the distance across the Atlantic Ocean, as I needed the briefing for my first public appearance on American soil. It was the first lecture trip for me outside Pakistan.

The phone bell rang in the lounge so I picked it up and said, "Hello".

Dr. Roy was on the phone calling from America he said, "Anese this is Dr. Roy here, I have to ask you a few questions, do you have the time to talk to me now?"

At once I said, "Good Afternoon Rusty – Yes! I have plenty of time. I'll do my best to answer all the queries you need me to answer or explain."

Dr. Roy was working out my itinerary and he wished to clear several topics, so he said, "Tell me do the Muslims have a special prayer day like we have a Sunday?"

I smiled as I informed him with "Yes indeed we do, the same as the Jews, who have a Saturday as their Sabbath, and they go to the Synagogue. The Christians have a Sunday as their Holy Day and they go to Church for "Sunday Mass", we Muslims also have a Friday as our Holy Day, and our men folk go just after midday to the Mosque for "The Friday Congregational Prayer."

Dr. Roy solicited a strange question, "Anese do you not go to Church or rather to the Mosque on Friday? I'm surprised! I thought you were really turned on, Islamically. Is it not obligatory for you to attend your mosque?" This defaulting appeared very strange to him.

My answers were very clear cut. I briefed him as to how the Islamic prayers are conducted, "According to the Holy Quran all Muslims are told to try and attend the Congregational prayer on Friday at the Mosque, because the community affairs could be discussed in open session and it also brings with it a bonding force of the brotherhood."

Dr. Roy posed me a direct question, "Anese do you go regularly to the Mosque on a weekly basis?"

I could neither agree nor negate his question so I replied, "No Rusty its not quite the same. Women are not forbidden to go to the Mosque by any Quranic Law. In the time of the Holy Prophet (PBUH) women did go to the Mosque, but remained at the rear, because they had children and babies with them. If the children needed attention, a lady could leave the Mosque with her child without causing a distraction or disturbance during the congregational service."

Dr. Roy inquired, "What about now? Do ladies go for their prayers together with the men, or are their prayers said later?"

I could understand Rusty's confusion due to segregation, so I explained, "No! The devotional prayers by ladies are performed at home, or wherever a lady is able to say them, when the call of the "Azan" is heard. This was introduced by the descendants of the newly born Muslim community much after the death of the Holy Prophet. It is not a Quranic Law but a social requirement for many centuries past and is accepted as a practical way for the Friday Service"

Dr. Roy desired to know about prayer timings, "Anese do you have a special time on Friday for a prayer meeting? When does it take place?"

I explained, "The Friday Prayer service is almost a mandate, recorded in "Sura Jumma" in the Holy Quran. As the rays of the sun change its course and time, according to the seasons, prayers are not conducted according to the change of clock timings, but rather follows the direction of the sun, when it is at the Zenith point, as the sun moves across the two Hemispheres. The time on the clock changes. The mid-day prayer is a "Mid-day" prayer."

Dr. Roy seemed to be satisfied with my answer and he observed, "Now all that information helps me to set up your Kirkridge Programme. I think if we start the "Retreat" at midday on Friday we could introduce you before we have your summary lecture on Islam. We could conduct your prayer service after midday and finish for the morning session. There will be a time space for lunch and we would be able to return for the afternoon session at 3:00 p.m. This would suit us fine, would it suit you?"

I thought I must indicate to Dr. Roy that I too needed time. I requested saying, "Rusty I would need some time space to meet the congregation, to feel their pulse, a kind of breaking the ice. It would help me to understand them and they could view me as a "Non Terrorist".

Dr. Roy must have been smiling as he brushed it aside, "Oh! Don't you worry regarding that, there is so much already on your platter here, you'll forget about spare time, except for the "meditation" time which we all use for a while after dinner. There will be almost three lectures with questions and answers everyday. But there will also be enough time for you to learn, to live, to eat, to play, and bridge a genuine respect, despite being from a different persuasion, one enjoys the perception of truth that brings and bond us together. If you are as perceptive and a spiritualist as your writing on religion reveals, you'll have no problems coping with the Spiritual retreat at Kirkridge. Oh! By the way would you require anything special to be arranged or put on the dais where you would be sitting. Just let me know."

There was a need and now I made the request, "Yes Rusty I do need something, if you can get it for me, or I shall make it here in London and bring it with me."

"Tell me what you want and we'll try to provide it, if it is possible …. Don't tell me you want an Elephant from India on the dais – we would if we could, but I have to draw a line there." he said with a laugh.

I was as ready as he was for playing with words and ideas, "Should I ask for a penguin from the Antarctic and if that is difficult perhaps a Kangaroo from Australia – leave it Rusty I'll compromise on a Koala Bear from Mongolia."

"Anese, I don't believe this – you are still the quick tongued girl, full of mischief, laughter and fun, as bright eyed and highly aspirated girl ahead of everyone else, but I hope, not the tomboy you once were. Your photograph makes you look like a lady – and I'll leave the rest unsaid."

But seriously, now I made the request I needed, "Rusty, behind my chair on the dias, I would like to have two drapes, one of green and one of white satin hung in the manner of drapes at the background behind the chair. I need the green, to represent the colour of Islam that I'm talking about and the white for the "purity" of spiritualism which is the ultimate good elevation of the mind for a soul seeking the spiritualism of purity."

This was of no problem to Dr. Roy so he said, "That's no problem. What about photographs, tapes etc."

I intimated to Rusty that I was self sufficient, "I'll be bringing my own camera, lights and videos. I'm sure someone from the congregation of over a hundred members could give me a helping hand with setting up the light equipment and the tripods. I also need some music played on a tape recorder. Is it possible for you to find just the music for "Abide with me". It is an ideal piece of spiritual rendition, in recognition that at the end, we all fade into a setting sun and the preparation should commence now."

Dr. Roy was most surprised at my request, "Anese you really amaze me. You are not remotely the tomboy sister of my best and life long friend. Who are you and what have you become?. . . and where have you been all this time?. This side of you is a complete enigma to me."

Trying not to remember the past I said, "Let it be Rusty. Whatever I am and whoever I have become today, time has made me so, and I'm happy, peaceful and content today the way I live my life."

We were nearing the end of our conversation, Rusty said, "I'll be calling you again in a couple of days. If you need anything or just to get briefed up, I'll be at the other end of the phone. Thank you for agreeing to come to us at Kirkridge. An Insight into Islam is badly needed at this time - Adieu my friend..." and he was gone.

Time slips away and lost memories return with amazing swiftness, time is dissipated plucking decades away, as we remember scenes returning, we relive the days of our by gone past. I stand back now smiling upon the importance we devolved by lavishing importance to the smallest, perhaps the most insignificant and unimportant details. Fine tuning became the pivot of our lives in the autumn of 1939. Every aspect of our harmonious living was orchestrated with an organized scenario, while our world spun round making us puppets of a play, in the war drama that appeared to be far from real.

Only a Divine but Benevolent Power could possibly have bequeath to mankind the blessings of nature, with a conformity to the rhythm and cycle of the seasons that encircle the earth, bedecking it with a panoramic order, season after season and decade after decade. There I sensed an emotion of belonging, amongst those indescribable vistas unravelling themselves, as we blazed in and out and round about curves and hair pin-bends, staggering our way through dark tunnels, leaving our eyes without vision, with my mind refusing to accept the present state of darkness, as it refuted the hackneyed commonplace statement as an empty promise of "light at the end of the tunnel". Realizing that my tongue was somewhat paralyzed as I had withdrawn into some remote unnamed world or undiscovered galaxy, Dr. Roy broke my ponderous silence, re-assuring me that, the end of the tunnel was in reality not so far away. I was galvanized into the present, exiting out of my unaware trans and returned once more to the earthly boundaries of the car. I said "No need to be, you seemed to have receded into another world." Perhaps it was true, as he appeared to be a reader of minds, or our system of telepathy was working overtime.

As we emerged out of the darkness and I adjusted to the blinding glare of sunshine, I was filled with a deep sense of gratitude towards nature. With amazement and admiration, I watched and marvelled at the cosmos harmony in its simplicity, yet a complex perplexity, blended the vast and abundant spectrum of nature's colour, that flowed into a kaleidoscopic perfection of harmony. For me, it was a strange multifarious synthesis that made no real sense. Was it nature that made the artist, or was an artist a mere pawn controlled by nature, as a single colour on any palette that was devised by an artist. The artist remains a mere deliver, who delivers the colours presented before him, bestowing a botanical creation and a cultural endowment gifted by nature.

As we drove over and out, between the winding hills, before we entered a long tunnel, the scenario was engulfed by magnificent trees robed in bronzes, burnished copper, golden festoons of leaves with shades of old gold that tipped the russet foliage, verdant autumnal leaves, now ranged from deep claret with bursting crimsons, wines, and plums were interspaced with variegated browns, burnt Siennas and dying dried leaves in retreat, unable to face the on coming winter that would claim it's sway over arenas beyond the sun-kissed hills. The tall verdant coniferous trees commanding in their dignity stood sentinel to the darkened depths, that displayed swaying branches in defence of their precious raiment, as gusty tearing winds attempted to deprive them of their veiling and their evergreen attire. As winter would progress so were the contrasting scenes of beauty that would emerge, devoid of the spectrum of spring and autumn colours, while their summer glory would be stripped off their raiment and left naked in a poignant touch of winter desolation. As I admired and contemplated the rich and unbelievable adornment of the Pennin hills, embellished by the generosity of natures salutary endowment presenting stunning vistas that fanned across the hills like the contents of a treasure-chest spilling out, an abundance of gold, enriched ornamentation, precious stones, or perhaps a harmonious well-balanced hand-crafted patch-work quilt, created by nimble hands, with an imaginative perception of colour and an incomparable blending of delicate hues.

Little did I perceive that in a very short time I was to reside for almost two weeks in a simple but immensely pleasing cottage, with its picturesque backdrop of autumn, amidst the "Appalachian Trail" of the Pennin Hills. The cottage was provided for the 'spiritual leader' of the group, it was set aside at a small distance away from the main building at Kirkridge. It was customary for the spiritual leader to reside in the cottage, away from the members of the group who were accommodated in the main building. The small but comfortable cottage rested on a large ridge of terraced rocks beside a rippling stream. Alongside it was a small natural garden, above there were rocks over which fell a beautiful waterfall, tumbling over boulders and smooth rocks creating a cascade that sparkled and shone while catching sunbeams, as they fell into the watery shadows to bury themselves in the murmuring water, that whispered its adoration, that rose giving birth to spiritual thoughts within the soul of a sensitive listener, so whatever time I spent in the cottage I was never alone. There was a small kitchenette located at the rear of the cottage, stocked with all that I could ever need or even desire, but cups of coffee, fruit juice, and a cracker were the only fare that passed my lips in that spiritual haven, for my spiritual soul was fully supplied with all the sustenance I needed. A new form of spiritualism penetrated my soul, I saw it as synonymous with nature and the purity of benevolence from the Master Creator. Recitation and ritual in any religion is not spiritualism and spiritualism is not just a conformation of varying physical modes of prayer. Pure religious guide-lines of spiritualism are stepping-stones towards preparation of the ultimate Paradise. Rituals of religion, keep one fit and physically trained, while spiritualism purifies your thoughts and elevates your soul to advance, into higher ideals. Both are inseparably, entwined and require to be merged to recognize the ultimate Truth and find the exalted path to the Commander of the Universe.

After traversing through the winding Pennin Hills, I eventually arrived with Dr. Roy at Kirkridge, I had already been briefed by him, as to what the meeting at Kirkridge was all about, but as I was to later learn or deduce, that it was in fact a haven and meeting-place of intellectual groups with various ideologies of spiritualities who shared their own individual and specific perceptions, with the people of other denominations, persuasions and religious concepts. Kirkridge was a self-built spiritual centre which had been built by a group of open minded and dedicated spirituals, individuals who lived out their careers and lives on highly elevated and dignified platforms. They were intellectuals, coming from all walks of life, ranging from the creditable scientists and religious presenters. Yet, even those at the height of the world's six most honoured and exalted scientists bowed their heads in acknowledgement of some theories in regard to spiritual perception, as Science had failed to unravel or reveal a great many, or even conclude correctly, the theories of numerous topics that are still unsolved by the scientific giants of our universe. None can refute that a Super Power controls the cycle of nature by an unknown system, with an unknown name, so we call this, "highly significant" source of power Allah, God, Jehovah, Lord, Brahma and a great many other names, adopted by different creeds, in fact there is only a single Power in control of the universe and the name bestowed by Muslims on this Supreme Master Power and Creator of the Universe is the benevolent name of "Allah" as revealed in the Holy Quran, a benefactor delivering His bounties of graciousness and beauty for Mankind, this is evident in the unlimited produce with the multitude and limitless variety of nature that has been provided for the benefit of man.

I was to discover that Kirkridge is in fact an elevated "Spiritual Forum" that has its doors open to all religions. I with all humility state, that I was the first "Muslim Spiritual Leader" for the spiritual group in "The fall of 1993". The group has over a hundred members and other visiting guests are invited who are mostly of the same elk, seeking the higher dimensions of spiritual perception. The members meet together for a period of two weeks several times a year. There are no words to describe the simple presentation and honesty of faith, the depth of devotional acumen, the true search for spiritual perception, the search of Sufism and the idealism that is shared with respect, during these interchanges of religious creeds. There are no hard and fast rules to acquire spiritual grace, there are no contentions, there is no acrimony, no self elevation, nor the presence of a religious hierarchy. It is a marvellous and a heart embracing opportunity, to unfold and harmonize ones thoughts, religious sentiments and then flow in the common effort to discern religious commonalities from the Spiritual Leader, based on the foundational belief that there is only one Supreme Power that rules the Universe, keeping the rhythm of life, in a consecutive sequence, the sound balance of the Universe by the elevated Power that moves the hands of nature's clock in the rotations of seasons, the flow of the tides and the power of life and death.

The haven and dimensions given to these spiritual lectures and discussions is greatly energizing. There are pertinent questions that are posed and appropriate answers, delivered without bigotry, individual opinions are proffered with relevant clarifications. There emerges a bonding by understanding and co-relating, there is acknowledgement for the freedom of worship, reward and punishment is not an issue – elevation and recognition of the Truth is the real issue. There are rules and laws to be followed in every community, for the benefit of our common and mutual existence. What is phenomenal at the retreat in Kirkridge is that despite the distinct separation amongst the codes of various religions that are always present, it transpires that there are commonalities that bond followers of "The Holy Books". The Muslims, the Jews, the Christians and the Sabians have a great deal in common where religion is concerned, but very little exposure has been given to reveal, or expound their basic commonalities, hence the vagaries and the misunderstood ambiguities exist. In the non Muslim areas where I lecture on Islam, from the point of view of our commonalities, such as the "Five Pillars of Islam", the Revealed Religions have their own fundamental pillars of balance. In the other two Revealed religions namely Judaism and Christianity there are a great deal of commonalities with Islam, besides having only one Divinity of a Monolithic God.

As the Spiritual Leader for a very large group of people, I was to reside in a reasonably small and compact cottage, set aside as the peaceful haven for the leader of the retreat. I found a new atmosphere for meditation and an inward search in the solitary cottage, resting beside a gentle flowing stream amongst those gold and russet leaves of the Pennine hills. The cottage displayed no religious symbol, no literature of any particular faith, it was devoid of any singular denomination or persuasion. The rooms were simple but comfortable and thoughtfully arranged – symbolic symbols of nature proclaimed the presence of a Super Power. It was ever present, it was seen and felt throughout the days I resided there. The proof that man is one with the earth is to be felt there – self image is dissolved, a new spirit is born in the heart of man. Members come to hear, see and imbibe emotions that had never emerged or experienced before. There at Kirkridge the ice thawed, the leaves burst into colour, birds sang and man came alive planting a new sapling in the heart of every nurturing emotion of spiritualism. Here the sapling grew by meditation by retreated solitude and an unexpected Spiritual aura.

As I emerged from the retreat I was no longer the being I was, when I arrived a fortnight earlier. I lost my own image, I had negated myself, discarded my prejudices, dismissed the falsehood and abanded the falsified social norms. I helped nurture new members joining the retreat, I lectured on the core issues of Islam, I unfolded the commonalities of the Revealed religions, I elucidated on the fundamental issues of Islam, I elaborated on the misguided norms attributed to Islam, such as Jehad, the misnomers of polygamy, revealed the benefits and protection given to women in Islam fifteen hundred years earlier. I taught the need, to seek the truth of Islam before condemning it. I shall record the letter of acknowledgement from a founder member of the Brotherhood at Kirkridge, where I had been honoured as their Spiritual Leader.

I delved fearlessly into the common use of malpractices in all religions as the weakness of man, not the imperfection of the Religious Creed itself. Degraded social behaviour, illicit relationships, malicious gossip, mal intent to destroy another. It is not condoned by any Creed the fault does not lie in the malpractice of the religion, it is infact the straying weakness of the defaulters themselves. All spiritual religions attempt to teach, to lead and guide their flock into the avenues of green and nourishing pastures, not into fields abounding with poisonous clover and eventually drugged oblivion.

After my private retreat in the silent Pennine Cottage, I returned as a different person. My deep ideals of sanctified spiritually were stronger, but also more purified. My religious tolerance as taught to me by the Holy Quran, the injunctions are not only tolerant, but enhanced by a deeper purer concept of human understanding. To be a Spiritual leader, I had to make a very deep commitment within myself, I was not to be just a leader for a short two weeks, I needed to keep myself forever, garbed in the cloak of commitment. Through the next twenty five years I never ever regretted or lost sight of my commitment, it was my commitment and my submission. Going back to how I found myself working for Islam across the globe I myself am amazed.

It was less than two years later that I found myself taking the road to Niagara Falls in Canada. As Peggy Dean and Christopher Waymark drove me in a speeding Mercedes that made its way through the wide but almost empty streets, through the suburbs of Toronto with their small compact little houses one after the other, I was reminded about the game of monopoly with little houses and an occasional Hotel that spread across the Monopoly board, but these little doll houses were for real, with prideful owners behind each front-door, where trim garden patches were still covered with fading flowers as Autumn claimed and applied her rights before the harsh winds of the coming winter. Neat tidy gardens with sloping lawns rolled down to meet the on rush of the highway traffic that emitted and ejected poisonous smog that donned a cloak or rather a shroud that squeezed the breath of life from the waning flowers and leaves. Behind this beautiful scene, despite the approaching tragedy of winter, hung a back-drop of once verbose trees, now making way for the unceasing demand of autumn, that swiftly converts the multiple shades of green into the varying colours that revolve in a spectrum of yellow bronze, to copper gold, then striking mustard and old gold leaves. But there was also the beauty of purple blended with plum, red bright maple trees dominating in its vivid spectrum of enriched colours, of startling reds sobered by the dignity of wine and shades of dark burgundy. Even here there was some of nature's stubborn streaks, for the evergreen carnivorous trees stood erect, like sentinels arresting the one continuous stream of violent colours that spread across the horizon.

We arrived in Niagara, parked the car, then stood gazing for quite awhile across the mammoth "Niagara Falls" as it cascaded from its gigantic slabs that projected over - hanging rocks, leaving a huge space creating a passage behind the water fall that works as a tunnel for boats to cross behind the falls, leaving a clear passage for, "the maid of the mist" a large tourist ship carrying hundreds of visitors in a joyous ride, that enters at one end, moving across to the Canadian embankment. There is no place in the world that could so effectually make one feel that one is moving through a cloud, thrilled by the knowledge of where one is, then once again out of the misty water tunnel and back to land.

After reaching Niagara on the American side I had a completely new view of the falls that I had never seen before. Even though the falls from the American side had lost its Imperial grandeur, it still presented an impressive view. The two sides of the falls, not only divide the land structure, but the two identities of a divided population. The contrast of life and culture was extremely clear with each clinging to its own prestige, forming their own identity and mode of living, Individuality was in strong evidence.

As Dr. Roy and myself crossed the bridge into the U.S.A. at Niagara, I had to step into the Visa section to show my passport, but Dr. Roy had no such duty, yet he hung around waiting for me to come out. Since it was taking time he aimed to come to my rescue. He entered the rooms and was surprised to find me having a friendly chat with the immigration officer, who was very concerned that I wanted only a two month entry card, as I was holding a British Passport. He seriously informed me if I was sure I wanted only a two months visit and why not a six months visa, when I said "No thank you" to his query he wanted to know if I could use a one year stay permit, but when I once again declined his offer he was most perturbed, as everyone was seeking to enter America for some reason or the other. Immigration was the most basic reason of all. He wondered how Dr. Roy had not succeeded in persuading me to come and stay in America.

We left the passport control office with some joking and laughing but also with a six month permit for me to reside in America and an extension of six months if I desired to do any "course" in the U.S.A. As we drove out of Niagara Falls, Dr. Roy questioned me saying, "Do you do this all the time?" I looked at him in a most confused manner. I could not find any words to answer for I had not understood his question.

"After reading your "Eternal Message" and hearing your graceful cultivated voice on the phone I thought of you more as a religious scholar who more or less lived in a spiritual world, but I can see you are not as I thought I would find you. You are not alien to the actual world we humans have created for ourselves."

I smiled as I answered him, "Rusty don't judge the book by its cover, but more important than that, is the fact that I have the ability to keep my two worlds apart. I need to function in a world full of some trust, some mistrust some dishonour, some virtue, some vice, some honour, some guile, some empathy, some callousness, some generosity and a great deal of selfishness. Truth and much diplomacy is needed, the litany of need is a long one and I could go on forever. Just take me as I am or as you find me, you'll not have to contend with duplicity."

After a long silence Dr. Roy gave me a long look saying, "That's a very deep assessment of the world and people. I wonder and would like to find out what really makes you throb."

The statement I returned was not a very involved one, it was simple and the truth, "I had to choose for myself the road I must take and I chose to embark upon a journey of parallel lines: a path of service in a world consumed by negativity, where material substance is in great demand. There is a paucity of sharing, humility and selflessness. On the other hand the doctrine of religious faith emphasizes the vital importance of brotherhood. This is to be found only in the values of a spirit born of deep spiritual perception. Invariably if the two parallels are to be converged, it requires the mechanism of selflessness like a magnet that works to draw the opposites together. This creates in man the ability to perform the obligations as revealed by the Doctrine of Islam and also the other Revealed religions that makes worldly purity easier to attain."

Dr. Roy was most interested in this, my theory of life so he questioned me, "Anese have you found the mechanism that you have searched for, do you feel that it will lead you to meet your goal? You already appear to have harnessed tranquillity - could you contract a marriage of the two imperative goals."

I replied with a simple statement, "Rusty I do not have a goal, I pray and I meditate to gain perception and guidance from my Benevolent Master. What hope I have, that my efforts should be able to keep my worldly life within the bounds of social respect in a materialistic forum, yet I have to be able to segregate my spiritual beliefs, that have enlightened my life and my Faith.

My spiritual life has always been a separate segment of my life. I've endeavoured to make them converge, keeping both my disciplines, to move forward together, creating the elevation that is contained in the core root of my mind and heart".

Dr. Roy made a very simple statement, "Anese I seem to be seeing you as a new person which requires me to search for new depths in you. You'll have me spinning if you present me in such quick succession, more of the shocking changes that I review in you, I shall have to re-evaluate now, discovering the other you, the real depth of values and how deeply you are involved. God be praised and may He keep you under His wing.

This observation by Rusty's in depth glimpse worried me so I said, "Rusty I never wanted anyone in the world to see the real depth in me, my thoughts and my deeds were to be a simple and personal prostrated symbol of my own submission, placed at the foot of my Beloved Master Creator. My personal views of life for all these long years have been in hiding, my communion with the Master has never been divulged to anyone, but now that I stand on the threshold of the dusk of my life, before my sun sinks into oblivion, I feel and know that I must flay my desire for privacy, of my inner being, I have to harmonize my life ensuring the carriage of advancing spiritualism."

There was total silence in the car as we both were engaged in our individual thoughts then Rusty commented, "I am now having to deal with a great deal of the new you. I recognized the spiritualism in you as soon as I discovered and heard your audio cassettes of "The Eternal Message". When your photographs arrived I saw a young lady as modern as the times we live in. I came to receive you and take you to our Penn State University before we began your lecture tour to Kirkridge. I was of the thought that the lecture tour was to be an academic subject of law and the living code of Islam. Now I find myself listening not only to a spiritualist but to a philosopher as well. I can understand very well how you function, because we are partners with the same line of thinking, that a man's life must be integrated with his worldly and religious brother, bonded in the unbending spirituality that is his submission to life."

My mind fled back decades and I reminiscence saying, "Rusty I grew up with the knowledge that you understood me well then, so now you should not find it difficult to understand me, even if it was half a century back."

He looked up at me aghast, "You must be kidding. No! it cannot be half a century. Where has time gone? Are you sure?"

Smilingly I assured him, "Yes it is or almost so – one may be given the liberty to call forty-nine years a half century."

By this time we had left the suburbs of Niagara and we were well on our way to Penn State winding round spurs, climbing hills that curved, dipped and rose again to duck once more and turn another bend. The sight was fascinating, I was awe-struck by the Kaleidoscopic panorama of variegated colours running from green in the north, while autumn claimed for the Penn Hills the bedecking garments of russet colours, lemons, gold fringed with yellow ochre, amber trees outlined by Vandyke brown burnt sienna, mustard leaves retreating into burnt amber, while obstinate coniferous pines and cypress trees retained their bottle-green and olive colours. As we moved forward it was apparent that nature had been busy with her brush of painting the scenic views with the warmth of colours that enfolded the undulating hills. The wide and far-reaching visions would rise with the all embracing colours, leaving within me a heartfelt thanks to Nature for such a vista of beauty.

Poems written in memory to my beloved friend,
Dr. Rustum Roy (1923-2010)

The Sword of Rustum

I thank thee for thy love and care
I send pure white lilies from my garden plot
I return to thee your ivory roses that are rare
And a decade bouquet of "Forget-me-not"
We prayed and walked through life's rugged path
Through bashing storms and bright sunshine
Sunbeams kissed our lives sublime
Your cherished love for me was wine
His "Spiritual Blessing" made our love Divine
We journey now to blue heavens above
Swiftly on the wings of a snow white dove
I hold your hand and still see your face
That shines with love from His Spiritual Grace
I'll seen you soon
In the garden of Bliss
For us there is all to come
We leave nothing here that we shall miss
'Adieu' Rusty my friend, until we meet

~ Anese

The Last Journey

I spoke with you in mellow tones
The evening before you silently slipped away
You whispered my name so tenderly
Then went into a slumber of Spiritual sleep
Taking your last and Eternal journey into the gardens of Paradise
Gabriel came for you in His verdurous light
Spreading his fleecy wings enfolding you
He soared with you through seven heavens
Into the garden of Eden for your Eternal Rest
And now that you have gone I my wakeful vigil keep
Amidst endless prayers as unbidden teardrops spill down my cheek,
My voiceless grief has banished sleep from my eyes
And in the darkness of the endless night I weep.
I see "moths" that dance around a flame
In a slow dance of death inviting me
To form a pair just me with thee
Leaving the world of mortal claws to set me free.
It is not my will.
But His be done
Till then I wait
My dearest love, my brother ,
And my "BELOVED FRIEND".

~ Anese

Unison

You told me once you would always walk beside
Yet you took this your last journey on your own
You left me to wonder in an empty space
A vacuum in a crushing world to face
Alone without your spirit by my side to guide me
I am doubtful that I can make this passage on my own
I need you here to give me strength – to gift me hope.
Perhaps you nurtured me too much and for too long
You have left me unprepared to walk alone
I need your spirit by my side
You gave me love with tender care
You cushioned me from worldly hurt
But left me with emotions unanchored and so bare
Cold oblivion called from emptiness comes to ensure me
From the chains of memory you cannot set me free
For survival I need you to glide beside me to the end
Until I too take my last and onward journey into Eternity.

~ *Anese Majid Khan, August 2010*

★ ★ ★ ★ ★

Truth Conquers the Universe

PARLIAMENT OF
WORLD RELIGIONS
A Unique Global Platform

PARLIAMENT OF WORLD RELIGIONS 1999
THE NORTH AMERICAN COALITION ON
RELIGION AND ECOLOGY
by
Anese Majid Khan

Since it is a forum of the Parliament of World Religions, one could presume that all attending the meetings would accept in theory the religious factor of a Super and Greater Spiritual Force. This force may be called by any name deemed fit, according to different beliefs. The means to achieve a 'spiritual state' is not important, the result and the effect it has on man and the Universe is and should be of primary importance. It is necessary to unify men of all civilizations, dichotomies, philosophies and beliefs, in order to forge a "New Global Ideology" for the benefit of the earth, the preservation of nature and all that pertains to the survival and benefit of man and the Universe.

This presentation is made in a simple straight forward approach by an individual who cares about nature, creature and creation, which is God's wonderful gift to man. This does not flow from the pen of a technocrat, nor intended to be a piece of scientific or architectural literature, it emerges from a genuine concern for man, the world and all of God's creation. This presentation does not touch upon the subjects of politics, the armament race, expansionism, world domination or even democracy, as these topics are not on the agenda of a religious session, but that does not mean that it is not responsible for the greater part of the world's turmoil.

Starting with "Global Stewardship" of which I am a member, When God created man He placed him above even the angels, giving man the august place as His vice-regent on earth. In this capacity it is encumbering on man to forge a unity that will ensure the preservation of the earth, the Global orbit, and the Universe for man himself, If man fails to shoulder his responsibility as "Steward and Custodian" of the earth, then he has failed in the reason for his own special creation, only animals live, bearing no responsibility. Can man really afford to ignore this Universal need of his responsibility to the earth? Should he not put his "Stewardship" above personal desires, personal ambitions and personal self gratification? Men must function together to preserve the earth, ensuring a good, sound and safe future for the coming generations. To this end a "New World Order" must be created and it must emerge by the concerted efforts of man himself.

At platforms such as the "Parliament of the World Religions", the "Congress, of Ideology" and philosophies, the big question is where and how would this "New World Order" be given birth? There is an urgent need that such platforms be given birth, and made to mature rapidly, thereby welding the links that bind and forge a chain of idealism and spiritualism. Through this strength, the universal, human cravings of materialism would be vanquished and a new ideology would emerge. Given the proper chance, these platforms would have man live by a philosophy that behoves the dignity of man. From these platforms, the "call" must be raised and the media of the world induced to expose the dangers of materialism, capitalism and consumerism. Grave dangers and even irreparable damage lies ahead, it has already anesthetised and subverted man's coherent sets of values, bringing Western and Oriental countries into a serious series of conflict and also into a phase of decline, morally, ethically, spiritually and discipline of human passion.

International insecurity makes it imperative to find and build a formula for a balanced coexistence of all global factions, with a differing of concepts, philosophies and individual cultural norms of civilization. Numerous questions emerge from this statement. Can the capitalists live with the Ayatullahs? Can the Donagons accept the doctrine of the

Dedarts? Can the Hindu, Muslim clashes be bridged to set aside their differences, to accept each other with their individual teachings? Can the West and the East stand together on one platform as equals, so that the generations to come may inherit the Earth? Will the West accept the philosophies of Islam and Confucius? The Chinese did a better job than the West to abolish materialism? Can Saudi Arabia and the Arab states ensure that their oil, would pass on a better world worth living in. Who or what in it's individual capacity can guarantee and ensure a safer tomorrow? This can only be achieved when aggression ceases and values are reformed, levels of conduct everywhere are respected and are allowed to function.

I quote from a Pakistani scholar Akbar Ahmed; "The clash with piety may help produce in the West a Post-scientific age, which re-admits the spiritualism presence, it once excommunicated." The west has already gone through a very advanced scientific phase and is now in an almost a post scientific era. This last phase in the West had spiritualism almost defrocked and made redundant, yet the West failed with its rhetoric, to find the answers to ensure peace with harmony and a safer world. Urgently needed today is that every effort be made for world preservation and the security of man himself. It is heartening to note that of late there appears to be resurgence in the seeking of spiritual values. Perhaps there is some truth to be found in the lament of the National Security Advisor Mr. Zebigneiw Brezezinster, "in our own self-corruption, self-indulgent and hedonistic society." And "Our moral consciousness has been corrupted by consumerism" and their difference we assign to all values, as if men were products on the supermarket shelf.

Analytically this brings into focus, the subject of materialism and consumerism which in fact are the off shoots of capitalism, which is like an octopus with arms of unbending steel. It suggests that values, ideologies and philosophies are consumer commodities to be traded or bartered. Values must be strengthened and secured by welding together these ideals, philosophies, civilizations and ethnic beliefs, in an effort to overcome man's never ending desire and hunger of materialism. The time has come for the world forums to use a multi-pronged campaign to proclaim a sound balance. The world media has a strange but strong masterful control over the human mind, then, should not the media be induced to use their power to assist and harness the degenerating values by propagating that "Enough is Enough". The media must stop now, to decide now, whether they will vote for materialism and world destruction, or will they throw in their lot with the reformers to forge a "New World Order". Let them contemplate on their own survival and their children and that of their children's children. There is faith that the media will come through waging war against "Materialism and Consumerism."

This brings me to the main body of a topic in which Islam may assist, in the development of ideology and values for the preservation of the globe and the environmental conditions that are being eroded and corroded by materialism and consumerism. Much is presented and authenticated by chapter and verse from the Holy Quran, but limitation of time makes for a shorter representation.

Initially I desire to point out, that in context to the subject there is a prototype awareness and a process of birth in eastern governments, such as Pakistan, India, Indonesia, Malaysia and other developing countries all over the world where a propelling awareness has need for the environmental preservation. To promote this, much material should pass through to the annals of the press and information from sound media presentations. To promote this, the press and information media must regard the current environmental conditions and lack of population planning. Any practical result is low, due to mass ignorance and gross poverty. The excuse of ignorance and poverty cannot condone the negligent attitude of the developed countries, where chemical contamination gets more dangerous with every passing year, consumer rubbish that cannot be successfully destroyed or recycled as fast as they are produced, thus have become a grave world problem. For example, in most western countries that proclaim proprietary right of advancement, the only safe drinkable water is commercial water, sold in commercial bottles. People use faster methods of feeding and caring for a family that so much more products come ready packed – with more garbage and more waste. Cameras, Videos, Electronics equipment, clothing and domestic equipment are built to be obsolete in two to three years and in 3-4 years even replacements become impossible to find – the new is ready for sale.

This continuous mesmerizing cycle of consumer-rubbish, leads to unused waste that clutters up the earth, creating a desperate need for waste disposal and of late there is talk to launch a programme that would send garbage into space. Unless the world media aids in a massive co-ordinated programme to stop the mercenary trend of "Keep up with the Jones" which has now moved to "Keep up with the new products" which is the prevalent cult of today. It will not stop until each individual sitting securely in their homes, fully realizes the gravity of the world's defacement. Organizations, forums, platforms, and societies cannot reach into the privacy of a home, but all public medias perform as inmates of a home, so are able to take up any campaign against the mirage of materialism.

Success within a family by a woman, even in a country like Pakistan has a fair share of what goes on within the family and the society. There are ladies like Ms. Benazir Bhutto-Ex Prime Minister of Pakistan, Miss Fatima Jinnah opposition leader against President Ayub Khan, Mrs. Liaqat Ali Khan, Lady Ambassador, Mrs. Khalida Zia, Prime Minister of Bangladesh and others such as myself who are not the exceptions. There are a very large number of ladies from all walks of life moving, working and attending to things that must be attended to. There are ladies who are fighting for women's rights, for their less fortunate sisters, others serve on the anti-drug committees, a large number work for population control, through "family planning" with child welfare organizations and environmental programmes are manned by ladies, Human rights has its fair share of ladies working for it. There are ladies working for environment institutes, doctors, teachers, professors, bureaucrats and governments, all are aware and working for a better environment.

At the School level, a great deal is being done to curb the flow of drugs into the schools, for an example there is the school system of the Esena Foundation with a large number of students that is run for students from the age of 3 to 17 years. All the students are trained to be simple and are required to conform to the basic school uniform, no make-up, no jewellery, no special privileges, no special books or special stationery. They are taught to be aware of the needs of others. They are encouraged to develop a control over self-desire and self-indulgence, when they leave school at the age of 17 and enter college they are exposed to a wider media of knowledge, distant horizons, high electronic devices and world-wide, T.V. programmes. Education means knowledge, knowledge means development and development means desire. This is where Islam in its true form plays a very vital part, to induce character formation and self-control of a human being. From the age of 11 years every Muslim is required to follow the doctrine of the Holy month of Ramadan which consists of 30 continuous days of fasting. This is for the development of the inner strength so a young person develops an integral strength to overcome intangible temporal temptations. This significant control saves man from chasing the pot of gold of a "material rainbow" which has no end, and it signs its own requiem.

As Islam develops a child's mind and character, morals and values become a part of the daily life. The pillars upon which Islam stands are; firstly Belief, spiritual awareness and responsibility; secondly Prayer –body cleanliness and spiritual contact five times a day; thirdly fasting – a continuous 30 days fast during day light hours to strengthen self-control; fourthly charity – which is 1/40 of ones wealth, to be given to widows, orphans and the needy, fifthly the Ultimate pilgrimage. If one is aware and carries out the responsibility that Islam has put as an injunction upon every Believer, then there is very little space for materialism, capitalism or any great need for the ever-increasing consumer luxuries. If Islam is followed in its true and pure form and emulates the dictum, as indicated in the Holy Quran without cultural trappings, it can encompass the adversary of materialism, that brings with it a pace without the ever consuming and entangled need to acquire, accumulate and become a slave, of the persistent drive for ambitious capitalism. Materialism as it is today engages the temporal world of this century. Man has learnt a great deal from the basic past, Islamic venues such as astronomy, medicine, architecture, geography, and, the art of trade, the beauty of poetry and literature and cultural ideology, have been used by the West, for development and advancement of their own techniques in these fields, but to-day stands as the prototype masters.

The world of the capitalist's materialism is based on the satisfaction of mans' sensual desire thus developing new horizons for advancement, materialism and self gratification, but in doing so it has destroyed the inner most peace of mankind. It is in the interest of the great consortiums, banks, amalgamating companies, drug barons, oil kings, finance corporates, industries and a million other capital orientated world organs that uphold materialism, realize that it stands as the greatest danger to man himself, it is significant to note that the great convenience of "Plastic money" the "buy now – pay later" theories have kept and served the aura of materialism throbbing at a dangerous level. When the bubble burst in 1990 and families fell under the hammer, due to unexpected recession, thousands were dispossessed of their homes, they came face to face with the devil of materialism at work. Most were unprepared for redundancy and succumbed to the total financial breakdown that followed with the result, that new problems emerged such as suicide, emotional disorder, mental derangement, broken homes, alcoholism, common theft and a million other human degrading problems. Too many facets of emotional problems spring from materialism and unfulfilled desires, which leave devastating effects on the human brain, destroying the emotional world of basically good human beings.

Moving to the subject of economics and capitalism one finds that it stops at nothing in the seduction of man. Every natural habitat has been raped and plundered to satisfy the ambition of man in his greed for wealth and power. Nothing has been left sacred. It must be called the "Rape of our time".

The first step to be accomplished was the rape of religion and spiritualism by the systematic subversion of religious ideology. Success in this was considered essential so a "laissez-fair" approach to moral and religion was introduced then publicly made acceptable and further given "legal status" such as "common law wife", "diminish responsibility", "homosexuality", "free sex" are some of the examples resulting from acceptance of a free society, hence the closing of Churches with the eschewing of religion, converting them into clubs and restaurants for pleasure. These erroneous and unequivocal steps have been made converting these once sacred grounds, in total disregard of the ideological, ethnic feeling or the adverse effect it would have on moral values.

The enormity of the second stage also proved to be successful in its unrestricted rape of moral and human values. Man became an equivalent slave to his desire of self-gratification. From there on different types of rape followed, as each had a requirement of its own kind – the rape of the earth for its mineral wealth, for the need of tycoons, with an insatiable desire to expand the circumstance of their possessions, the rape of the seas for the scientists and industrialists, polluting it with buried atomic waste, that has no guarantee against leakage in 50 to 100 years from now. The death and extinction of marine life by polluted water from burning oil spills. The rape of the skies for commercial use, satellite domination and the launching of garbage, making outer space a garbage dumping ground and polluting the skies and outer hemisphere, the rape of the ozone layers which is the earth's protective cover. The rape of the seasons as climatic changes are brought about by gross interference of the outer hemisphere, the rape and damage to natural food and crop rotation which is man's need for food to compensate this ravaging of nature and natural food.

Chemicals are used to improve what the earth has been robbed of by substituting chemical fertilizers to improve the quantity of production and visual appearance of food, in fact it has a devastating result on the nutritional values. Further, there is the rape of the wild animals that are becoming extinct, because ambition, greed and the need of experimental uses are more important and lucrative than the destruction that is being caused to animals in the wild. They are hunted, caught or killed for the high prices paid for them: the rape of the forests, the flora, the fauna, small animals and insect life; the rape of the land for more roads, faster highway housing enclaves and vast spreading shopping plazas. Nothing has been left untouched, undesecrated or immune by human desire and the epitome of man's blind selfishness.

So much has been gained by science and western technology, but also destroyed by Western Progress, that has done away with all ground rules of behaviour and many blind Easterns followed this call, but a halt is the need of our time. Every one must accept that "Enough is Enough" or else man will dig the pit into which he himself must fall. The wealthy, the ambitious, the capitalists and the thoughtless, would not have much use for their accumulated material wealth. Now is the time for the public and media to face their "Global Responsibility", and annunciate their disapproval of the ambitious rapists, to project a "New World Ideology". Today "The Stewards", "Custodians" of the globe are the public media, they are the voice of the world and have the ears of the people. The "Ideology Platform" needs an all out endeavour for the success of an independent world media. The real question is "will the media pick up the challenge?" or "would the media put the socio political problem above the Global need?"

* * * * *

- 258 -

Save the World

Musical Theme from Esena Dramatic Presentation

Standing here together we're guardians of the Earth
Yet Nature is adying by the hand of man
She waits for us to fight her cause
To save her seas, her air and trees.
She waits for you and me
She waits for you and me.

There beneath the waters sea-life quietly dies
Rivers are polluted by industrial waste
The air is thick with carbon smoke
The sky devoid of ozone layers.
So come and save the world
So come and save the world.

Scientists discover treasures for mankind
Man abuses God's gifts in his greed and pride
Men destroyed by ammunition blasts
Who then would brave the lion's "wrath".
That is for you and me
That is for you and me

Time is running out against the tide of life
Nature made unbalanced by its rape and strife
Man's greatest worry is food for life
No water left to quench his thirst.
So come and save the world
So come and save the world.

Children now are starving in lands around the world
Fields have turned barren producing no more food
The young will question "What is left for us"?
For gold we're sold now stand bereft.
So come and save us now
So come and save us now.

Hasten to join our forces to save this precious earth
Nature needs your help to fight her worthy cause
Protect the earth for the generations to come
Give them a world in which they can live.
So come and save the world
So come and save the world.

~ Esena

★ ★ ★ ★ ★

Truth Conquers the Universe

CONCLUSION
A Long Biography with Much More to Deliver

THE LITANY
My Promise

To my Beloved Counterpart Majid

When your mind is scorched from the fires of life,
I'll come to you like a mountain torrent.

When your mouth is parched from silence and waiting,
I'll come to you like a springtime shower.

When your heart lies bleeding from disappointment and grief,
I'll come to you like the radiant sun of the summer.

When your peace is lost in the bush of uncertainty,
I'll come to you like the joyous burst of a song.

When tumult arises like a dam in your work,
I'll come to you like the caressing waves on the shore.

When your eyes sting from the heat of frustration,

I'll come to you like a wafted breeze in the night.

When your mind turns blind from thunder and storm,
I'll come to you with the nimble steps of the dawn.

When your hearing is impaired by the roar of demands,
I'll come to you like the murmuring surf of the sea.

When your ambition lies crushed because you are lost,
I'll come to you like a guide-book of life.

When your will sits crouched in an unused corner,
I'll come to you with the throne of kings.

When you have been beggared with unfulfilled desire,
I'll come to you with a golden horn of plenty.

When your cup has been drained with bitterness and tears,
I'll come to you with a goblet overflowing with love.

When your tears have dried because your faith is lost
I'll come to you with a crowning glory of flowers.

When your friends have deserted you in the midst of a storm,
I'll come to you with my arms outstretched.

When your road is cobbled and strewn with thorns,
I'll come leading you home on a path made of sand.

When your world turns dark like the darkest night of the year,
I'll come to you with the midday sun in my hand.

When your steps are lagging from fever and strain,
I'll come to you with a magic portion of hope.

When you thirst to be loved because selfishness surrounds you,
I'll come to you with a bible of sacrifice.

When your desire is dead because passion betrayed you,
I'll come to you with a flood of fulfilment.

When religion eludes you because of life's weeds,
I'll come to you planting a bower of prayers in your heart.

If you would hold my hand and come with me,
We'll sing our litany of "Hope"
And angles will join in our chorus.

~ Syeda Anese Majid Khan, December 18ᵗʰ 1971

Today in the sunset of my life, I am honoured to be called a "Beacon of Light" and my experience of course is the fundamental base of this distinction that has been bestowed on me. It is a wonderful position of gratification, as I have become a trusted, well respected, and beloved matriarch, encircling me as the central figure around which the family, friends and associates revolve. Together we have been touched by happiness, tragedy, individually and as a family, but some questions are often unexpressed and the unanswered questions of "why?", they remain suspended in the air, for which there is no answer, only a sense of loss or joy encapsulating the entire family. Even while my beloved, my life's partner Majid passed on, he had enveloped us in the fulfilment of his devotion, which he so generously bestowed on all, giving us our strength as the "patriarch" of our extended family.

With me, our bonded life was not just a marriage, it was not just a flash of love, it became a fusion of both, a bonding through the precious five decades. We saw brilliant radiance of the dawn sunshine, the dark depth of midnight, yet again, sunshine as we moved together, in a singular harmony, blended in tune encapsulated in tone as one soul in one entity. It had the incomparable radiance of a star, beautifully gratifying our unselfish union, the melody played, like a harmonious orchestrated refrain. Its value was subtle, yet it bore the cleaving of a powerful magnet, co-ordinated and fettered in devotion, encompassing the whole family. Majid and I always moved first as a couple in a dance of ecstasy for, we both knew it takes "two to tango", thus it formed a sound balance for the fusion needed, that perfected the sequence of our exclusive tango. My life had been a series of discords, perhaps the compelling past of my life was complex, as it not only possessed a haunting theme, but far too often, it formed swirling waves that should have crushed me, dragging me down into a whirl-pool of disaster, but I survived.

The other part of my life with Majid was radiant as the bursting rays of the morning sun, bringing with it polka-dotted sunbeams that became the turntable of fulfilment of my days. I had never been given to dreaming dreams, yet all the dreams I could have dreamed, I was gifted in love, in dedication, in marriage, my service to man's life, my unanchored dreams, my unspoken desires that Majid gifted me, was a "Divine" gift from the Master for which I am ever beholden.

The past and the present for me were in dire contrast, as two definite eras of my life. They stand indelibly defined and separated and yet in the weaving, the two thus produced in me a unique fabric, each with its own singular design, woven together integrating a myriad colours and hues, some bright and radiant, some incandescent and others sombre, bleak with a dreary darkness, the result was, a picture of my life taking on the affinity and spectrum of the rainbow. Some areas were filled with the bright brazen flashy dramatic colours of spring, other areas, of my life's canvas was contrasted with the more heavy, doleful, drab hues and tones, that once too often even dragged in the sinister colours of darkness. This fabric of my life became the tissue that I myself had woven, with designs and figures of my own composition, so my destiny was the harvest of the field that I had inseminated. I had to reap as I had sown. The autumn of my life has been rich and colourful, winter has set in, but I am still glowing like a festive season as work never stops and the accolade is consistently making my life a worthy one.

The biblical span of life for man is three score years and ten, which is an abundance of time. I found, it is wise to winnow the grain from the chaff, as every competent farmer knows, thus gleans an abundantly rich harvest in return for his hard labour. Obviously all my dedicated work and vigilant supervision, has today been rewarded with my 'National Awards', and "International recognition" where I find that I am held with honour, esteem and respect.

Life for me has been a series of diverse challenges, the outcome resulted into making me the woman I am today. I have looked in hindsight, through the seven decades of life, the three decades of my early years, when I've had many occasions to do so, but I never regretted the challenges I took, nor did I remotely expect the homage that I have so generously received. To me it has been God's gifted privilege to serve Him and His people, to work for the needy and our national development, consummating the ideals of my youth, and the dreams of my desire.

I humbly state that I am a direct descendant of Nawab Imdad Imam the "Poet Laureate" of his time, a great and highly praised scholar holding the honour of being elevated as Master of the "History of Urdu Literature" incorporated as a part of the Urdu course in several Universities of India. His vast dedicated works and contributions to Persian and Urdu were laudable. Perhaps bearing his genes, propelled certain members of our family to rise to elevated heights in their own presentations, or professions above other good and sound writers. Perhaps the gift by some unfathomable chance flowed into my genes, giving me a slight edge over my penmanship. Most of my written work is in English, being the result of my need to deliver in a language I had the ability to Master. I was reluctant but unafraid to record my thoughts, nor have I need to stumble through words, in a search for appreciable expression in my presentations. Perhaps this is the manifestation of the early training received in England, where I acquired the form of good English delivery. My education was firmly grounded in the formal format of a British public school.

My maternal uncle Syed Mehdi Imam, a great scholar of Greek, had translated the holy Quran into Greek, he also was the sensitive author to produce two very important books in English as a part of the Masters English Course taught at Oxford for many, many years. His outstanding 600 pages, a volume of "Poetry of the Invisible" had outstanding success and its superiority was widely acclaimed by most of the universities and libraries abroad. My younger grand-daughter, Asma Majdoline has the uncanny ability to write fairly well, both in English and in Urdu. Unfortunately she did not have the confidence to believe that she had inherited this gift and with maturity she would achieve elevation. She married young and moved away from me, so lost the chance or perhaps, I lost the opportunity to inculcate the desire that would develop and drawn out the best of her talent. It does appear that several members of our family carry the noble genes of a "Poet Laureate" and we are the "gifted" progeny descended from him.

My parental Grandfather Sir Syed Ali Imam possessed a giant law brain, he was appointed as Law Minister to the "Viceroys Council" of India, his brother, Sir Syed Hasan Imam was my maternal grandfather and a member of the "Queen's Privy Council" and a participant of the Geneva Convention. Both brothers were lawyers, but deeply involved in politics and fought for the supremacy of Independence for India. Sir Syed Ali Imam was the founder President of the Muslim League Party in Bihar and Sir Syed Hasan Imam was the elected President of the Bihar Indian Congress. Together the two brothers made a "very powerful" unit creating a formidable political team, as a joint venture it bonded the two parties under the one canopy of "resistance".

I have had the opportunity to meet a vast number of politicians in real life, as a matter of fact I have known numerous Ambassadors and some very highly intellectual politicians in the company of my Father, when he was the Chief Justice of India. Dramatically, I have had occasion to see several performances of political cartwheels like dancing clowns, during the last three decades, turning their services of sacred trust, against the welfare of the masses that they represent, the silent spectators are the audience for the circus. Perhaps my experiences and such imagery has made me reject politics and my dominating genes prefer to perform, as an administrator, an educationist and a writer, these positions have become my life's goal.

I have enjoyed, discussing varied situations with my Father and my uncles, as I developed a clear vision of the local and also world politics, I watched the manoeuvres that are played like a game on the chessboard, yet I cannot find myself indulging in the tangle of serious local politics. Though I have been called upon and offered from time to time the coveted seats in the Senate, I have also been assured of holding a reserved seat for women, with the promises of Ministerial positions. I must admit I found the offers pleasing – they were a boost to my ego, but acceptance of these eminent positions failed to entice me. My position at any political level was bound to be dominated by the mandate of the political party, to which I would have to owe an allegiance. I do possess a deep and inherent desire to serve my nation to which I have unstintingly pledged my services. There will always be clashes within the members of any party, but the debunking of ethics, or compromising on principles would not be acceptable to me. The soliciting reasons for votes and party politics, may suit an individual's mode of operandi. I have worked and perceived that my consistent dedication to work should always be conducted on the basis of moral and legitimate sanctions. Since I am unable to be a "lota citizen" I would be obliged to remain with my founder "party" that enables me to retain my seat, even if my conscience denied the principles under which the party mandate functions. I have known from the inception of my working career, that the "Parliament Arena" was not the stadium in which I desired to play.

Apart from anything else I am convinced that I would be a complete failure as a politician, I would be inept, lacking the spirit needed to be embroiled in situations that fell below the acceptance of my conscience and ethical standards. Perhaps, by some I could be classified as a coward, but it is a matter of my personal and individual preference of living, for I do not have the stomach to indulge in somersaults or performing a political suicide.

For the last twenty five years or more of my life, I have been tied up with my Quranic World and intricate complexity of the doctrine of Islam. My time has been divided with the Parliament of World Religions and Mr. Mikhail Gorbachev's "State of the World Forum" I taught Islam all over Britain, Canada, U.S.A., and South America. In my written books, I have interpreted and translated from the Holy Quran. The books namely "The Eternal Message" and the two volumes of "Insight into Islam" have taken up an abundance of my time. Much of my time has been spent travelling, while doing a series of Islamic "lecture tours" every year, that range from Montreal in Canada right down to Mexico city in South America. The schedule of my lecture trips covered long periods of time lasting several weeks. These trips have extended through the length and breadth of continents, they were very fast and intense, flying almost three to four times a week and even sometimes daily, hailing taxies, going from one lecture hall to the next and then from one city to another, crossing continents, visiting twenty to twenty-five cities and towns in America during a period of five to six weeks. My participation in World Conferences has taken me from Pakistan, across Europe – to America and Canada and even into South America.

Most of my non-working time is expended indulging in the ambience of the incomparable philosophy to be found in the unrivalled "Message of Light", bestowing the philosophy of good living, to be found in the teaching of the Holy Quran. The beautiful Message and the doctrine was the revelations of Allah, not just the Message of Spiritual uplift, but a deep concern for man to live by a code of ethics, honour, with a dictum and a philosophy of good living. For over several centuries, Islam was not termed a "fundamental" doctrine, but Islam has now been degraded, vilified, and debased as it appears today, nor did it drop out of space to become the pedestal, for the clergy of fundamentalists who use it to stand on. Each sect expounds its own interpretation of the Divine Message. The revelation was necessary at that time, so that the human race could learn from the Holy Quran a moralistic way of life, then in turn teach the philosophy of Muslims, as instructed and learnt from the Eternal Message, it is the beauty of love, the blessing of peace, and the sanguinity of harmony, the search for knowledge and the advancement in all things was the fundamental requirement of life.

It is the revelation for a life of good against evil, which had been preached from time immemorial. This has been a consistent acknowledgement by all the revealed religions, that God has bestowed on some, such as the Prophets and Saints, the Gift of greater minds than on others – these are the philosophers, the teachers of faith, the special chosen speakers gifted by Allah to deliver and elucidate the doctrine of religious norms, and the duties incumbent on man, for the benefit of mankind, for the Divine Creator needs nothing from man, He is sufficient unto Himself. Prayers are not for Allah, they are "to" Allah for one's own amelioration and for the benefit of one's own soul. Those who have been specially gifted must be aware, of just how much to teach, neither introduce their own interpretations, nor may they become a self-elected clergy, or the guardians of man.

Those who have become the spiritual leaders and teachers of today, have acquired power, have taken upon themselves the position of preacher, and also the judge and executioner. Sura Qiyamat says that at the "judgement" sentence or reward will be given by Allah alone on the Day of Judgement. He alone is the Spiritual Judge to award, a reward or punishment in the after world.

I have not long to go as I am already eighty-three with declining health, and I am eager to go, as I know that Majid awaits my arrival. I too desire to join him. He has been the kindest man that I have ever known, his nature was benevolent, his speech dipped in consideration, gentle to the hearing. He had healing hands that caressed the pain out of an aching heart. While his generosity was abundant, his emotions without rancor, his philosophy was forgiveness and understanding, his honesty was without question, his morals draped in purity, his ethics undeniable, his trust without doubt, his words without rankle, his self respect without compromise and his honour without sale.

I was the luckiest woman who bore his name. When he gave me his name to wear, he was sure that we could journey the road of life together. For half a century we have loved, cherished and honoured each other. And our lives found fulfilment.

With these untarnished memories I bid you adieu.

Yon rising Moon that looks for us again –
How oft hereafter will she wax and wane;
How oft hereafter rising look for us
Through this same Garden – and for one in vain

And when like her, oh Saki, you shall pass
Among the Graves star-scatter'd on the Grass,
And in your joyous errand reach the spot
Where I made one – turn down an empty Glass!

~ Omer Khayyam

★ ★ ★ ★ ★

Truth Conquers the Universe

Letters of Recognition

CONSORTIUM ON RELIGION AND ECOLOGY
INTERNATIONAL

Begum Anese Khan   9 December 1993
69 Maitland Court
Lancaster Terrace
London W2 United Kingdom

Dear Mrs. Kahn:

With great pleasure it is my privilege to invite you to become a member of the Board of the Consortium on Religion and Ecology-International (CORE-Int'l).

As you know, the CORE-International is an organization whose principle aim is to promote the values of Global Stewardship of the environment and the related social value of Sustainable Development. These values are crucial to the future of the planet as a whole as well as the sustainable development and health of individual nations and peoples around the Earth.

CORE-International had a significant role to play in the preparation for the United Nations Conference on Environment and Development. It also was involved in several important activities during the Earth Summit and has continued afterwards to work with promotion of the Stewardship ethic through a variety of social education programs.

During the recent Parliament of the Worlds Religions, held in Chicago, you showed excellent leadership qualities which we will find of great value for Board members. Moreover, your presentation on the panel sponsored by CORE-Int'l and the North American Coalition on Religion and Ecology (NACRE) was an important contribution to this global event.

As chairman of the Consortium, I personally welcome you to the board and we are deeply honored by your openness to accept this position.

Sincerely,

Donald B. Conroy, Ph.D.
Chairman

PENNSTATE

The Pennsylvania State University
University Park, PA 16802-4801

December 30, 1993

Begum Anese Majid Khan
Esena Foundation School
24-C,Gulberg II
Lahore, Pakistan.

Dear Begum Majid Khan,

REPORT ON THE FALL' 92 MEETING

It is not an exaggeration to say that most Company Members felt that the Fall 1992 meeting was one of the most upbuilding and harmonious events that we have ever held.

She interpreted the Koran and pointed out the many parallels and similarities to the Bible. She also interpreted for us many of the key points of the Koran which have been misinterpreted in the West such as Jihad (Holy war), and the attitudes women. There were surprises in store for many.

Anese Majid Khan was such a surprise and delight to all of us that she made it much easier for us to listen to her message. A soft-spoken scion of one of leading Muslim families, she came to America at her own expense to interpret her own positions as a contemporary Muslim woman.

The prominent role that women had in writing the Koran and shaping the early history of Islam and Mohammad's Introduction of polygamy as being based on a concern for outcast and deprived women were eye openers. She pointed out that much of the doctrines and actions attributed to Islam are not to be found it the Koran at all.

DR. RUSTUM ROY

May 1 1995

Mr. Begum Anese Majid Kahn
24-C, Gulberg -11
Lahore
Pakistan

Dear Mr. Kahn,

It is my personal honor to invite you to participate in an historic and timely endeavor, the State of the World Forum, to be held in San Francisco September 27 - October 1, 1995.

As we leave the Cold War behind, we face many complex problems whose solution will require not only physical and financial resources but also political and moral will. We need a critical reassessment of all our assumptions and a new combination of players to envision the next phase of human development.

We are inviting to the Forum those individuals whose expertise and concern enable them to critically analyze and constructively shape the issues pertinent to the future of our planet. They include senior statespeople, current political leaders, business executives, scientists, spiritual leaders, intellectuals, artists and youth. Each has an important and complementary part to play as we enter the next century and a new millennium.

I have invited as Co-Chairs for the Forum several friends and colleagues who are particularly interested in these issues: President Askar Akaev, President Oscar Arias, Prime Minister Tansu Çiller, President Václav Havel, Prime Minister Ruud Lubbers, Nobel Laureate Rigoberta Menchu, Prime Minister Yasuhiro Nakasone, President Julius Nyerere, Secretary George Shultz, Mr. Ted Turner and Archbishop Desmond Tutu.

It is my hope that those of us who gather for the Forum will consider how we might collaborate in the future.

Please allow me to present as a gift the enclosed selection of my personal reflections on humanity's future, which I hope will prove useful as you review the materials and consider your personal participation.

I believe you would make an important and valuable contribution to this international endeavor and I look forward to meeting and working with you at the opening of this initiative in San Francisco.

Sincerely,

Mikhail S. Gorbachev

MSG/jb
Enclosure

LA ROCHE COLLEGE

Office of the President

January 14, 1994

Begum Anees Majid Khan
Director
Eaena Foundation
24-C-Gulberg-II
Lahore (Pakistan)

Dear Mrs. Khan:

Although we have had a number of telephone
conversations and enjoyed the pleasure of your company
when you visited the College last Fall, I find that I
have not formally welcomed you to the Board of the
Pacem In Terris Institute. I do so now, belatedly,
with a great deal of pleasure.

Please accept my gratitude for your willingness
to serve as a member of the Institute's Board. While it
has been just a few months since you joined us, you have
demonstrated a remarkable dedication through all of your
efforts on behalf of our international students. I look
forward to our association as we continue to work for
the success of this project.

I send you our best wishes for a blessed and
successful New Year.

Sincerely,

Monsignor William A. Kerr
President

WAK/bmm

9000 Babcock Boulevard   Pittsburgh, PA 15237-5898 • (412) 367-9300

CONSORTIUM ON RELIGION AND ECOLOGY INTERNATIONAL

Begum Anese Khan
69 Maitland Court
Lancaster Terrace
London W2 United Kingdom

September 25, 1993

Dear Anese,

      Trusting in Divine Providence, which has so blessed your work and our collaborative work at the Parliament of the World's Religions, I have prepared this Action Plan for your reflection and approval prior to my sending it to our Executive Board and Board of Directors.

DONALD B. CONROY
President NACRE
Chairman CORE-Int'l

5 Thamas Circle, NW Washington Dc 20005
202 462-2591

. . . .

The Global Commission to Fund the United Nations

October 31, 1994

Mrs. Begum Anese Majid Kahn
c/o Mrs. Sibi Shah
9163 Forest Lawn Court
Springfield, VA 22152

Dear Ms. Kahn:

With this letter, I would like to invite you to become a member of the Advisory Council of the Global Commission to Fund the United Nations. You are among a distinguished group of people who have joined with us to study the important area of finding appropriate and independent funding for the United Nations. The Global Commission to Fund the United Nations follows up the work of the Commission on Global Governance and also the Yale Report on the United Nations in its Second Half-Century.

I am enclosing for your information more detailed information about the Global Commission.

I hope you accept this position and that, at your convenience, you will be willing to help us in our major goals of studying and creating global dialogue on the general topic of making the United Nations accountable and capable of handling the ever-increasing role it is being called upon to play in this Era of Global Interdependence. This is the first Commission of which I am aware that was begun, not by a large institution such as the United Nations, but by the global civic society made up of people like yourself anxious to make a contribution toward sustainable human community.

Let us stay in touch as we work together to further our mutual goals. May I add that it has been a cherished personal pleasure to meet you and to spend time talking with you. Please call me if you need any information or have suggestions for the Commission.

Sincerely yours,

Diane E. Sherwood, Ph.D.
Director

Director: Diane E. Sherwood, Ph.D.
1 K Street. N.W. Suite 1120 · Washington, D.C. 20005 USA · (202) 639-9460 FAX: (202) 639-9157

- 277 -

COMITÉ NATIONAL FRANÇAIS
de liaison pour la
RÉADAPTATION des HANDICAPÉS

71, Avenue de Breteuil, Paris 15ᵉ

SECRÉTARIAT :
103, Rve du Fg St Honoré PARIS
Tél. BAL. 16-76
Après-midi (sauf samedi)
de 14 à 18 heures

Nº 112
DR/DJ

March 25, 1965

Mrs Anese Rashid
Le Cadeau
24-C. Gulberg
LAHORE
                    Inde

Dear Mrs. Raschid :

        I am so pleased that you have accepted to speak
on Thuesday June 25th.

        Your lecture will last 15 minutes. Could you send
me before the 15th of April the text of your conference to
have it published in Copenhagen ?

        "The means of solving problems for the handicaped
with voluntary participation in Pakistan" is the title of
your lecture.

        Looking forward to seeing you soon.

                        Sincerely

                        Diane de Rouchy

GOVERNMENT OF PAKISTAN
MINISTRY OF WOMEN DEVELOPMENT

No. 5-1/2006-Coord/Council.   Islamabad, the 15th January, 2008.

From: Ms. Samar Ihsan Beg,
          Deputy Secretary,
          Tele: 9201075.

To: Begum Anese Majeed Khan,
          Chairperson,
          ESENA Foundation,
          24-C, Gulburg-II,
          Lahore.
          Tele: 042-5755523.

Subject:-   **PAKISTAN CIVIL AWARDS 2008-INVESTITURE CEREMONY.**

Dear Madam

        I am enclosing a Citation regarding the Pakistan Civil Awards – Investiture
Ceremony 2008, wherein you had been recommended for an Award on the basis of your
contributions in the field of Education, Muslim Culture and Girls Education with the request that
you may kindly go through the Citation and vet the same as desired by this Ministry and return
the same urgently but not later than 17th January, 2008 as Cabinet Division has to be informed
about the same.

                                              Yours sincerely,

                                              (Samar Ihsan Beg)
                                              Deputy Secretary

Enclosed as above:

Begum Anese Fatima Majid Khan

Award	:	President's Award for Pride of Performance
Field	:	Education

Begum Anese Fatima Majid Khan, is a known educationist and has contributed a lot in the promotion of education, culture and Islamic values. She had started a private educational institution called "ESSNA Foundation School" in Lahore providing best education to the girls along with Islamic Knowledge. She has written a number of books. T.V. Channels of Europe and America telecast her educational programs. She has delivered more than 6000 lectures in prominent universities of Europe, America, Africa and Middle East. On the basis of her contribution, she was nominated as member of the Board of Governors for the Global Steward Core International, Bosnian Trust, State of the World Forum in San Francisco. She has received the President of USA Award at Laroche College in Petersburg, USA. She has also earned many gold medals and life time achievement Awards. She was awarded "Jerusalem Star" by President Yasser Arafat for her substantial assistance in Palestine cause during Islamic summit, 1974. She has also been the recipient of several International Merit Crystal Awards for the cause of Islam from 1998-2007

In recognition of her outstanding services in the field of Education, the President of the Islamic Republic of Pakistan has been pleased to confer on Begum Anese Fatima Majid Khan the Award of **President's Award for Pride of Performance.**

In August, 2007 she received the 'Best Performance Award' bestowed by the Government of Greece for her cultural and Islamic services.

In November, 2007 she has been awarded the International Crystal Award in Dubai for her Islamic Quranic work and the field of Education.

Begum Anese Fatima Majid Khan

Award	:	President's Award for Pride of Performance
Field	:	Education

Begum Anese Fatima Majid Khan, is a known educationist and has contributed a lot in the promotion of education, culture and Islamic values. She had started a private educational institution called "ESSNA Foundation School" in Lahore providing best education to the girls along with Islamic Knowledge. She has written a number of books. T.V. Channels of Europe and America telecast her educational programs. She has delivered more than 6000 lectures in prominent universities of Europe, America, Africa and Middle East. On the basis of her contribution, she was nominated as member of the Board of Governors for the Global Steward Core International, Bosnian Trust, State of the World Forum in San Francisco. She has received the President of USA Award at Laroche College in Petersburg, USA. She has also earned many gold medals and life time achievement Awards. She was awarded "Jerusalem Star" by President Yasser Arafat for her substantial assistance in Palestine cause during Islamic summit, 1974. She has also been the recipient of several International Merit Crystal Awards for the cause of Islam from 1998-2007

In recognition of her outstanding services in the field of Education, the President of the Islamic Republic of Pakistan has been pleased to confer on Begum Anese Fatima Majid Khan the Award of **President's Award for Pride of Performance.**

In August, 2007 she received the 'Best Performance Award' bestowed by the Government of Greece for her cultural and Islamic services.

In November, 2007 she has been awarded the International Crystal Award in Dubai for her Islamic Quranic work and the field of Education.

Pakistan Muslim League
(Women Wing)

Farrukh Khan
Secretary General

20 August 2007

Mohtarma Sumaira Malik
Federal Minister for Women Development and
President, Pakistan Muslim League
Women Wing
Islamabad.

Subject: **Life Achievement Award for Begum Anese Fatima Majeed Khan**

Respected Madam,

    This is with reference of Programme Committee meeting of the National Centenary Committee of Muslim league which held under the Chairmanship of Senator Mushahid Hussain Sayed, Secretary General, Pakistan Muslim League. It was decided that Cabinet Division will be requested that Special Citizen Award be given to Begum Anese Fatima Majeed Khan for her meritorious contributions for women development in last 60 years. Begum Anese Fatima Majeed Khan is a daughter of late Sir Justice Dr. Imam, Chief Justice, Supreme Court of India and granddaughter of Sir Ali Imam, Chief Justice and Member of Privy Council of Viceroy of the India. She rendered valuable contributions for development of women folk. She established ESENA Foundation School in Lahore 45 years ago. This is the first English medium school for girls of Lahore. She is a great philanthropist and patron of almost all the literary and cultural organizations of Lahore. She is Visiting Professor or more than six international universities and has delivered more than 6000 lectures on Islamic values and Pakistani culture. Recently, President of Pakistan has conferred President Pride of Performance Award for Begum Anese Fatima Majeed Khan. She is 80 years old legendary lady scholar.

    Senator Mushahid Hussain Sayed told her that Women Division will celebrate her 80th Birthday Anniversary on 5th September in which a Life Achievement Award will be given by the Women Division. Raja Zulqarnain Haider, Senator Mushahid Hussain Sayed, Mr. S.M. Zafar, Dr. Ghazanfar Mehdi will pay tribute to her life long achievement. Senator Mushahid Hussain Sayed has left for USA and he will return on 1st September. It is requested that a special function may kindly be arranged by Women Division on 5th September at Islamabad or Lahore in which Life Achievement Award may kindly be awarded to her.

    Submitted for necessary action please

Yours Sincerely

(Farrukh Khan)
Secretary General

CC to: Mr. Mahmood Salim, Secretary, Women Division with request to arrange the above programme accordingly as announced by Senator Mushahid Hussain Sayed, Secretary General, Pakistan Muslim League and Chairman Senate Standing Committee on Foreign Affairs

(Farrukh Khan)
Secretary General

بسم الله الرحمن الرحيم

حکومت پاکستان

کابینہ ڈویژن

سیکرٹری کابینہ

اسلام آباد، تاریخ ۲۸ فروری ۲۰۰۸ء

حوالہ نمبر ۵/۱۴ء۲۰۰۷ اعزازات

محترمہ بیگم انیس فاطمہ مجید خان

السلام علیکم!

میں آپ کو مسرت کے ساتھ اطلاع دیتا ہوں کہ صدر پاکستان نے ۱۴ اگست ۲۰۰۷ء کو یوم آزادی کے موقع پر آپ کو "صدارتی اعزاز برائے حسن کارکردگی" عطا کیا ہے۔ یہ اعزاز پاکستان کے خصوصی گزٹ میں شائع ہو چکا ہے۔

۲۔ پروگرام کے مطابق ۲۳۔ مارچ ۲۰۰۸ء کو یوم پاکستان کے موقع پر منعقد ہونے والی تقسیم اعزازات کی تقریب میں گورنر پنجاب آپ کو "صدارتی اعزاز برائے حسن کارکردگی" پیش کریں گے۔ تقریب اور پروگرام کی تفصیلی آپ کو انشاء اللہ مناسب وقت پر متعلقہ صوبائی حکومت کی طرف سے ارسال کر دیا جائے گا۔

مخلص

سید مسعود عالم رضوی

محترمہ بیگم انیس فاطمہ مجید خان
چیئرپرسن
ایسنا فاؤنڈیشن، ۲۴۔ سی، گلبرگ ۔II،
لاہور

FEDERATION MONDIALE DES ANCIENS COMBATTANTS / WORLD VETERANS FEDERATION
HEADQUARTERS: 16 RUE HAMELIN, PARIS 16

Major. GHULAM HUSAIN, T.Q.A.
HONORARY VICE-PRESIDENT
OF THE W.V.F.
11, GRAND HOTEL,
EDWARDES ROAD,
RAWALPINDI.
TELE NO. 517-Gng.

Ref. No. WVF /200.
RAWALPINDI.
(PAKISTAN)

23 April, 1963

My dear Anese,

Further to my letter of even No. dated the 28th March, 1963.

2.   I am pleased to forward, herewith, a copy of the "World Veteran" for the month of February, 1963, containing an article on the International Picture Sale in Paris.

Kind regards,

Yours sincerely,

(Sd)

No.14/ ~ /62/PASB
Government of Pakistan
Ministry of Defence(PASB)
Rawalpindi, the 9 May'63

To

Mrs. Anese Fathima Rashid,
La Cadeau, 24-C, Gulberg, Lahore

Subject:-   WVF Picture Sale

Attached letter No.2462 dated 18th April'63 from WVF Secretary General, received in this office, is forwarded for necessary action.

(Ghulam Ghaus) Major
A/Secretary
Pakistan Armed Services Board

Fédération Mondiale des Anciens Combattants
World Veterans Federation

16, RUE HAMELIN
PARIS · 16 ·

TEL. POINCARÉ 31 70, 11·64
CABLES : WORLDVET PARIS

Paris, April 18, 1963

Mrs. Anese Fathima Rashid,
La Cadeau,
24c Gulberg,
Lahore,
PAKISTAN.

At this time, therefore, there are two alternatives before us.
We are planning in the next few months to hold our biennial Charity
Sale, at which handicrafts and other items from all parts of the world
are sold for the benefit of the programs of the Federation. We intend
to include a section of works of art in this sale and, if you agree
we would be pleased to exhibit your work with a price fixed on the basis
of expert judgement as to its reasonable value in Paris at this time.

Alternatively, if you would prefer to have your work returned to
you, we will dispatch it immediately at our expense.

In either case, I can assure you that we are deeply grateful for the
generosity which prompted you to contribute your work to our sale and,
while I regret that the results were not more in keeping with our
anticipations, I do feel that, with your cooperation, we have added in a
small but important way to the progress of international appreciation of art

Sincerely,

SECRETARY GENERAL.

From:- Maj Gen Sahabzada Yaqub Khan
MC
Headquarters 1 Armoured Division
Kharian Cantt
30 Aug '62

Dear Anis,

I gather from Daffadar Aziz ur Rehman – the bearer of this note, that you are now working, with your usual efficiency no doubt, in the Institute of Prosthetics at Lahore.

As you may perhaps know, Aziz ur Rehman lost his leg recently, having been badly gored by a wild boar, during the wild boar shooting operations in which the area was engaged earlier this year. This young and promising NCO belongs to my division and showed great devotion to duty during these operations.

He tells me that there is a vacancy in your Establishment for disabled men. I am therefore giving him this letter and commend him to you.

With every good wish for success in your new appointment & in the fine and noble work you are doing.

Yours sincerely
Yaqub

Mrs Anis Rashid,
Armed Forces Institute of Prosthetics
Lahore

- 286 -

TEL: ...
...

POST WAR SERVICES RECONSTRUCTION FUNDS
PAKISTAN

TRUSTS CREATED UNDER THE CHARITABLE ENDOWMENTS ACT, 1890, FOR THE
BENEFIT OF EX-SERVICEMEN AND THEIR FAMILIES

HARLEY STREET,
RAWALPINDI CANTT.,
P. O. BOX 84

Date 11 October, 1963.

I have known Begum Anese Fatima Rashid, nee Imam,
ever since she joined the Rehabilitation Centre for
Disabled Veterans at Lahore, then known as the Red
Cross Home, in December, 1959, as a volunteer Welfare
Worker.

. Begum Anese's work at the Centre was of the highest
order. She never spared herself and gave devoted service
to it and its inmates. She showed great organisational
and administrative ability, and helped to train the other
lady workers at the Centre. High dignitaries in Pakistan
and foreign VIP's who have visited the Centre during the
last 3 years have been struck by the high standard of
administration, training, games and other welfare activities
there, and the credit for this must largely go to Begum Anese.

3. In April 1963, Begum Anese found it necessary, for
domestic reasons, to cease her connection with the Centre,
and this has been a great loss to it.

4. Apart from her work, Begum Anese has a most impressive
and engaging personality, and it has been a great pleasure
for me to have known her.

Major (Retd.),
Director,
P.W.S.R. Funds.
(GHULAM HUSSAIN).

"*We must involve youth in our lives, we must involve them in our quest, in our search for the solutions to the problems that the world is facing.*"

-- *Mikhail Gorbachev*

The Presidio
P.O. Box 29434
San Francisco
California 94129
Tel 415 561 2345
Fax 415 561 2323
forum@worldforum.org

Co-Chairs

Askar Akaev
President, Kyrgyzstan

Oscar Arias
Nobel Peace Prize Laureate

Jean-Bertrand Aristide
President, Haiti (1991 1994)

James A. Baker, III
U.S. Secretary of State
(1989 1992)

Tansu Çiller
Prime Minister, Turkey
(1993 1996)

Marian Wright Edelman
President
Children's Defense Fund

Jane Goodall
Primatologist

Mikhail Gorbachev
Nobel Peace Prize Laureate

Ruud Lubbers
Prime Minister
The Netherlands (1982 1994)

Federico Mayor
Director General, UNESCO

Thabo Mbeki
Deputy Executive President
Republic of South Africa

Yasuhiro Nakasone
Prime Minister, Japan (1982 1987)

Leo Rabin
First Lady of Israel (1992 1995)

Jehan Sadat
First Lady of Egypt (1970 1981)

Ted Turner
Chairman
Turner Broadcasting System, Inc.

Desmond Tutu
Nobel Peace Prize Laureate

Elie Wiesel
Nobel Peace Prize Laureate

Muhammad Yunus
Managing Director
Grameen Bank

"*We have come from different nations. We have come from the furthest ports of the Earth. We have come because we have a vision. We have come to save our home.*"
-- *Melonie Parris, '96 Youth Delegate Tobago Trinadad*

June 19, 1997

Anese Majid Khan
Esena Foundation
24/C, Gulberg-11
Lahore, Pakistan

Dear Anese:

I hope you will consider joining us at the 1997 Forum November 4 - 9 in San Francisco. We have many exciting and innovative program plans this year which will allow Forum participants increased ability to interact and examine critical global issues among other social innovators and leaders. However, one of our most important goals for the 1997 Forum is to expand youth participation by bringing over 50 Youth Fellows representing outstanding and emerging young leaders from around the world.

The mentoring of the next generation, both our own children and youth with whom we interact during our lives, is one of the most critical task that we as adults share. Because of this, the State of the World Forum has included youth in its annual international gathering in San Francisco. Most recently, a delegation of youth also participated in the Forum's inaugural regional gathering in Guanajuato, Mexico.

At the 1997 Forum, Youth Fellows will have an unprecedented opportunity to engage directly with world leaders on current global challenges, and to create new models of cross-generational problem solving and cooperation. Youth participants will form the cornerstone of the Forum dialogue regarding the state of the world's youth

Hoping that you will be participating in the Forum this November, we ask that you or your company also consider sponsoring one or more youth participants. While we are well aware that you will be covering the costs of your own participation, we extend the request in an effort to "match" adult mentors with the youth participants and facilitate increased dialogue among youth and adult participants during and after the Forum.

I ask that you give thought to the life experiences you would like to pass on to the generation which will follow us and how you can share your wisdom with a Youth Fellow at this year's Forum. As the father of two young sons, I have been giving considerable thought to this very question, realizing that the combined wisdom of experiential learning and true empathy can only be passed from one person to another -- one experience at a time.

Please give serious consideration to this request to support Youth Fellows at this year's State of the World Forum.

Thank you.

Sincerely,

Jim Garrison
President

Truth Conquers the Universe

Awards and Honours

AWARDS EARNED BY BEGUM ANESE MAJID KHAN

1. **AWARD SITARA-E-BAIT-UL-MAQDAAS-1974**
   given by Mr. Yassar Arafat, Chairman P.L.O. to Al Mujahid
   Bint-e-Palastine.

2. (a) **AWARD FOR LITERATURE-1987**
   Given wirting:
   1) An Anthology of Poetry
   2) History of the Arab World.
   Complied from the lectures given in the Government College
   for Post-Graduate students by Bolan Academy.

   (b) **AWARD FOR EDUCATION-1987**
   Given for being pioneer of private education for girls in
   Pakistan. "Esena Foundation" was the first private school for
   girls started in 1964.

   (c) **AWARD FOR ARMY SERVICE FOR THE DISABLED-
   1987**
   Begum Majid Khan did not only help to organize and head an
   army department programme which rehabilitated the disabled
   but also organised the 1st ever "1st Asian Games" for the
   disabled, played on the courts of her army unit in Lahore
   1961.

   (d) **AWARD FOR SOCIAL SERCVICES-1987**
   Given to Begum Majid Khan for her services in the various
   social organisations that she has launched and worked for
   since 1958.

3. **AWARD GIVEN IN ISLAMABAD-1988**
   Given to Begum Majid Khan for the interpretation of the
   Holy Quran in her audio cassettes titled "The Eternal
   Message" for use in foreign countries of Muslim.

4. **AWARD BY THE BALUCHISTAN GOVT. 1989**

   For the writing and recording of "The Eternal Message" and
   for her social service to Pakistan in different fields of work
   and education.

AWARD BY THE ARTS INTERNATIONAL UNITED ARAB EMIRATES 1990 (Awarded in Dubai)

For 'The Eternal Message" (on recorded cassettes) of the interpretation of the Holy Quran and the Divine Message.

THE ABOVE AWARDS WERE GIVEN BY VARIOUS GOVERNMENTS AND ORGANISATIONS THROUGH THE BOLAN SOCIETY.

6.   The All Pakistan Private School Management awarded Begum Majid Khan four separate shields for services in the Educational Field.

7.   Bazm-e-Danish awarded three medals on separate occasions for her contribution in the field of Literature, Social Work and Education. 1991.

8.   The Bolan Society gave five of their own personal awards to Begum Majid Khan for her service in the educational field and various social fields and for her contribution to Literature, Religion and Education. 1987-1993.

AWARDS IN 1993

9.   Bolan Cultural Society gave "Crescent Group Award" to Begum Majid Khan in 1993 for her religious services in different countries i.e. America, England and Canada.

10. Bolan Cultural Society gave an Award to Begum Majid Khan for her Meritorious and dedicated services in the field of education, religion, social services, literature and army services

Begum Majid Khan toured different countries in 1992 for the teaching of Quranic Islam. The different associations have awarded shields for her services in the religious field and teaching of pure spiritualism "Spirit of Islam".

1. Writers Association of Pakistan presented a shield in 1993 for her religious services.

2. Rising Youth Pakistan Council presented a shield in 1993 for her religious services.

3. Anjuman-e-Tafaaz-e-Haqooq-e-Pakistan presented a shield for her religious services.

4. Paksitan Film Producers Association presented a shield.

5. Bolan Cultural Society presented a shield in 1993 for her religious services and teaching of Islam in England, Canada and America.

6. Human Rights Society presented a shield in 1993 for her services to Islam and the teaching of Quranic Islam to children, students and Christians and multi religious groups in England, Canada and America.

1. Award Sitara-e-Bait-ul-
Maqdaas - 1974 given by
Mr. Yassar Arafat, Chairman
P.L.O. to Al Mujahid
Bint-e-Palestine

۱۔ محمد سیسا ه بیت المقدس میں ۱۹۷۴ میں جناب یاسر
عرفات چیئرمین پی ایل او کے چیئرمین جماأ مجرید نے
المجاہد بنت فلسطین دیگر میڈ گذر آ من فلسطین کے
خدمات کے سلسلے میں دیا

2.a) AWARD FOR LITERATURE-1987
Given for Writing:
1) An Anthology of Poetry
2) History of the Arab World.
Compiled from the lectures
given in the Government
College for Post-Graduate
students by Iolan Academy.

۲۔ع انگریزی ادب کے میدان میں خدمات
ہیر ۱۹۸۱ میں لولان تکمیل سرہانی نے
تکیم مجید کو تحفہ دیا

b) AWARD FOR EDUCATION-1987
Given for being pioneer of
private education for girls
in Pakistan. "Esena Foundation"
was the first private school
for girls started in 1964.

۳۔ب تعلیمی میدان میں ۱۹۸۱ میں ۔ پہلا تعلیمی
پرائیویٹ ادارہ بناکر الیسانا فاؤنڈیشن کے ۱۹۶۴ میں شروع سرت ہیر لولاں اعظم کی جانب
سے الوارڈ دیا گیا جبکہ آب اس میں جاری ہیں
پرائیویٹ ادارہ اس کی پہلی جانب تھیں

c) AWARD FOR ARMY SERVICE FOR
THE DISABLED - 1987
Begum Majid Khan did not only
help to organize and head an
army department programme
which rehabilitated the
disabled but also organised
the 1st ever "1st Asian
Games" for the disabled, played
on the courts of her army
unit in Lahore 1961.

۴۔ج معذور فوجیوں کی خدمات کا الوارڈ ۔
۱۹۸۷ تکیم صاحبہ نے ۱۹۶۱ میں معذور فوجیوں
کے جیب اسٹنٹ فیمر سمیت جرو نے کا اہتمام اس
ماحول میں لولاں سوسائٹی پہ ماسا کھیل پر
کے دوسرے خدمات بھر تحفہ دیا گیا

d) AWARD FOR SOCIAL SERVICES-1987
Given to Begum Majid Khan for
her services in the various
social organisations that she
has launched and worked for
since 1956.

۵۔ سماجی خدمات بھر الوارڈ ۔ ۱۹۸۷
تکیم مجید ۱۹۵۶ سے سماجی خدمات میں اہا
مصروف جن اور سرگرم ہیں۔ ان سماجی خدمات
بھر لولاں سوسائٹی کی جانب سے ایس الوارڈ
دیا گیا

3. AWARD GIVEN IN ISLAMABAD-1988
Given to Begum Majid Khan for
the interpretation of the Holy
Quran in her audio casettes
titled "The Eternal Message"
for use in foreign countries
of Muslim.

۶۔د مذہبی خدمات بھر الوارڈ ۔ ۱۹۸۸
تکیم مجید نے قرآن مجید مسلمانوں کا انگریزی زبان
میں ترجمہ وتفسیر سرتے تاکی اوہی ممالک میں آ ڈیوکیسٹ
بنار سرتے ۔ اور آبیس مسرف محاسب میں بھیجا

4. AWARD BY THE BALUCHISTAN GOVT.1989
For the writing and recording of
"The Eternal Message" and for her
social service to Pakistan in
different fields of work and
education.

۷۔ بلوچستان حکومت کی جانب سے نوابی
مذہبی اور سماجی خدمات دسمبر ۱۹۸۹ میں تکیم
بیٹ کو صوبی الوارڈ دیا گیا

(P.T.O.)

AWARD BY THE UNITED ARAB
EMIRATES 1990 (Awarded in Dubai)

For "The Eternal Message" (on
recorded cassettes) of the
interpretation of the Holy
Quran and the Divine Message.

THE ABOVE AWARDS WERE GIVEN BY
VARIOUS GOVERNMENTS AND
ORGANISATIONS THROUGH THE
BOLAN ACADEMY.

6. The All Pakistan Private School
Management awarded Begum Majid
Khan four separate shields for
services in the Educational
Field.

7. Bazm-e-Danish awarded three medals
on separate occasions for her
contribution in the field of
Literature, Social Work and
Education. 1991.

8. The Bolan Academy gave five of
their own personal awards to
Begum Majid Khan for her service
in the educational field and
various social fields and for
her contribution to Literature,
Religion and Education.
1987-1993.

AWARDS IN 1993

9. Bolan Cultural Academy gave
"Crescent Group Award" to
Begum Majid Khan in 1993 for
her religious services in
different countries i.e.
America, England and Canada.

10. Bolan Cultural Academy gave an
Award to Begum Majid Khan for
her Meritorious and dedicated
services in the field of
education, religion, social
services, literature and
army services.

Begum Majid Khan toured different
countries in 1992 for the teaching
of Quranic Islam. The different
associations have awarded shields
for her services in the religious
field and teaching of pure
spiritualism "Spirit of Islam".

Messages

I was delighted to learn that the sports day was a great success. It is a great joy to me to see that sport for paraplegics is going so well in your country and this gives me a great satisfaction."

—Dr. L. Guttmann, CBE, MD, FRCS, MRCP.
Director, National Spinal Injuries Centre.

I thank you very much for your kind invitation. Unhappily as you know, the 3rd of May, I will be in Paris in view of the meeting of the board of the W.V.F.
Expecting to have the pleasure to meet you later in Lahore or in Europe, meanwhile, I remain, Dear Sir.
Sincerely yours.

—Mr. G. M. Cordier,
World Veterans Federation, Paris (France)

Your work in organizing these Sports is of particular interest to me, as I am trying to do a similar organizing job in Canada for our fairly large number of Paraplegics. They have their own organization but it is on an individual group basis and their has been little or no effort to make them into a national organization, which would give them greater numerical strength and ability to take part in either national or international sports, such as yours and the Stoke Mandeville Games.
If you have organizational data on how you went about organizing your Paraplegic Sports at Lahore I would be most grateful if you could send me a copy for my personal information and use. The fact that Pakistan has organized such sports for the disabled might be just the incentive we need.
My warmest best wishes for the future of your excellent work.

—Mr. K. M. Guthrie,
*Air Vice Marshal (ret), World Veterans Federation,
1459, West, 38th Avenue, Vancouver 13, Canada*

First Games in Asia

LAHORE, West Pakistan, is the first Asian city where a national sports meeting for disabled ex-servicemen has ever been held.

The event took place last May, when 22 inmates of the Home for Disabled Ex-servicemen — mainly paraplegics — competed in various events which included table tennis, archery, badminton, javelin throwing, shot put, a wheel-chair relay race and basket ball.

The competition was watched by five delegates to the Ninth General Assembly of the World Veterans Federation; four from Laos, one from Nepal.

The enthusiasm shown by members of the Armed Forces for the welfare of their disabled comrades was the most striking feature of the colourful sports programme adapted to the capabilities of the invalids.

In basket ball, the disabled were not far from equalling able bodied sportsmen in their good play and command over the game. To spectators it was interesting as well as strange to witness the disabled steering their wheel chairs to chase the ball and fighting hard to score. The match between the "yellow" and the "red" teams of five players each was won by "yellow" with the score of 7 to 1 points.

(The above are the extracts from the article, "First Games in Asia" appearing in the "World Veteran", July 1961.)

Truth Conquers the Universe

Notes About the Author

Anese Majid currently resides with her family in Lahore Pakistan but also has a home in London. She has to her credit published many books, her paintings exhibited internationally and she is recognized as competent a writer of both prose and poetry in the English Language.

A camel may find it difficult to get through the eye of a needle; or a rich man to enter into heaven; but this fascinating book shows that a woman born to wealth and privilege is not disqualified from seeking after truth, and putting it into practice. From silver spoon to hard knocks, Begum Majid Khan has become her own woman; firm in her faith, yet open to the best that East and West can offer. She is Pakistan's best ambassador.

~ Mr. Eric Payne, England

"An inspirational autobiography. It teaches us how one can live several lives, successively, in the course of a single lifespan, in various countries. Simultaneously spiritual and worldly, the author has provided others with intellectual and practical aid, regardless of age or station."

~ *Mrs. Antonia Payne, England*

"A truly remarkable story of one woman's courage and integrity. Born into a life of privilege Anese Majid Khan reaches out across a wide chasm of 'Class and Tradition' determined to help those less fortunate than herself.

As a devout Muslim and a true humanitarian, she succeeds in breaking down the obstacles that beset her of class and gender.

Her story set in the turbulent times of the birth of a Nation, her book moves at a fast pace delivering a feeling and insight into the political and social environment after the birth and division of two nations India and Pakistan.

She guides us through jungle adventures, emotional traumas and psychological issues and political tit-bits that provide us with fascinating glimpses of the lavish life styles of the aristocratic upper eschelons and the suppressed indigent class during the time of the British Raj in a rapidly changing world.

She is a sound Islamic Scholar and a recognized authority on Islam and its philosophy which is a code of 'good living'. Having translated The Holy Quran into English with clear interpretations which she has produced and also appeared in several series on T.V Programs across the globe. She recently lost her husband. She has two grand daughters and six grand children, but she is still vital and very active in her Educational and philanthropic endeavours, such as providing tube-wells to villages of dry barren areas that spread across hundreds of waterless villages where the mortality rate is very high. She still conducts the educational and cultural programs of the Esena Group of Schools."

~ Mrs. Peggy Dean, Canada

"The Title Page of the book informs us: 'The One that Got Away', 'The Truth Revealed', and the first page tells us: "An Unusual Story by an Unusual Personality'. Having known Begum Anese Majid Khan since 1970, I have heard various episodes of her life and experiences from her but nothing compares to the story of her life revealed here!

There are revelations that make one wonder: 'What a Lady! Has she really experienced all that she narrates!' As I said before, I have known Begum Anese Majid Khan since 1970 and since then have participated in a few of her activities with her and I know first-hand that she is a most unusual person who has had some most unusual experiences and she has some most unusual ways of dealing with situations.

The biography deals with numerous aspects of her life spanning seven decades. The reader becomes aware that the child who returns from England develops into a personality that is quite of her own making as she spars with one situation after another. One views the broad spectrum of her life as it develops through each decade. The autobiography reveals Begum Majid Khan's wit, wisdom and wealth of knowledge. Her love of poetry is evident from the poetry pieces the reader finds in several sections and all the chosen poems are self explanatory for that particular section. Begum Majid paints pictures in words. Her apt descriptions of scenes or a lone tree, the convent, gardens, railway stations, the tiger and elephant shoots, the private swimming pools of fish are all so clear that one seems to be witnessing the scenes. She is a born builder and like she has built her house and school, she constructs poetry, scenes and pictures too.

Begum Majid's biography shows her love for her husband and partner, Group Captain Majid Khan who was a calm and gentle person and loved by all. In short, he was a gem. He had a special bond with Begum Majid. Another special bond was shared by him and Tahira Nazira (Bunny) , Begum Majid's daughter and later on with her grand daughters, Natalia and Majdoeline. He was a peaceful soul who wanted ideal conditions for all living beings. There is an intense family bond between Begum Majid, her grand daughters and her great grand children.

'The One that Got Away' tells exactly what it says: The one that got away from the double standards of various eras. With exposure to two kinds of education, dress and culture- English and local the book divulges to its readers the plight of a girl who begins to compare, sift and then choose to adapt her own culture.

The story unfurls the various time periods: the olden days of gracious living, the social set up, double standards, various phenomenon, norms , change in social behaviour after the entry of the British, the borrowed dress-code, style and mannerisms that were forced upon the locals. There are some potent pieces of historical information that are from her personal environment. The narrations about Jinnah, and the views on The East India Company correlated with the current situation in our country are all very interesting and informative. About the fight for freedom, there are some episodes not found in any book of history as they were personal observations and experiences of Begum Majid.

The Independence of Pakistan and India, and the new social set up in a changing society is another eye-opener for the reader.

On the lighter and social side the reader is taken on adventures and escapades with Begum Majid: the tiger and elephant shots are written as though shot on film. Begum Majid's vault full of specific vocabulary for hunting clothes and various guns, elephant hunts and shooting sites can be experienced. The art of description comes naturally to her and she uses precise language to describe places and events e.g. specific layout, crockery and cutlery for various meal times and events. She uses a 'mental autopsy' for every thing seen and heard and comes to her own conclusions. All this, perhaps, is due to the nurturing and grooming of a bud by the parents, the environment and a host of relevant factors of time.

Through the biography the reader comes to know the multi-faceted personality of Begum Majid. Her empathy for the less fortunate, her quiet efforts to relieve the miseries of those wounded in war, the have-nots and her never ending efforts for the service of Islam are but a very small aspect of her life.

There are words of wisdom and an insight into life as Begum Majid writes about the philosophy we tend to have about ourselves, the colourful pictures we paint for ourselves, and then shattered dreams awaken us to a rude reality.

The reader experiences the hardships, heart aches and the travails of a young girl; of a young bride who was left on her own even during confinement and child birth; of the black sheep, and the ugly duckling that turned into more than an accomplished swan, an acclaimed beauty queen; an entrepreneur who glides, and will forever glide in the realms of the Esena Foundation, and who will live in the hearts of those who received wisdom and sustenance from her.

At the international level, on various platforms and forums like The Parliament of World Religions, Congress of Ideology and Global Stewardship Begum Majid has displayed that she is well versed in Commonalities of Religions where the New World Order envisages 'humans to live by a philosophy that behoves the dignity of humans' where humans should form a New Global Ideology for the benefit of the Earth, the preservation of nature and the preservation of global and environmental conditions.

It is amazing to see one person living through so many factors, who has endured so many changes in life, emerged successful and has the ability to coordinate all these multi-faceted lives into one. One could dub her story as 'The Five Faces of Eve'. This Eve feels for people. She has done and continues to do what is in her power, by personal philosophy, to alleviate the distress of *others by providing material and monetary assistance to families so that they become productive citizens rather than beggars on a monthly pay-roll. She has an on-going project to supply drinking water to villages that have less access to water channels, and equipped villages with hand pumps and tubewells for this purpose.*

Briefly, the biography tells of Time and its vagaries, the emotional and psychological state of the author, as a developing person and the cycle of enrichment throughout her life. She chose to rise rather than succumb to adversity. That is why she is what she is today! And her signature song is: 'I did it my Way!'"

~ Shaheen Ajmal

Truth Conquers the Universe

Editorial Reflections

Working with Begum Anese Majid Khan, has been a tremendous opportunity to learn more about her and others around the world.

In memory and honour of Rustum Roy, I am grateful to him for introducing us. Anese and I share in efforts for global education, whole person awareness, sustainable global change and bridging science and spirituality. May Anese's efforts continue in the name of truth, hope and freedom to impact generations to come. May blessings of love, peace and joy light within you and shine throughout the world.

~ Dr. Heather E. McKinney
Managing Editor, United States of America

I find myself fortunate to have the opportunity to edit the personal autobiography, of such a dynamic personality as Begum Anese Majid Khan, who does not emanate as merely a single individual, but as a multi-dimensional institution of herself. She is a writer who has travelled extensively across the globe enabling her to pen her extraordinary and phenomenal experiences. As an author, she has generously shared her widely gained knowledge as she has introduced and revealed the life of not only the variable cultures of the east, but also of the west without drawing comparisons. The author possesses an uncanny privilege of an insight with an in depth knowledge of both worlds.

While editing this biographic book, "The one that got away", I discovered that it certainly was not merely a biography, but a biographical travelogue, through which one travels traversing lands, oceans, far off countries, ancient cultures, universal religions, slight of hand politics, philosophy, ethics, and even changing emotions with different aspects of psychology and psychological diversions.

What I found truly amazing, was that one person's biography of a lifetime, could cover so extensively such a vast diversity of aspects, subjects and scenarios, all described with a depth of correct and related vocabulary needed for the intricate details of penmanship. There is an unusual transference of vision, as the image of oneself identifying with the written presentation, be it culture, religion, politics, ethics or even something as prosaic as crockery or cuisine, the writer left nothing to the reader's imagination, instead created a picturesque, diversion, elaborating each topic with the ultimate details in a magical aura of delivery.

It is truly amazing that the author's memory could span over seven and a half decades, to record with precision, events, conditions, episodes, and even fleeting emotions in such detail. I find this not only fantastic but quite unique.

The book is a treasure-trove of knowledge, an unparallel personal encyclopaedia of multiple subjects, a presentation that reveals the pure essence of seventy-five years of action and experiences with accume and even indepth concept of "policy" manipulation.

As a master of literature, a unique political observer, a social reformer, a philosopher and a philanthropist, she is the unrelenting champion of "Human Rights". She uses her "pen" as her sword and through the sharp sword of her penmanship, she unfaulteringly analyses and forcibly denounces, all the negativities of social, cultural and humiliating norms with degrading rituals, causing the disastrous outcome of senseless wars with the debilitating impact on the human mind, with life and emotions shamelessly axed, creating traumatic mental paralysis through the annals of materialism.

She has devoted her life to educational development as the basic requirement of human development, creating a successful platform for Human Rights and progressive societies.

Begum Majid Khan is a powerful writer with a masterful submission which is no easy task. To extend and propound an issue with both, a flawless quality of vocabulary, and expression she competently depicts the sensitivity and diversity of an untrammelled author, who contrived to dispel the unnecessary or incompetently captured projection of some very important topics.

Begum Anese Majid has no dirth of words at her command, knows their apt usage, proving that her masterful command of the English language is ever present. She has a dismaying concept of Human Psychology, seasoned by philosophy encompassing all ages and diverse circumstances. She appears to have been blessed with a "psychic", or sixth sense as she zeros into a correct analyses for whatever she handles.

The needs of the "less fortunate" is of paramount concern to her, as may be observed through her personal work with the "Disabled" the "Village Tubewell" programme and "free education" to the underprivileged. She is not a social worker but a serious and dedicated reformer during an era of social decline.

While working on the editing of the biography, I was totally immersed in the manuscript, that when I completed it, it left me with one deep regret – I had not had enough. In her life of over seven decades she must have done far more, seen a great deal, suffered and endured much, loved with happiness, enjoyed life's gifts, met a multitudes of people across the world, but we could not be the beneficiaries to enjoy those absent episodes from her biography which would run into at least two or more volumes. I do request that she gives us the benefits of those missed out experiences in at least one more volume. She really needs to divulge more.

The author depicts the lavish life style of the aristocratic upper echelons, but also highlights the miseries of the oppressed indigent class and one can observe from her book, the total lack of social human empathy as she is a true humanitarian. For a healing process of the indigent and the absence of rights she advocates that all must work for "Human Rights".

She remains a devout Muslim despite her western training, yet she is spiritually highly elevated due to which she was bestowed the honour of representing Islam as a "Religious Leader" at the two week "Retreat at Kirkridge", Penn State U.S.A. in 1995.

This biography is a masterpiece of an unusual kind, both in its presentation and the undivided interest, as it races ahead moment after moment, leaving one breathless and eager regarding the material yet to come. It is crowded sometimes with startling new information that one is amazed. One is also amused by the quips in between the writing form, which makes the reading most enjoyable. Serious topics are handled logically, yet there is a continuous beauty of language at the same time ensuring that facts have been sincerely revealed with authenticity. On the title the words, "The Truth Revealed" are unfolded with honesty without censure, or criticism, hence one flies with the writer, on the winds of change to destinations unimagined yet made simple to comprehend and enjoy because of the competent delivery.

For a book to stand on the pedestal of "Good", the writing requires to be consistent with three basic and fundamental avenues of writing. First knowledge, the other, expression and lastly the writer's ability to synthesize the material. While editing I observed that the book encompasses a wide range of comprehensive and knowledgeable subjects, that have been expressed in an unusual manner and characteristically in a form that captivates the reader's deep interest, leaving one momentarily unaware of one's surroundings.

To sum up this, the book unfolds itself as a "Rare Book" and is a challenge in itself, choosing and submitting material that is as captivating, while it traverses the globe passing through avenues of knowledge, unlocking doors to numerous frontiers of information and probing the revelations of self assessment, at the same time revealing the purity of truth despite splashes of darkness and describing the beauty of life through the benevolence of "Nature" and the generosity of presenting its own individual piquancy, setting it apart from the normal format of biographical writing.

Here, I should like to whole heartedly congratulate the author for producing such a wonderful autobiography and giving me and I am sure, a multitude of readers, the same delight I experienced while it held me in captivity.

This is my humble submission as one of the editors.

~ Miss Naheed Yousaf
Editor, Pakistan

★ ★ ★ ★ ★

Truth Conquers the Universe

LEGACY REFLECTION
A Genius Personality

Syeda Anese Majid is not a single person but a dynamic personality who emanates variegated colours of a rainbow revealing multifarious facets each one of which inspires the people surrounding her.

She is a distinguished poetess of the English Language and a scholar par excellence. She is a well-reputed historian, who divulges concealed facts of history in a most revealing manner. She is a well-known educationist who has established the most modern school system in the shape of Esena Foundation for educating the Muslim girls of Pakistan on modern lines. As time passed, years lent recognition to the name of Esena Foundation. Parents came from abroad bringing their young daughters from America, Canada and England to be educated in Pakistan. She came in contact for the first time with these students at school and was shocked to find that the girls knew very little about Islam in the true context of the Holy Quran. She resolved to investigate this serious deficiency, so followed this up by visiting Birmingham, Bradford, Tooting and other Muslim areas in Britain.

On her trip to Canada and America, she found that many of the children were unable to read or comprehend the Arabic of the Holy Quran or even read the Urdu text. She guided the teachers and students to Dinyat, Islamiyat and the development of an Islamic approach in all matters concerning behaviour, decorum, moral values, and simplicity bonded by a high sense of integrity. Later on many more educational institutions were established imitating Esena Foundation, but they could not excel the standards laid down by her as Chairperson of Esena

Foundation. She has always taken personal interest in the affairs of the Foundation and guided the people concerned with its chores and routine matters.

Besides this, she is a great Muslim revolutionary and a reformist who practically participated in the Palestinian struggle for the liberation of Palestine from the clutches of foreign oppressors. She provided material and social succur to the forlorn children of the Bosnian refugees, many of whom have been settled in Pakistan by our government.

Syeda Anese Majid is the direct descendant of the Ahle Bait of our Holy Prophet and belongs to the most revered Imam family of the sub-continent. Her father, Jaffar Imam, was the famous Chief Justice of the Supreme Court of India. Her grand fathers, Sir Ali Imam and Sir Syed Hassan Imam, had the distinction of being the founders of the Freedom Movements for Independence and were the close associates of Quaid-i-Azam Muhammad Ali Jinnah, the founder of Pakistan, Mr. Allama Iqbal and Mr. Nehru.

Being the sincere devotee of Islam, Syeda Anese Majid has composed the commentary of the Holy Quran in the English language by the beautiful poetical title "Echoes of Eternal Message" which truly represents the scope and depth of her erudition and knowledge. Before embarking upon this holy project of Quranic commentary, she visited the holy places of Mecca, Medina, Najf-i-Ashraf and Karbala-i-Moalla in order to acquire full knowledge and comprehension of the background of the various events as depicted in the holy Quran.

The poetical and prose rendering of the Holy Quran was commenced in the holy month of Ramazan in 1987 A.D. She completed the assignment within the record time of three months. Then came the turn of video cassette recording the commentary in her own voice. She spread the holy message of the last revealed Book of Almighty God by distributing these video cassettes free of cost to thousands of people in Pakistan and various school, colleges and universities in U.S.A. and Canada as well as to the Church Groups, Islamic Centres many other institutions and organizations interested in this venture.

All the expenditure in this regard was borne by Begum Sahiba herself, because she does not believe in accruing any financial benefit by selling the commentary of the Holy Book. She says she will bear all these expenses as long as she can and she hopes her grand daughters Natalia Zainab and Asma Majdoline will continue the publication of this project after her and that she has trained them well on these lines. According to Begum Sahiba, her attachment to Islam and the Holy Quran is God gifted and a true inheritance of her predecessors. When going for higher education to England, her Mother had presented a beautiful copy of the Holy Quran and advised her to recite it daily.

"Echoes of the Eternal Message" is a marvelous and scintillating commentary of the Holy Quran which has received universal ovation and consequently she received bouquets of tributes from all over the world. In Tokyo, the international Conference held on behalf of the world religions, was highly impressed by her translation and commentary of the Holy Book and bestowed upon her the title of "Soofi Dervesh".

She is well-known to the Western World as a philosopher and the scholar of Islam. She toured extensively throughout the world and delivered meaningful lectures on the teachings of Islam to the selective gatherings of distinguished research scholars and well-reputed intellectuals introduced by Dr. Rustum Roy of Penn State U.S.A.

She was greatly applauded for her lectures at Research Centre of America, Islamic Centre of Canada and Islamic School of Canada. Begum Sahiba painted the true and real picture of Islamic ideology and cleared the minds of the Western fanatics of any distortions created about Islam.

In 1992, Begum Sahiba authored a beautiful book "Insight into Islam" comprising 400 pages and elaborated important topics which had been the burning issues in the Western World. In August, 1993, she was invited to address the "Parliament of World Religions" which represented 137 various religions of the world. Around six thousand delegates arrived from all the corners of the world and took part in the proceedings of the Parliament. She had the unique honour of representing Islam and addressing the gathering nine times. In September, 1993, Dr. Donald Conroy of Washington nominated her as a member of the Board of Governors for "The Global Stewardship Corps International". In October 1993, she was nominated "Trustee" on the American Board which caters for the educational needs, clothes and articles of daily needs and requisite funds and dispatched them to America from London for the Bosnian students of the "La Roche College" Pittsburgh U.S.A.

In February 1993, Begum Sahiba initiated "Global Stewardship Network" in Pakistan and helped organize environmental protection programme in the country. In May, 1994, she was bestowed the "International Merit Crystal Award" and the "Diamond Award from the U.A.E. in recognition of her services to the cause of Islam. She also received the President Medal in Pittsburgh for Bosnian students.

Like a true fighter, she sacrificed spiritually and materially for the cause of Palestinian Students Organization and was awarded a Sword and Model of "Al Aqsa Mosque by Yasser Arafat himself in recognition of her services. The PLO honoured her with "Jerusalem Star" in view of her enthusiastic efforts for the students of Palestine.

She managed to send food, clothes and medicine to Palestinians in Beirut by air, and patronized the Palestinian students in Pakistan in all respects throughout those difficult years.

In fact, Begum Sahiba has played a key role in enhancing the prestige of Islam throughout the world and achieved with limited resources at her disposal, what others could not achieve inspite of their extensive and wealthy resources. She has dedicated herself wholeheartedly in the service of Islam, and some of the tributes paid to her by the eminent scholars and celebrities of the world are an ample proof of her dedication to Islam.

~ Khawaja Nazir Ahmed

★ ★ ★ ★ ★